IMAGES
of America

TYLER COUNTY

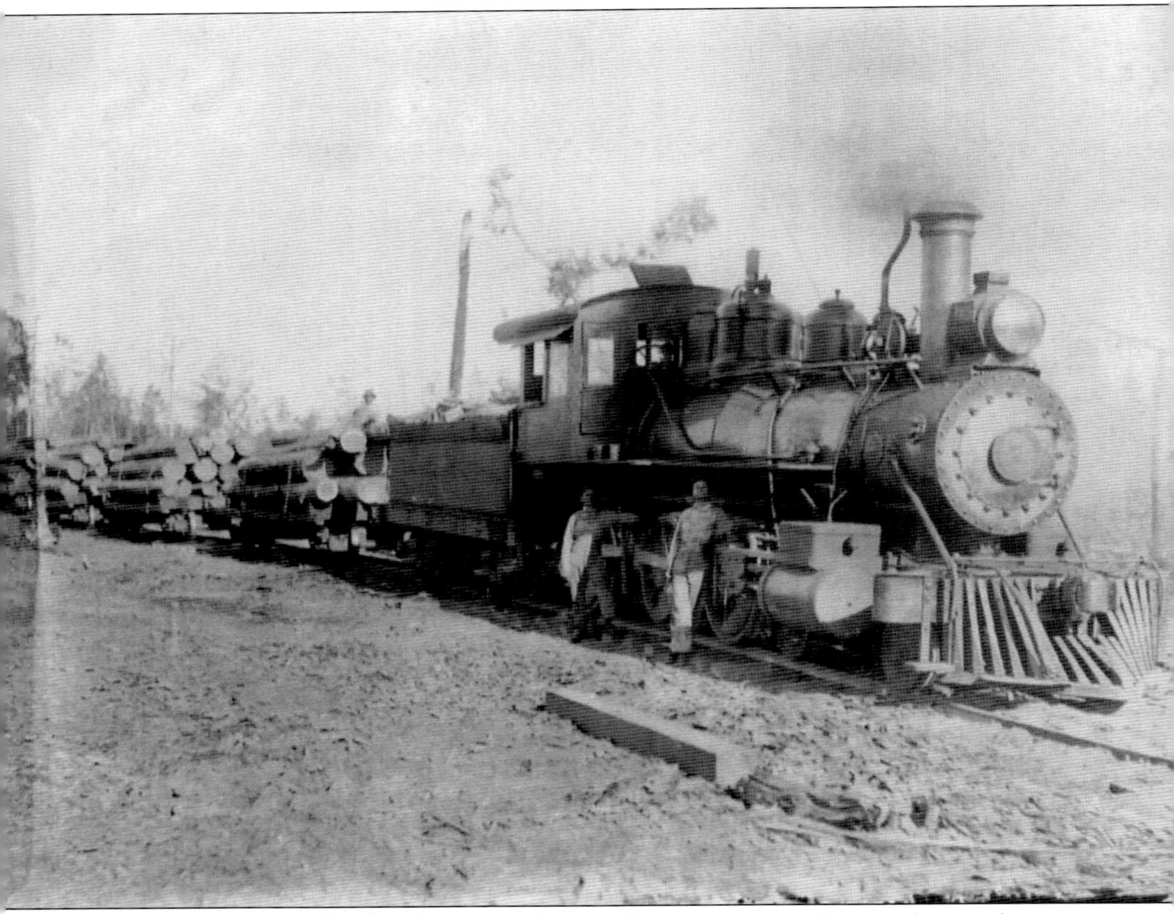

In 1882, commercial railroads stretched across Texas, and privately owned steam locomotives rolled through piney woods in Tyler County on portable logging-tram roads. Loggers built, used, removed, and rebuilt these tram-road railway systems as they crisscrossed the forests and delivered logs to company sawmills. The Trinity and Sabine Railway (T&S) and Texas and New Orleans Railroad (T&NO) networks delivered finished lumber and other wood products to far-reaching markets. (Courtesy of Texas Forestry Museum.)

On the Cover: Beginning in 1959, the Dogwood Queen, her court of princesses, and ladies-in-waiting were selected by a group of county businessmen called the Kingsmen. These men also took responsibility for raising funds to produce the Tyler County Dogwood Festival—a task previously shouldered by queen candidates. Pictured on the front cover are queen Beverly Standley Reese (left) and princess Patsy Daily Boden. On the back cover is lady-in-waiting Jean Richter. (Courtesy of Beverly Standley Reese.)

IMAGES
of America

TYLER COUNTY

Tyler County Historical Commission
and Tyler County Heritage Society

Eleanor Holderman
Researcher and Compiler

ARCADIA
PUBLISHING

ISBN 978-0-7385-8498-0

Published by Arcadia Publishing
Charleston, South Carolina

Printed in the United States of America

Library of Congress Control Number: 2011927146

For all general information, please contact Arcadia Publishing:
Telephone 843-853-2070
Fax 843-853-0044
E-mail sales@arcadiapublishing.com
For customer service and orders:
Toll-Free 1-888-313-2665

Visit us on the Internet at www.arcadiapublishing.com

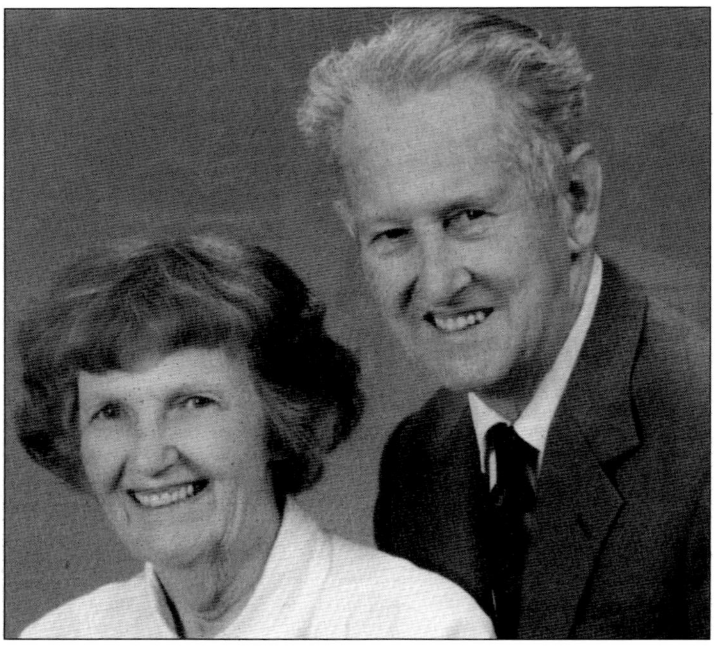

Our friend Jack Whitmeyer fully embodied the title jack-of-all-trades. From designing museums to constructing, wiring, and painting them, he owned the process of preserving Tyler County's history. To honor this geophysical engineer turned genealogist and leader of our organizations, the Tyler County Historical Commission and Tyler County Heritage Society dedicate this book to honor the memory of Jack Whitmeyer. (Courtesy of Tyler County Heritage Society.)

Contents

ACKNOWLEDGMENTS

Without the vision of James E. Wheat and Dan Utley, this publication would not exist. The late Judge Wheat applied his lifelong appreciation of history to a writing project that analyzed county events of the 19th and early-20th centuries. Utley, a contemporary historian, challenged the Tyler County Historical Commission and Tyler County Heritage Society to bring the story into the 21st century and served as project mentor.

Mary Nell Rainey, Yvonne Goss, and Eleanor Holderman, members of those organizations, outlined the story to be told and collected photographs to do the telling. They began with archived photographs in Whitmeyer Genealogical Library at Heritage Village.

Debbie Walker combed a network of friends to retrieve boxes of photographs. Others sharing large collections of photographs include Bob Boykin Photography, Matt Trahan, Marvin and Kathy Mott, and Gladys Best. School librarians from all five districts shared scrapbook and yearbook images. Many other contributors are credited inside the book.

Every photograph tells a story, and for this project, county storytellers shared willingly. They include J.C. Clark, Jeannine Hicks, Jackie Brown, Mayme Canada Brown, Johnny Ruth Wilson, Brenda Goode, Josh David, Billy Jack Jordan, Tom Dick Mann, Maxie and Joyce Young, Jean and Buddy Spurlock, Herbert Branch, and Toby and Shirley Spurlock.

Texas Department of Transportation staff provided information and archived pictures to enrich the story. They include Amber Cauthren, Marc Shepherd, Bruce Jenson, and Anne Cook. David Young of the Texas Forestry Museum shared photographs and historical documentation. County commissioner Rusty Hughes and county clerk Donece Gregory shared official county documents.

Eleanor Holderman organized images, conducted research, and wrote captions. Finally, Beth Allison and Mary Nell Rainey proofread with helpful eyes. Simone Monet-Williams and Winnie Rodgers, both acquisition editors, and Kristie Kelly, publisher for Arcadia Publishing, guided and encouraged our team to bring the book to a rewarding conclusion.

Some images in this volume appear courtesy of Tyler County Heritage Society (TCHS), Tyler County Historical Commission (TCHC), Allan Shivers Library & Museum (ASLM), Tyler County Booster (TCB), The Woodsman (TW), Tyler County Dogwood Festival (TCDF), Texas Forestry Museum (TFM), Texas Department of Transportation (TxDOT), Texas General Land Office (TGLO), and Colmesneil Independent School District (CISD).

Introduction

For more than 170 years, the towering pines and graceful hardwoods of Tyler County have welcomed travelers and encouraged settlers. As early as 1834, Americans with an appreciation for nature and a strong work ethic began carving their livings from this rich land and called it home. Some of those hearty folk joined Alabama and Coushatta Indians who had migrated from Louisiana, making their homes near the Neches River at Peach Tree Village. Others settled lower on the Neches at the site that would later be named Town Bluff.

Images of those earliest days under the Mexican government must be drawn from maps and words recorded in historical documents. With the birth of the Republic of Texas in 1836, the Liberty County boundaries included the area that would become Tyler County. The Menard Judicial District, carved from Liberty County, included the soon-to-be-formed Tyler County, whose official boundaries were set by the Texas legislature on April 3, 1846. The legislature named the new county in honor of Pres. John Tyler.

Images of America: *Tyler County* offers a peak through the windows of time to celebrate the people, places, and events that brought that simple, agricultural county into the modern age. It offers a visual tour easily taken from the reader's comfortable chair. Turn the pages to travel from the days when families farmed their land and raised livestock for home use and consumption, to an era when they shipped dairy and farm products to markets as far away as Houston. Observe the transition of a logging-and-wood products industry as it moved from one that relied on beasts of burden to one supported by mechanized harvesting and milling equipment.

Town Bluff served as the earliest seat of government for the new county. Later, state legislation encouraged counties to establish county seats close to their geographic centers. Three sites competed for the designation, and Dr. Josiah Wheat's 200-acre tract in the forks of Turkey Creek won the title. Surveyors laid out a plat for the town of Woodville, where a series of courthouses occupied the town square. From the beginning, the courthouse formed a hub for activities of all kinds, expanding beyond its use for traditional governmental activities. Early and recent photographs tell the stories of evangelistic revival meetings, Bible classes, memorial celebrations, and even the occasional meting out of justice at the hanging tree.

Photographs document the improvements in transportation and technology that have created new opportunities for all of Tyler County. While early doctors rode to their patients on horseback, patients now drive themselves to medical appointments and receive treatment in state-of-the-art clinics and hospitals. With refrigeration, merchants now offer perishable items as well as staples from their inventories. Dangerous railroad and highway crossings have been replaced with underpasses and overpasses, and slippery clay hills have been paved, promoting safe travel and spawning a new industry: tourism.

Much of Tyler County's culture developed from church, school, and civic-sponsored activities. In the beginning, each community operated as a self-contained unit—a single building functioned as school, church, and lodge. Somewhere near that building, a cemetery offered a peaceful resting site. Often a gristmill, cotton gin, or sawmill became part of the picture. Sometimes, the settlers even added a general store with a post office. Photographs from these settings tell more than the simple story of who did what, when, and where. These images reflect the commitment made by families across several generations as they shared the work and recreation, the burdens and blessings, and the challenges and celebrations involved in growing a successful community.

While communities expanded and roads improved, state legislation focused on improving education for all Texas children. Thus began the development of normal schools to train teachers and the consolidation of community schools. The number of county schools decreased from 54 in 47 common districts to a total of three or four schools each in five independent districts. The consolidation process brought rural children to town. Barriers came down slowly, but they did come down. No longer did separate doors, water fountains, and seating arrangements divide African American and white students at school or their parents in the communities.

From 1850, when the population reached 1,894, until the year 2000, when it exceeded 20,000, the people have made Tyler County a special place to live and work. At first, the county court formed citizens into road crews that maintained the roads connecting their farms to the nearest settlement. This arrangement meant that work on the farms or plantations waited for the men to return home with their mules, equipment, and time. Later, the county began collecting taxes to pay for such maintenance. In both settings, the people gave whatever was needed to help their communities prosper.

As one of Texas's oldest and most rural counties, Tyler County is distinguished by being home to many statewide leaders, such as the following: Allan Shivers, governor of Texas; Clyde E. Smith, supreme court associate justice; Judge James E. Wheat, charter member of the Texas Historical Commission; and John Henry Kirby, a businessman who arguably was the largest lumber manufacturer in Texas. In more recent times, such leaders as Clyde Gray, Mayme Canada Brown, and James White stepped out to use Tyler County's rich heritage as a springboard for continued growth and improvement. Contributions from family albums depict the personal and professional sides of these leaders' lives.

Readers of Images of America: *Tyler County* may find unexpected treasures among its pages. Perhaps the reflection on a long-forgotten event will bring pleasant memories to mind. Hopefully, an inspiration will also come to those who observe how natural resources sparked the pioneer spirit, bringing opportunity and people together. Certainly, this pioneer spirit lives and is seen across generations as it guides improvements that respond to changing economic patterns.

Tyler County and her people share a story far too rich to be captured in a book. Just as a rainbow spans the breadth of a horizon, so a heritage spans the life of a community. A colorful, majestic arch enriches our view, and a powerful, human story enhances our vision. Both hold promise and hope for the future.

One

Foundations for the Future

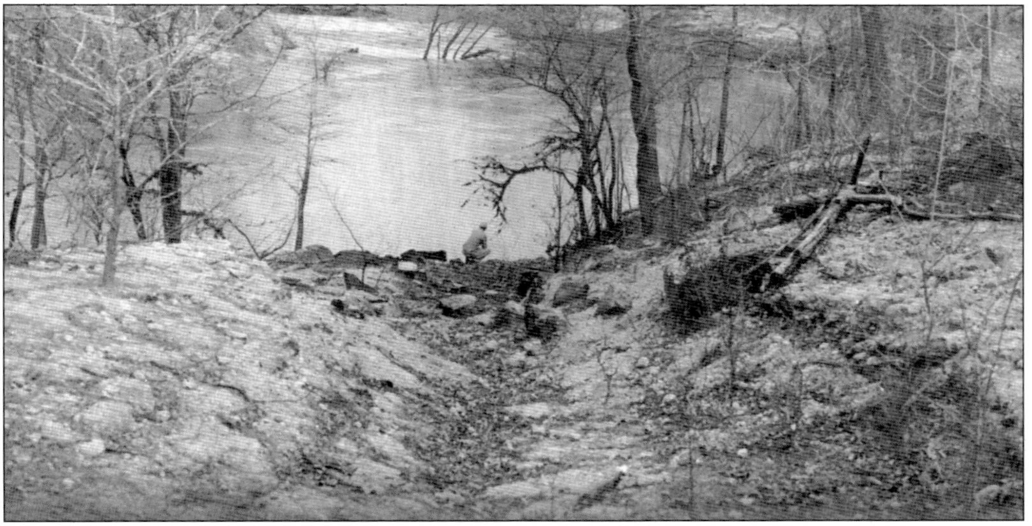

In 1830, the Mexican government built Fort Teran to help stem the tide of gringos entering Texas via the Coushatta Trace, which connected Texas to the United States and Louisiana. In 1835, the newly formed Republic of Texas issued Tyler County's first land grants. At the Fort Teran site, S.T. Belt operated a ferry, trading post, and shipping point, which he continued until the coming of railroads in the 1880s. (Courtesy of TCDF.)

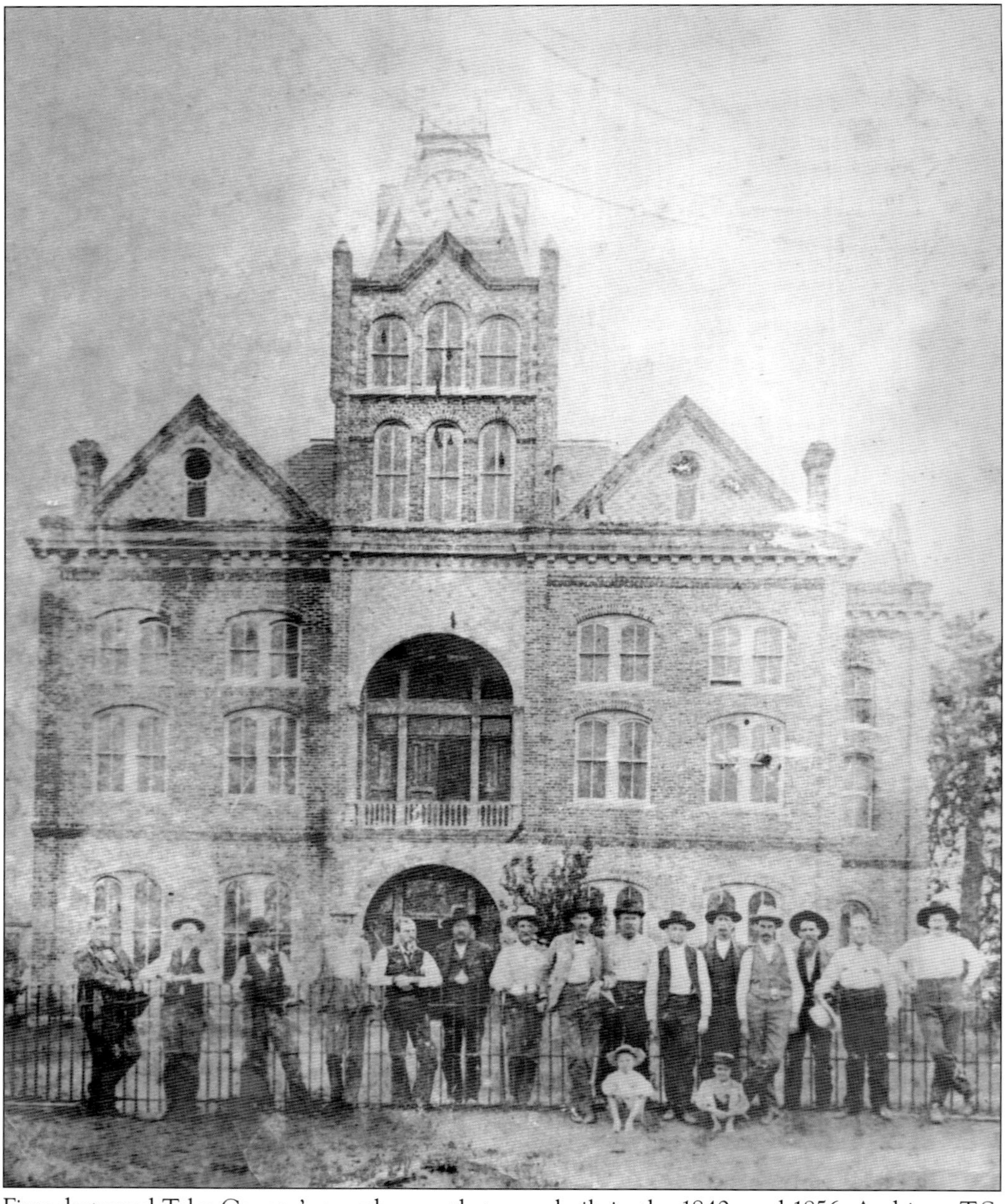

Fires destroyed Tyler County's courthouses that were built in the 1840s and 1856. Architect T.S. Hodges chose an Italianate style for the structure built in 1891, and it featured graceful arches, columns, and gables. Citizens could overlook the entire town from behind iron railings on the balcony of the ornate bell and clock tower. Pictured near that building, from left to right, are B. Kennerly, A.G. Reid, J.D. Collier, Aldridge Minter, W.A. Johnson, J.M. McDonald, J.F. Isbell, T.C. Crews, Bud Barclay, J.P. Mann, G. Holt, E.T. Parsons, A.E. Harison, D.P. Rock, and D.W. Rhodes. Boys seated in front of the fence are Carrol Rock and Barto Mann. Though the purpose of this c. 1900 photograph's gathering remains unknown, the names of men in attendance indicate a wide representation of county communities. Later, as Tyler County entered the 21st century, many of those family names continued to be recognized for county-wide leadership. (Courtesy of ASLM.)

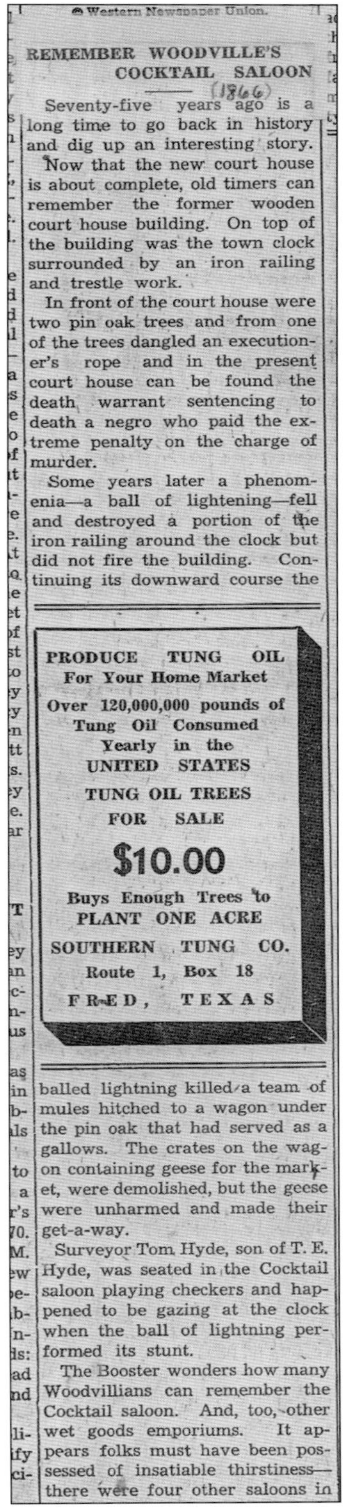
© Western Newspaper Union.

REMEMBER WOODVILLE'S COCKTAIL SALOON

(1866)

Seventy-five years ago is a long time to go back in history and dig up an interesting story.

Now that the new court house is about complete, old timers can remember the former wooden court house building. On top of the building was the town clock surrounded by an iron railing and trestle work.

In front of the court house were two pin oak trees and from one of the trees dangled an executioner's rope and in the present court house can be found the death warrant sentencing to death a negro who paid the extreme penalty on the charge of murder.

Some years later a phenomenia—a ball of lightening—fell and destroyed a portion of the iron railing around the clock but did not fire the building. Continuing its downward course the balled lightning killed a team of mules hitched to a wagon under the pin oak that had served as a gallows. The crates on the wagon containing geese for the market, were demolished, but the geese were unharmed and made their get-a-way.

Surveyor Tom Hyde, son of T. E. Hyde, was seated in the Cocktail saloon playing checkers and happened to be gazing at the clock when the ball of lightning performed its stunt.

The Booster wonders how many Woodvillians can remember the Cocktail saloon. And, too, other wet goods emporiums. It appears folks must have been possessed of insatiable thirstiness—there were four other saloons in

A 1941 edition of the *Tyler County Booster* reported the completion of courthouse renovations that had begun in the late 1930s. That work had transformed the stately 1891 courthouse into a box-like structure. Before covering the building with stucco, designers chose to remove the gables, columns, and ornate ironwork from the landmark and expanded the building toward the south. While celebrating the "new" structure, the reporter also captured an old-timer's recollections about the wooden courthouse that stood on the square in 1866, a mere 75 years earlier. In addition to describing the second courthouse building, the news story also provided a glimpse into the life and times of its era. All signs of the hanging tree and cocktail saloons of the 19th century disappeared through the years, but checkers and domino games played in the courthouse shadows continued into the 21st century. Currently, citizens interested in preserving the county's rich heritage seek grant funding to help restore the historic building to its original grandeur. (Courtesy of TCHS.)

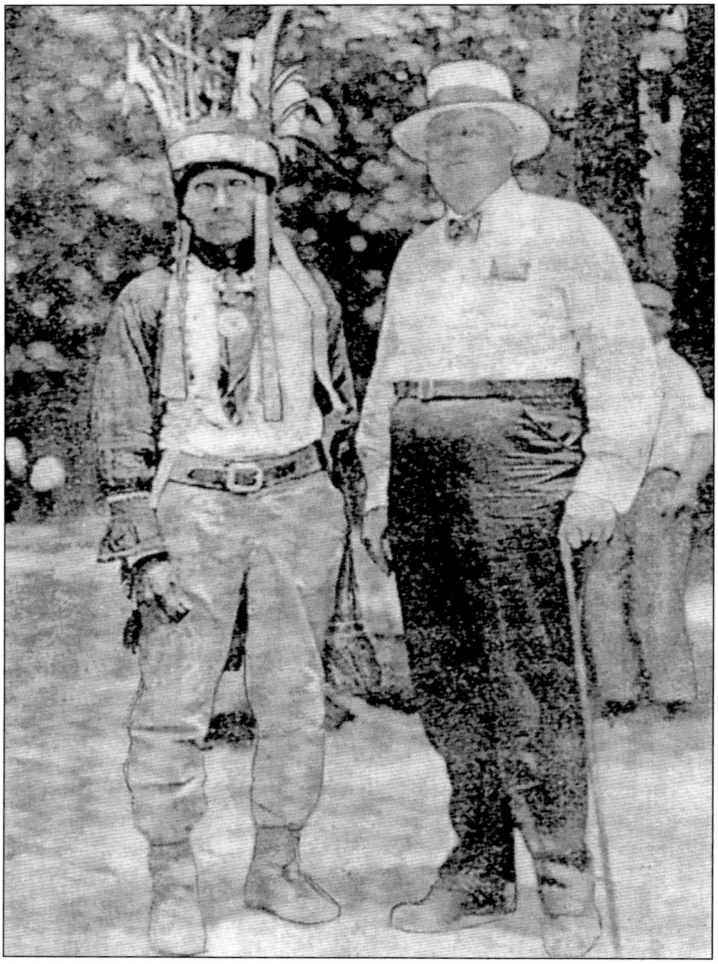

John Henry Kirby earned the respect of all kinds of people from his beloved piney woods. National leaders of government, business, and industry consulted with Kirby regarding Texas's economic development matters. Alabama Indian chief Sun-Kee joined the celebration at the dedication of Peach Tree Village Hall—a memorial to Kirby's late parents. Others in attendance included Oscar Branch Colquitt, who was the 25th governor of Texas. In all, more than 3,000 guests attended the ceremonies performed by Mount Hope Lodge 121, which was the first Masonic Lodge established in Tyler County. All the guests arrived by train on the Trinity and Sabine Railway, except the locals who came in wagons or on foot. (Both, courtesy of TCHS.)

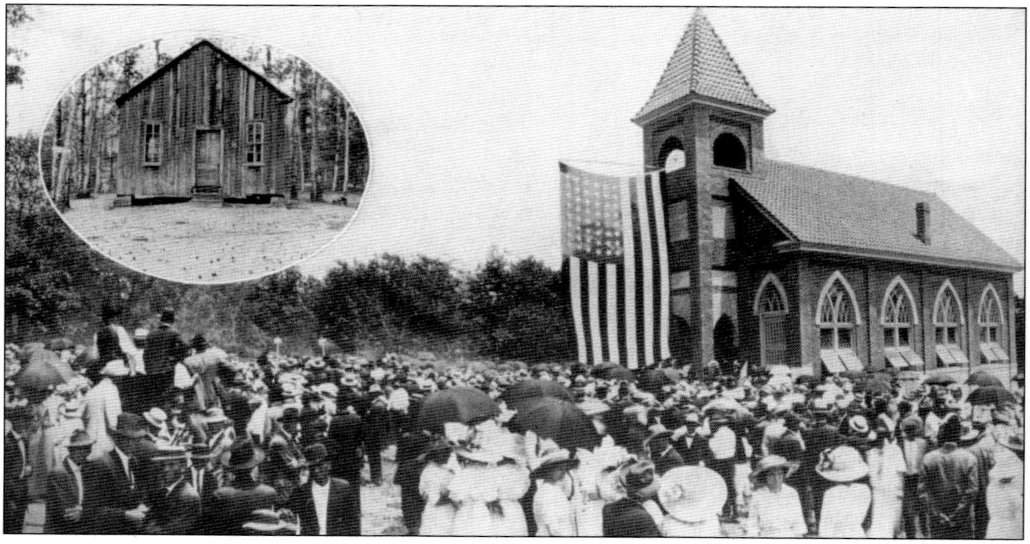

In 1907, John Henry Kirby's timber and logging empire reached its peak. As an attorney, oil baron, and capitalist, he owned thousands of acres and dozens of sawmill camps in Texas and Louisiana. His enterprises provided jobs for more than 16,000 men and women. He entertained such notables as Franklin D. Roosevelt at his mansion near downtown Houston. Yet, as Texas's first homegrown millionaire, Kirby valued his country upbringing and treasured his country friends. On one occasion, he made arrangements for a group of 12-year-old boys to travel by train from Chester to Houston. They stayed overnight at his mansion and served as ushers at the Democratic National Convention. Kirby endeared himself to his friends with his annual Christmas letters and frequent gifts of Bibles, which he personally inscribed. (Right, courtesy of TFM; below, courtesy of TCHS.)

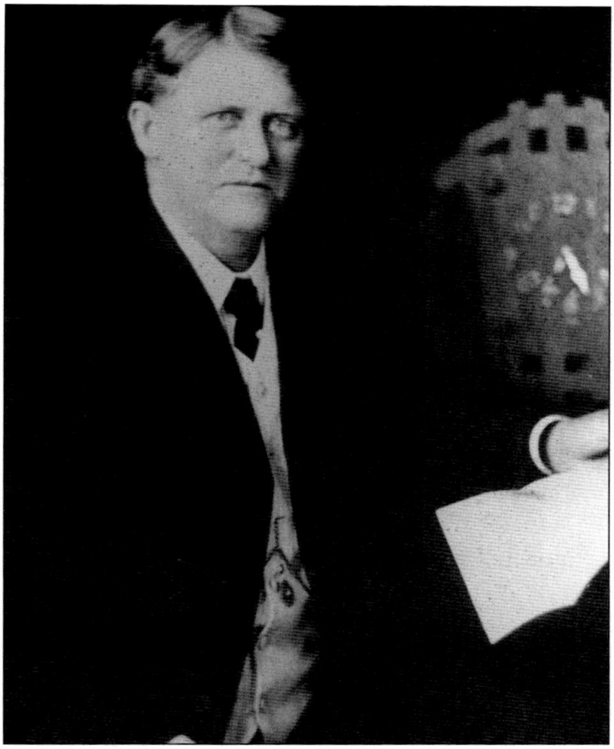

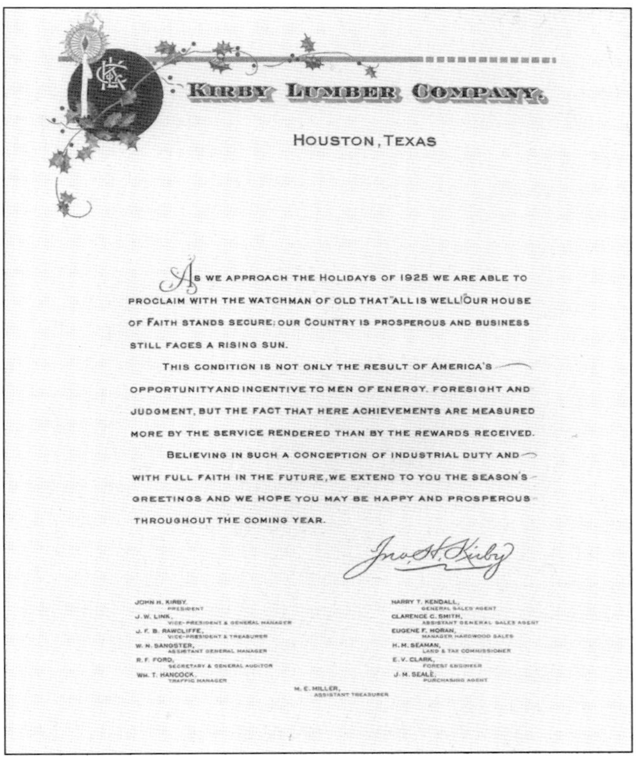

KIRBY LUMBER COMPANY.

HOUSTON, TEXAS

AS WE APPROACH THE HOLIDAYS OF 1925 WE ARE ABLE TO PROCLAIM WITH THE WATCHMAN OF OLD THAT "ALL IS WELL." OUR HOUSE OF FAITH STANDS SECURE; OUR COUNTRY IS PROSPEROUS AND BUSINESS STILL FACES A RISING SUN.

THIS CONDITION IS NOT ONLY THE RESULT OF AMERICA'S OPPORTUNITY AND INCENTIVE TO MEN OF ENERGY, FORESIGHT AND JUDGMENT, BUT THE FACT THAT HERE ACHIEVEMENTS ARE MEASURED MORE BY THE SERVICE RENDERED THAN BY THE REWARDS RECEIVED.

BELIEVING IN SUCH A CONCEPTION OF INDUSTRIAL DUTY AND WITH FULL FAITH IN THE FUTURE, WE EXTEND TO YOU THE SEASON'S GREETINGS AND WE HOPE YOU MAY BE HAPPY AND PROSPEROUS THROUGHOUT THE COMING YEAR.

Jno. H. Kirby

JOHN H. KIRBY, PRESIDENT
J. W. LINK, VICE-PRESIDENT & GENERAL MANAGER
J. F. B. RAWCLIFFE, VICE-PRESIDENT & TREASURER
W. N. SANGSTER, ASSISTANT GENERAL MANAGER
R. F. FORD, SECRETARY & GENERAL AUDITOR
WM. T. HANCOCK, TRAFFIC MANAGER

HARRY T. KENDALL, GENERAL SALES AGENT
CLARENCE C. SMITH, ASSISTANT GENERAL SALES AGENT
EUGENE F. MORAN, MANAGER HARDWOOD SALES
H. M. SEAMAN, LAND & TAX COMMISSIONER
E. V. CLARK, FOREST ENGINEER
J. M. SEALE, PURCHASING AGENT

M. E. MILLER, ASSISTANT TREASURER

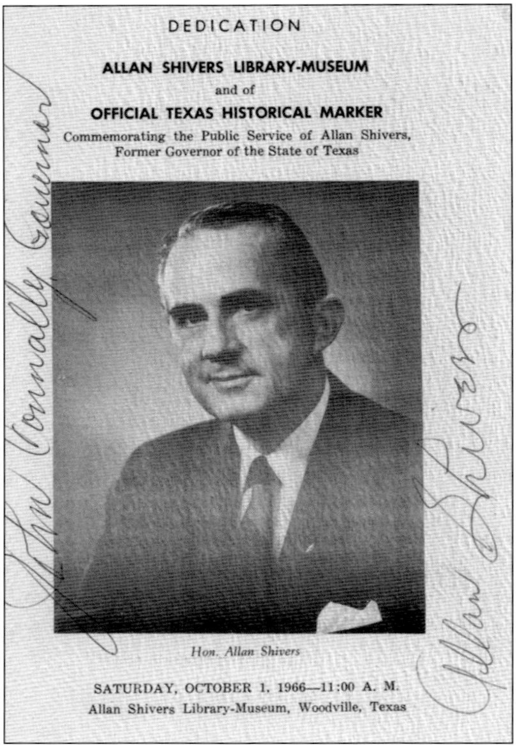
DEDICATION

ALLAN SHIVERS LIBRARY-MUSEUM

and of

OFFICIAL TEXAS HISTORICAL MARKER

Commemorating the Public Service of Allan Shivers, Former Governor of the State of Texas

Hon. Allan Shivers

SATURDAY, OCTOBER 1, 1966—11:00 A. M.

Allan Shivers Library-Museum, Woodville, Texas

In 1966, the Honorable Allan Shivers held the distinction of being the longest-serving former governor of Texas. Having entertained national dignitaries at the governor's mansion in Austin, he still maintained his home near Woodville. There, he established a library and museum that was accepted by officials of Woodville Independent School District, the city of Woodville, and Tyler County. W.H. Risinger Sr. chaired the Tyler County Historical Survey Committee, which sponsored the dedication. (Courtesy of ASLM.)

Hon. Allan Shivers and his wife, Marialice, acquired the historic R.A. Cruse home, which was slated for demolition. They arranged for it to be moved, restored, and furnished as a museum holding papers and artifacts from his years of public service. Additionally, they built an adjoining, state-of-the-art library for general use. Friends of the Allan Shivers Library, a nonprofit corporation, continue to support expansion and improvement projects for the facility. (Courtesy of TW.)

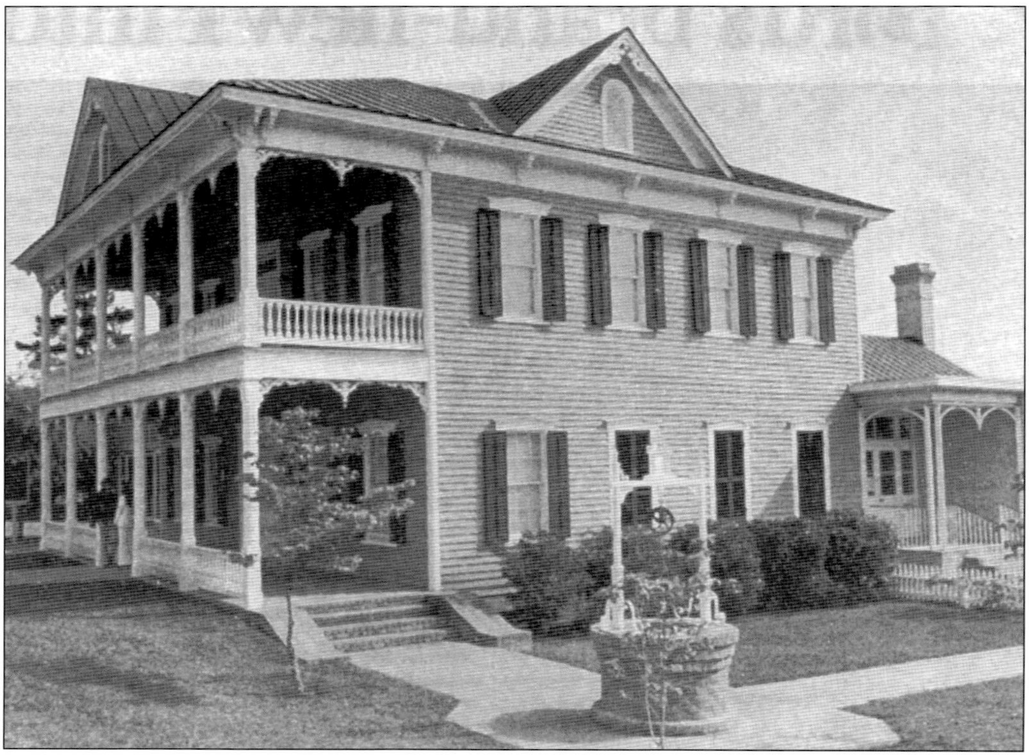

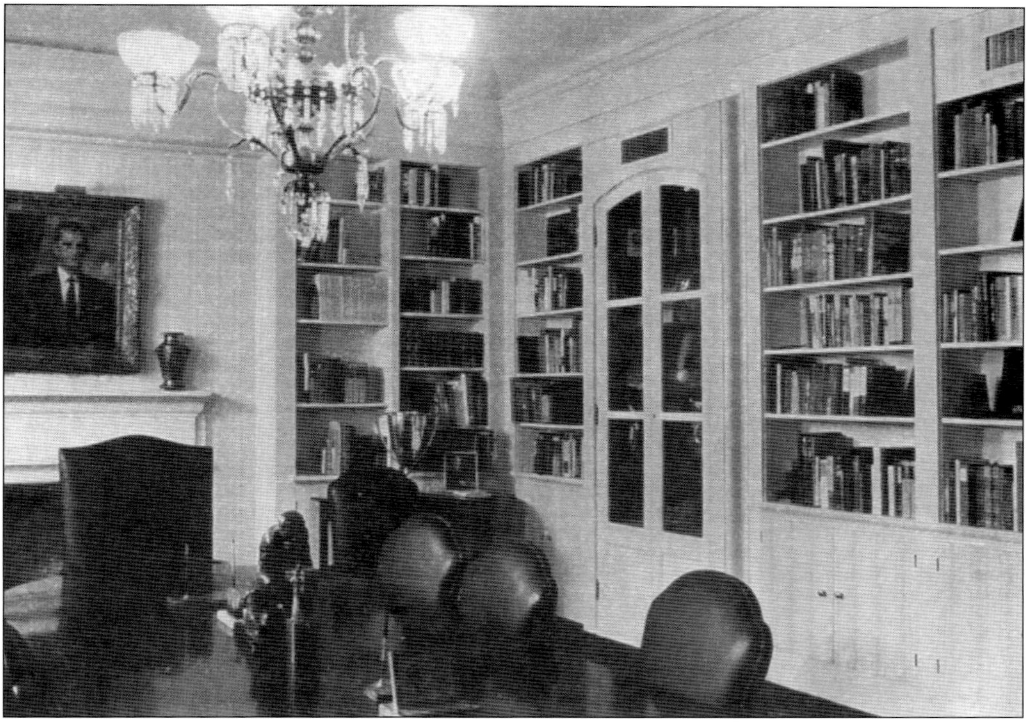

Allan Shivers's collection of books and papers reflects his wide-ranging interests and activities. His early career included a three-year stint as a union laborer in the Texaco refinery before completing his undergraduate and law degrees at the University of Texas. He went on to become Texas's youngest senator, then lieutenant governor, and governor. He served as president of the US Chamber of Commerce and on numerous boards of trustees. (Courtesy of TW.)

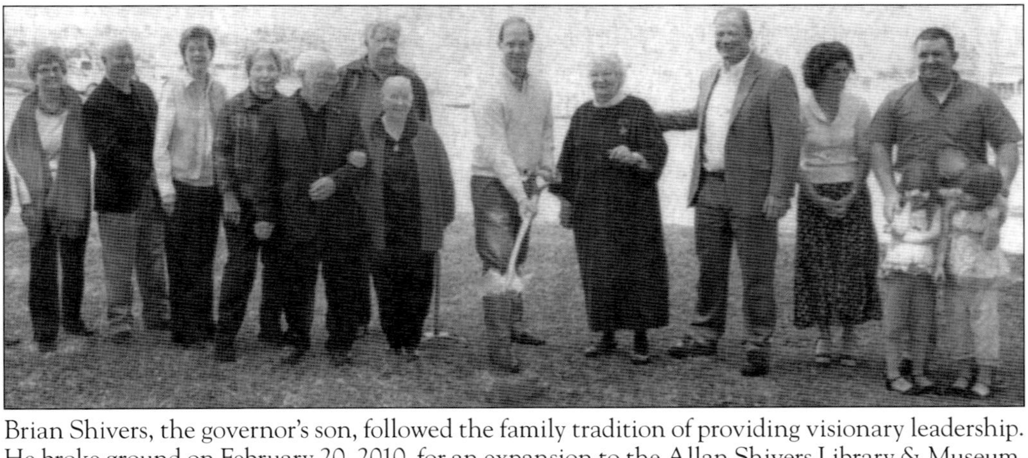

Brian Shivers, the governor's son, followed the family tradition of providing visionary leadership. He broke ground on February 20, 2010, for an expansion to the Allan Shivers Library & Museum. Librarian Rosemary Bunch led a campaign to raise the $330,000 needed for construction. Shivers, along with the library board, honored her service and the encouragement of her beloved husband by naming the new facility the John and Rosemary Bunch Room. (Courtesy of ASLM.)

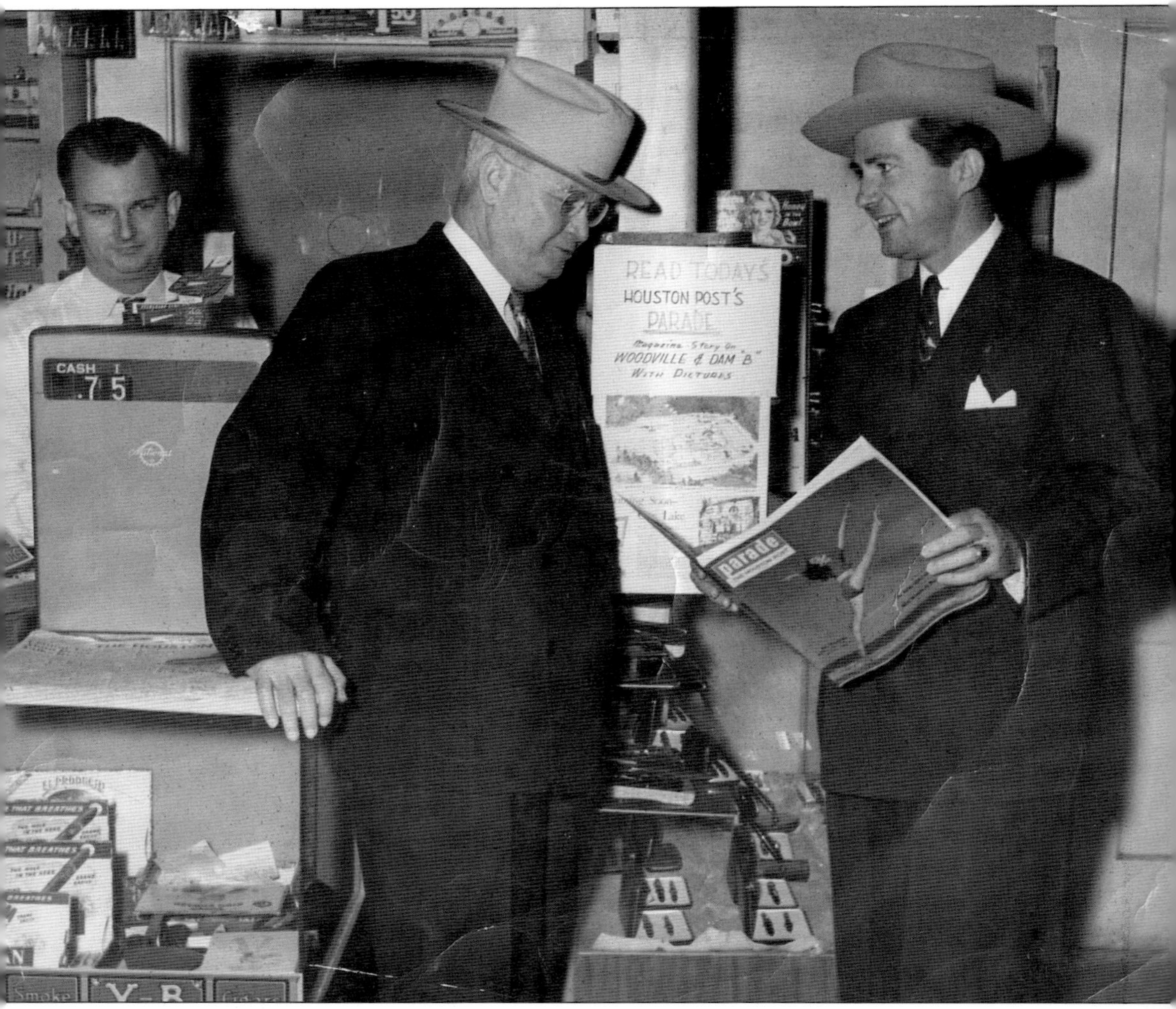

James E. Wheat (center), born in a log farmhouse near Chester in 1887, had a vision that exceeded farming. He worked various jobs (including teaching) to prepare for a career doing more than "walking behind a plow and a mule." A graduate of the University of Texas Law School, Wheat clerked for and became partners with attorney Joe Thomas in Woodville. He established his own law firm and the first title and abstract plant in Tyler County. Wheat served as county attorney from 1914 to 1918. As captain, he led an infantry company in World War I and a state guard company in World War II. After his election as Woodville's first mayor in 1929, Wheat's administration levied the first city taxes. Joining businessmen like Bill Jarrott (left) and statesmen like Allan Shivers (right), he supported ventures that would improve the quality of life for his fellow citizens. (Courtesy of George Jarrott.)

James E. Wheat's influence extended far beyond his law practice. He organized and served as Scoutmaster for Tyler County's first Boy Scout troop, director of the Beaumont district of the Boy Scouts of America, president of Woodville Independent School District's board of trustees for 30 years, and secretary and chairman of the state democratic organization. He was a director of the Houston branch of the Federal Reserve Bank, the East Texas Chamber of Commerce, the state prison system's board, and the State Bar of Texas. He was a charter member and first president of the Texas State Historical Survey Committee. He helped charter Woodville's Rotary Club and served as president. He led activities in the American Red Cross, Masons, Shriners, and Woodville's First Christian Church. He founded the Tyler County Dogwood Festival to celebrate the beauty of springtime in East Texas. Below, Wheat is pictured with his wife, Ruby. (Both, courtesy of TCDF.)

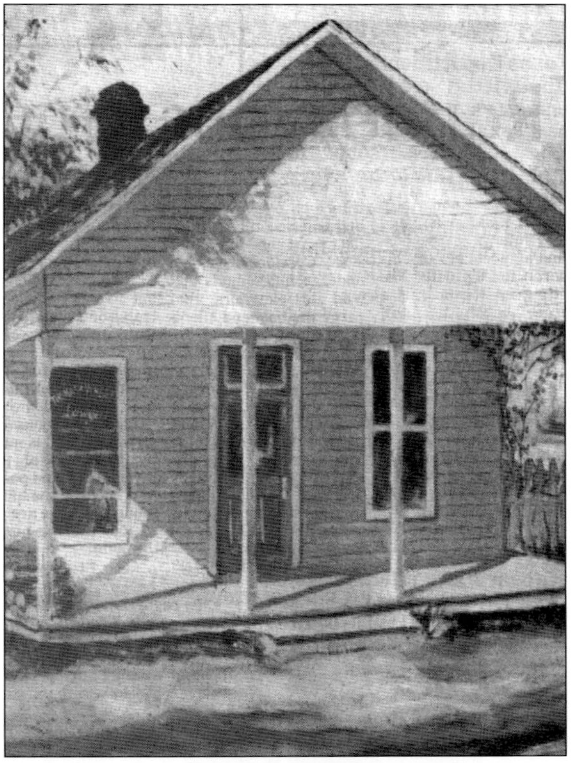

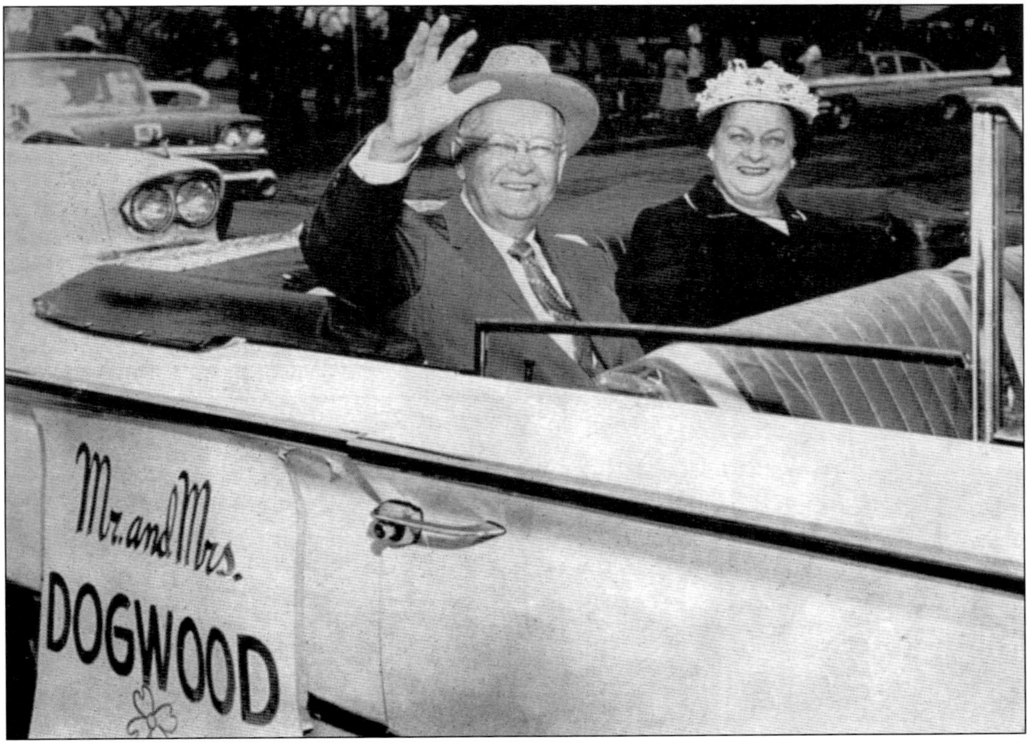

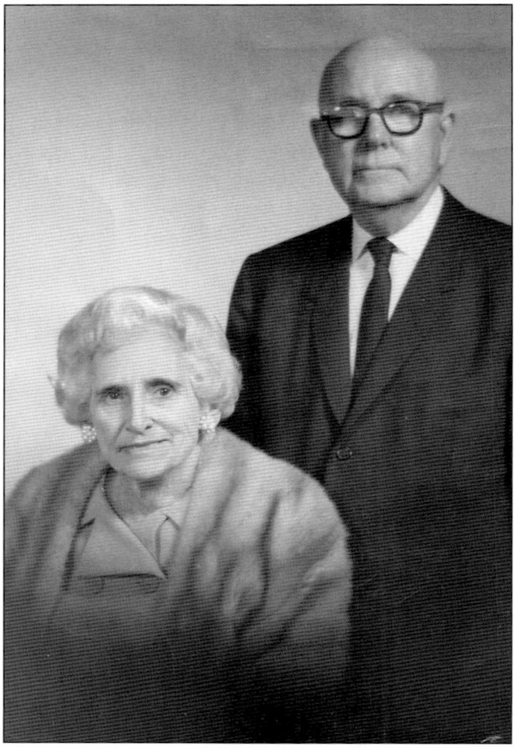

Clyde Earl Smith Sr. spent his early life on a tenant farm and in an orphanage. Returning to his family, Smith completed school in Woodville, studying law at night and working as a telephone operator. In 1919, at age 22, he passed the Texas State Bar. Smith practiced law, serving as county attorney, district attorney, and district judge. From 1950 to 1970, Smith served as the associate justice of the Texas Supreme Court. (Courtesy of Tessa Smith Sullivan.)

James White, a Republican from Hillister and a teacher at Woodville High School, made history when he was elected as Tyler County's first African American representative to the Texas Legislature. As one of his first official acts, he invited a Tyler County economic development team to discuss its needs with Gov. Rick Perry, pictured in the center. (Courtesy of TCB.)

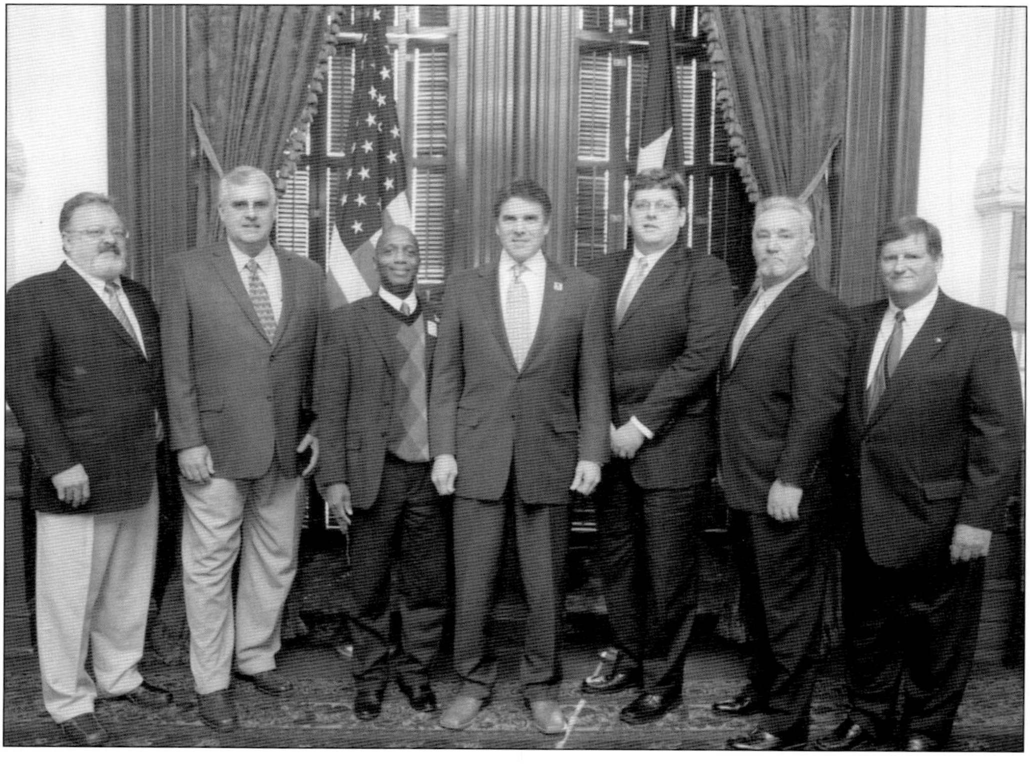

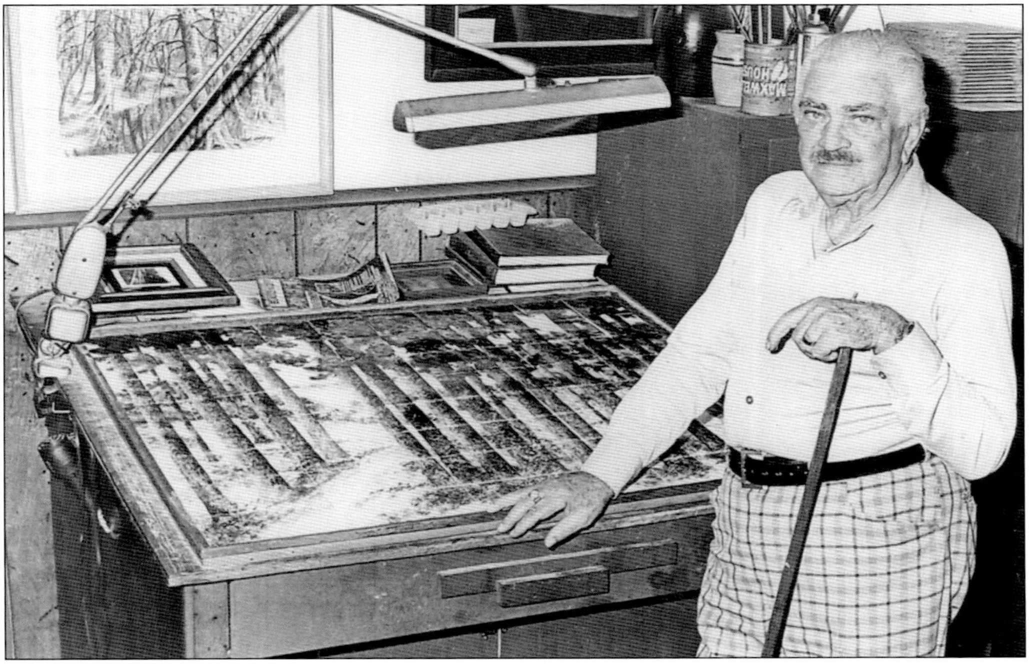

Clyde E. Gray pioneered the art of recording Texas history on ceramic tile and established the Heritage Garden Museum to attract tourists to Tyler County. In 1957, he received the Texas Heritage Foundation National Medal for "distinguished and meritorious service in preserving Texas heritage." He continued to paint on canvas and tiles while operating the museum until he retired and sold the museum to the Heritage Society in 1981. (Courtesy of TCHS.)

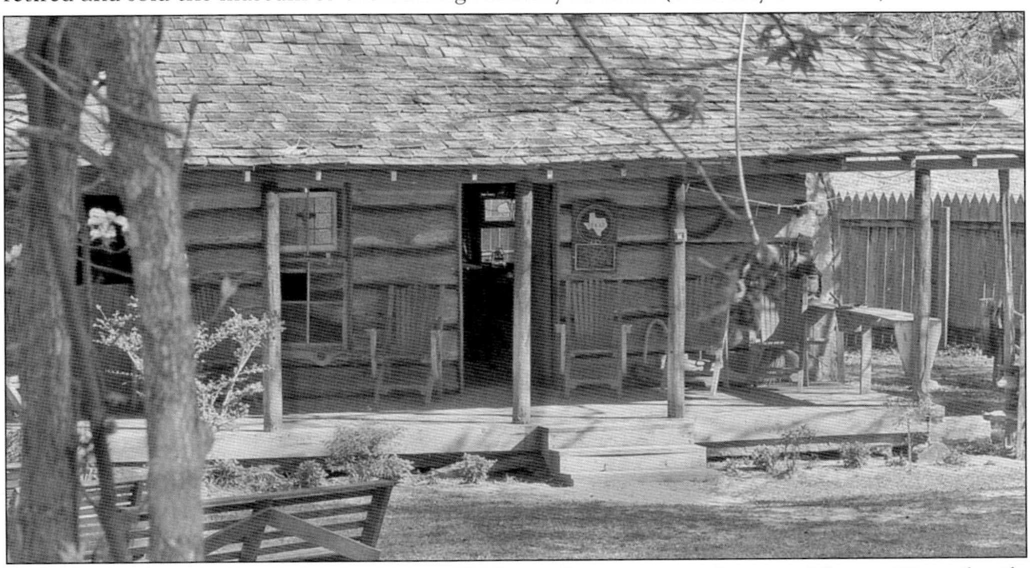

In 1866, Robert Tolar built this log home, which was later converted to a cookhouse. Here, family meals were prepared over an open fireplace with a mud cat chimney until 1960. In 1964, Clyde Gray accepted the Tolar Kitchen as an exhibit for the Heritage Garden Museum. The squared-and-notched log structure, with a roof made of hand-rived shakes, provides tourists with a window into 19th-century lifestyles. (Courtesy of TCHC.)

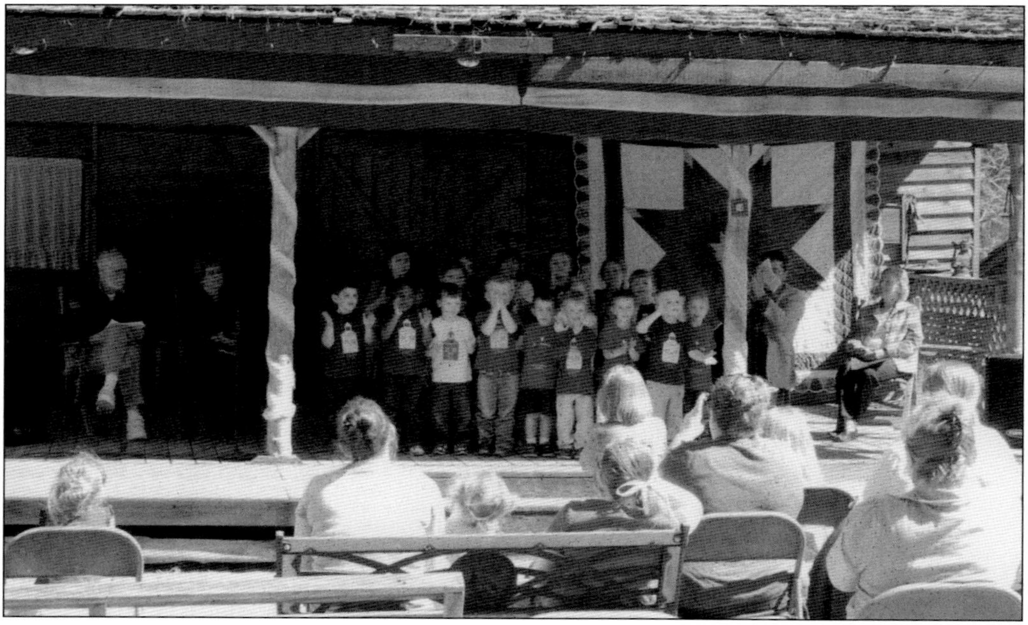

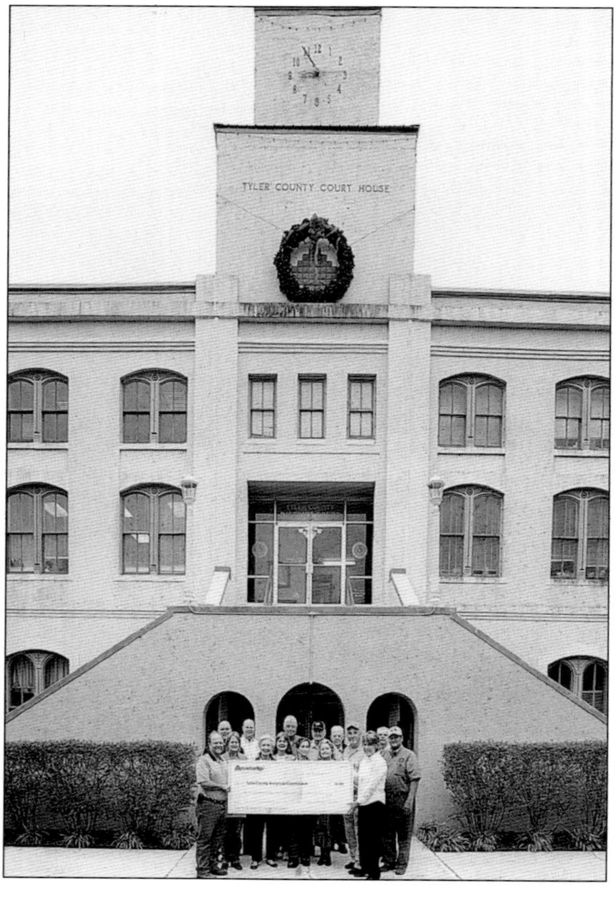

Since its establishment in 1953, the Texas Historical Survey Committee has provided guidance for appreciating, recording, marking, and preserving Texas heritage. In Tyler County, Judge James E. Wheat and W.H. Risinger led in the preservation of the county's early history. A state action in 1981 changed the survey committee's name to "historical commissions." At that time, the Tyler County Historical Commission created a nonprofit corporation, the Tyler County Heritage Society, so that charitable contributions might be received and acknowledged. The Heritage Society raised funds to purchase Clyde Gray's Heritage Garden Museum and renamed it the Heritage Village. The society has provided perpetual management of the village, expanding it into a major tourist attraction. The historical commission continues to promote the preservation and restoration of historic structures, most notably, the Tyler County Court House. (Above, courtesy of TCHC; left, courtesy of TCB.)

Two

LAND, LABOR, AND LIFE

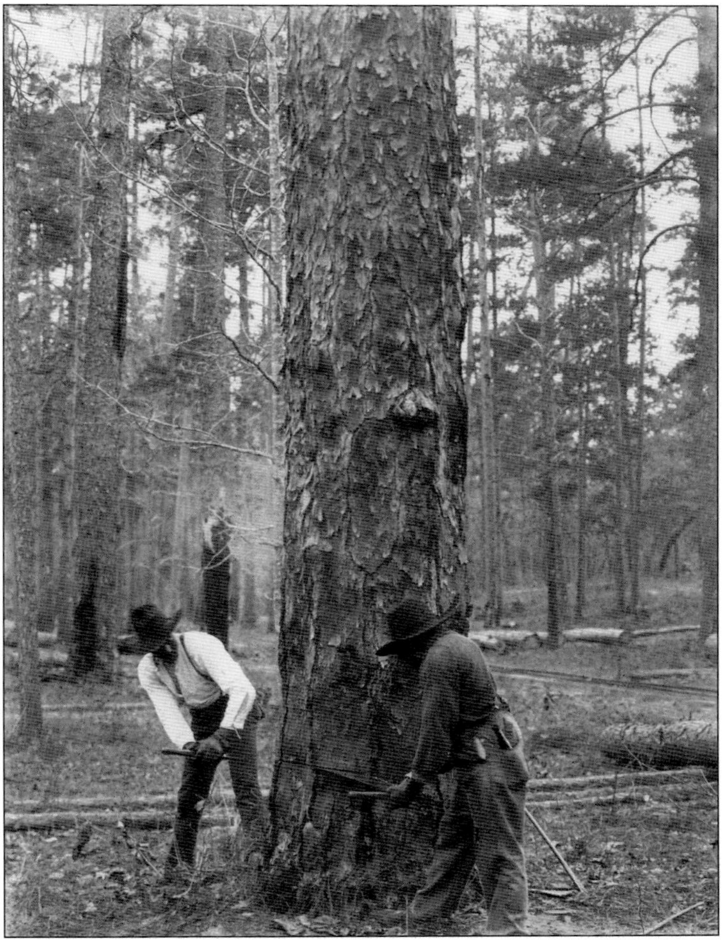

Following the Civil War, longleaf yellow pine trees revolutionized Tyler County's economic base, shifting it from farming and cotton plantations to timber and wood products. Reconstruction demanded building materials, and Tyler County farmers responded. The forests, once a nuisance to be cleared away, now provided resources for economic growth. Flatheads—the nickname given to some men working in the logging woods—manned crosscut saws and brought down the giant trees, receiving as much as $1.50 per day for their labor. (Courtesy of TFM.)

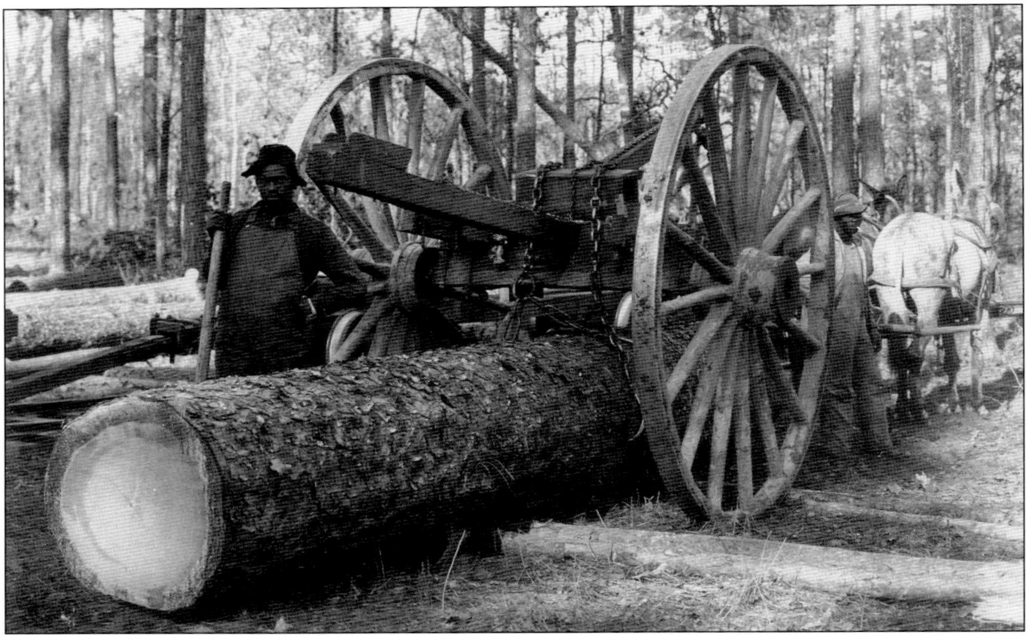

Skidding felled trees to the loading deck required the "just right" combination of tools and power. Mules resisted heat better than oxen and could maneuver through the woods, pulling logs hooked onto chains. On the other hand, oxen could pull more weight than mules. Skidding the heaviest logs for long distances required the use of slip-tongue or eight-wheeled wagons. (Courtesy of TFM.)

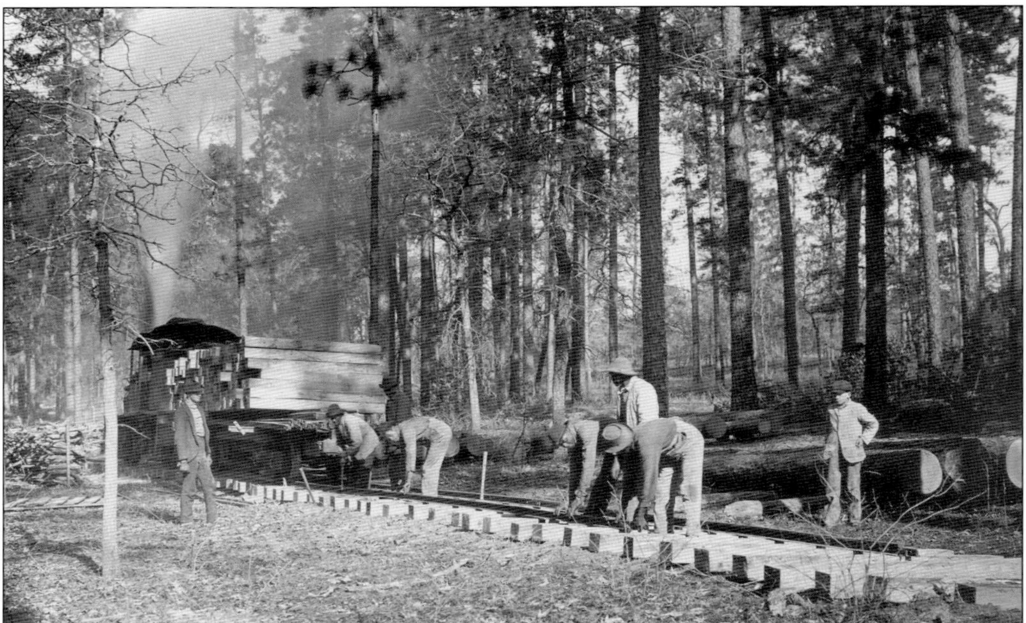

Steel gangs performed the hardest work at logging sites. Workers knew as they laid the cross ties and rails at one location that it was just a matter of time before they would undo their work and relocate the whole scene to a new site. They often chanted to help ease the monotonous, tiring routine. "Pick 'em up and lay 'em down. Jint 'em back! Swing 'em high!" (Courtesy of TFM.)

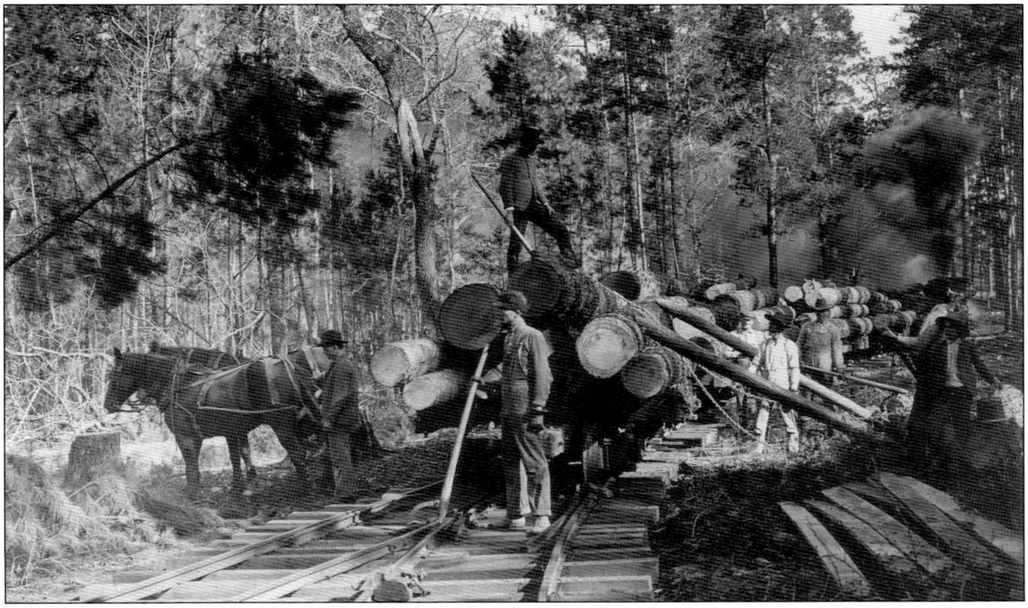

The logging process started when flatheads felled the trees. Logging continued as choppers delimbed and bucked the timbers into manageable-length logs. Then, bullwhackers guided mule teams to skid the logs to the loading deck and cross-haul those logs onto railcars. Finally, the locomotive hauled the load of logs to the mill. Sometimes, one engine pulled as many as 10 carloads of logs. (Courtesy of TFM.)

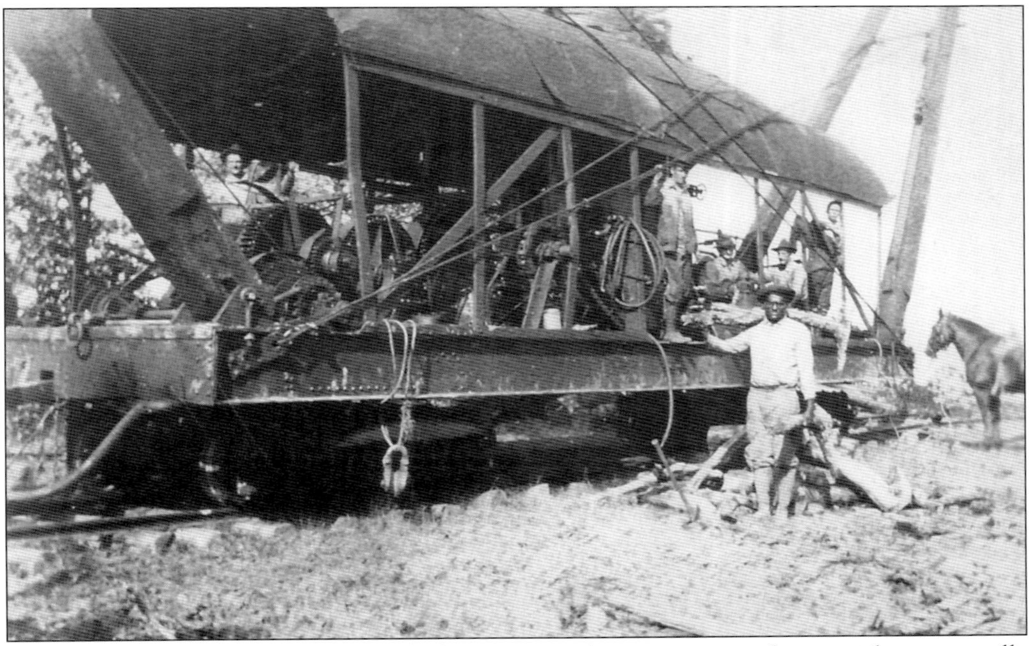

Logging activities created an extremely dangerous work environment where accidents generally considered to be caused by carelessness were commonplace. In 1912, new workmen's compensation laws began to require companies to take responsibility for industrial accidents. A modern invention, the steam loader, improved both the safety and efficiency of logging practices. (Courtesy of TFM.)

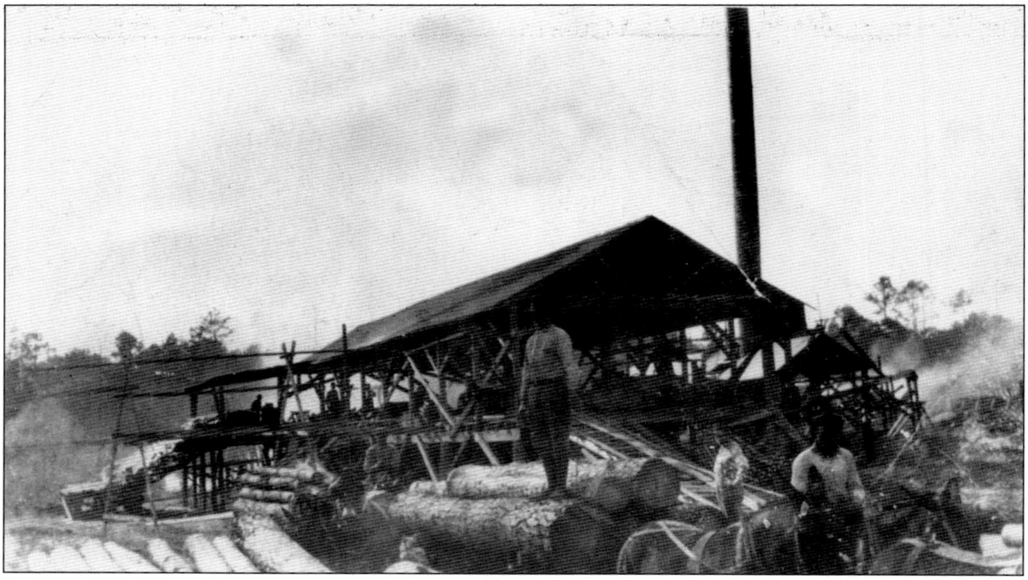

In 1927, T.O. Sutton and Sons crossed the Neches River at May's Ferry near Rockland to relocate its sawmill from Louisiana to Texas. Beginning at Holly Fork, the Suttons later expanded to Chester, Chireno, and Nacogdoches. Each son specialized in an area necessary for a successful logging, sawmill, and lumber business: Willard in banking, Herbert in sales, Harold in trucking, Bill in machinery, and Robert in surveying and timber management. (Courtesy of TCHC.)

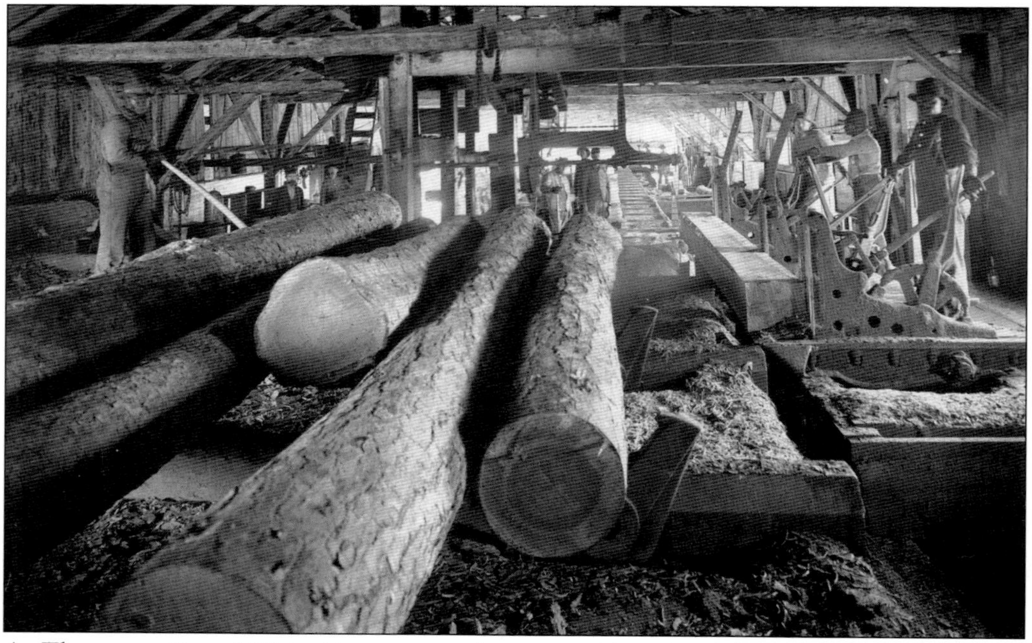

At Thompson Bros. Mill in Doucette, workers moved logs from the jack ladder to the deck with log kickers, then positioned and blocked them into the carriage for the sawyer's first cut. Men repeatedly repositioned the cut log (called a cant) with cant hooks for additional cuts that converted it into rough boards. Conveyors moved boards to the planner to be dressed as finished lumber, flooring, paneling, or trim pieces. (Courtesy of TFM.)

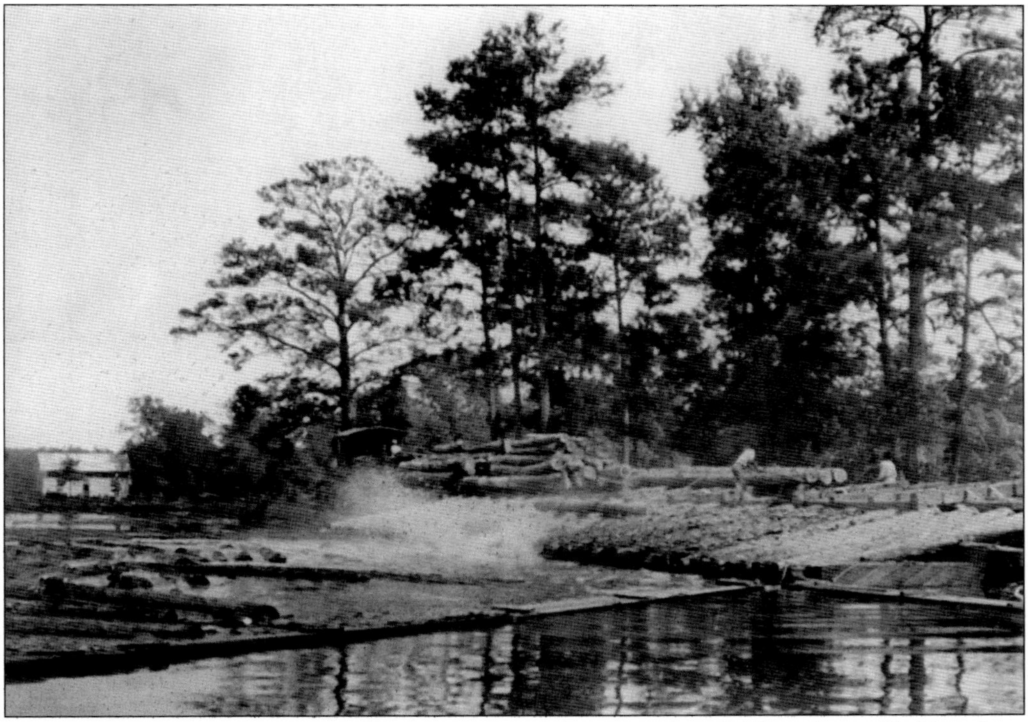

Water played a vital part in sawmilling enterprises. Thompson Bros. Mill workers rolled logs from railcars into the millpond to remove debris that might damage saw blades. Boilers heated water, making steam to run the engine that powered the machinery and heated the kiln. Water tanks on high towers created pressure needed to force water toward the inevitable fires. Still, mills often burned to the ground and were rebuilt. (Courtesy of TFM.)

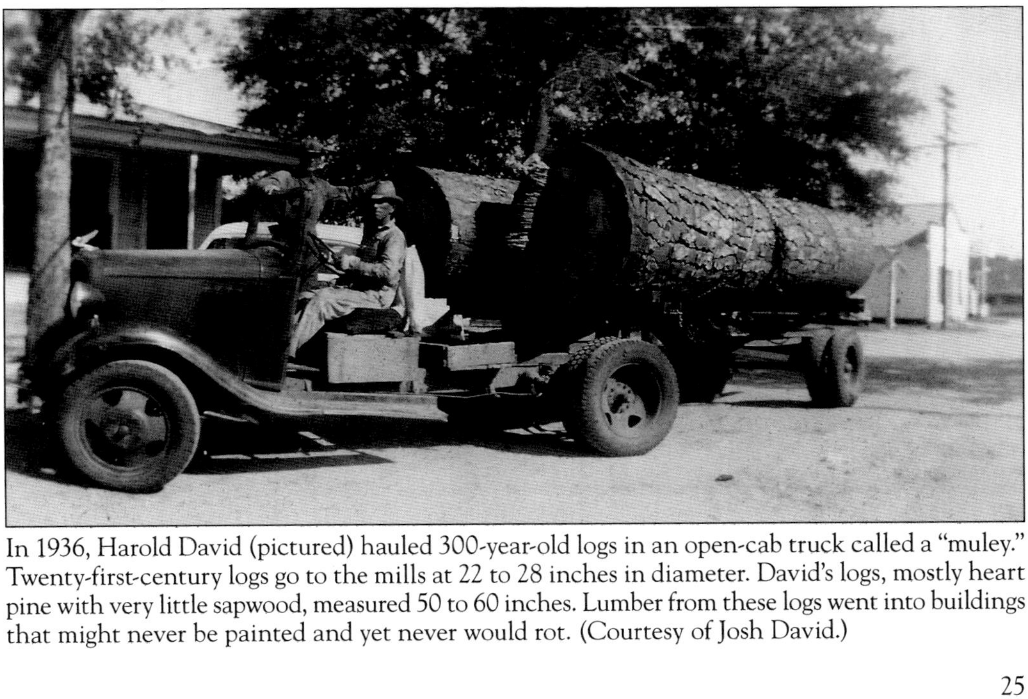

In 1936, Harold David (pictured) hauled 300-year-old logs in an open-cab truck called a "muley." Twenty-first-century logs go to the mills at 22 to 28 inches in diameter. David's logs, mostly heart pine with very little sapwood, measured 50 to 60 inches. Lumber from these logs went into buildings that might never be painted and yet never would rot. (Courtesy of Josh David.)

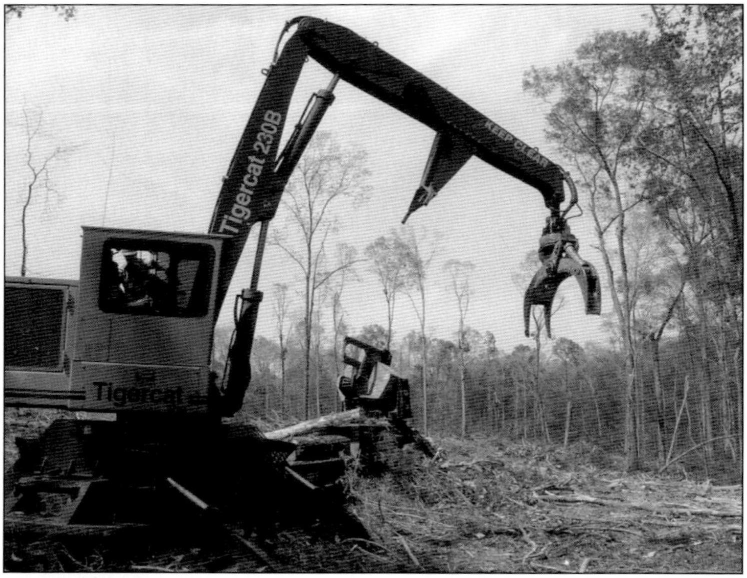

As the 20th century drew to a close, modern logging equipment included a diesel-powered loader to replace mules and steam loaders. Hard hats replaced straw-and-felt headgear, and steel-toed boots took the place of leather brogans. Shears, delimbers, and chain saws replaced crosscut saws and axes needed to fell and trim the giant pine trees. (Courtesy of TCHC.)

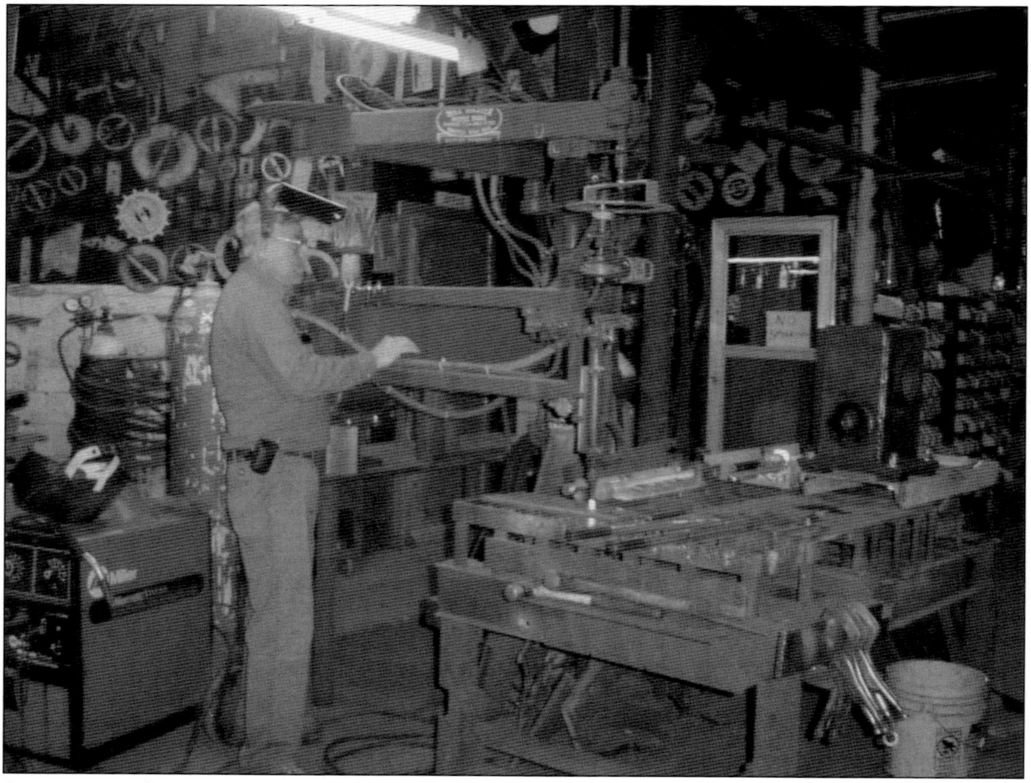

Since 1946, when Harold Pryor opened Mill Master Machine Works in Doucette, three generations of one family have built and repaired sawmills and sawmill equipment at this location. Unlike his father and grandfather, who designed machinery by hand, Ronnie Pryor (pictured) uses computer-assisted drafting programs to craft designs for steel parts that he will cut, form, assemble, and weld together. (Courtesy of TCHC.)

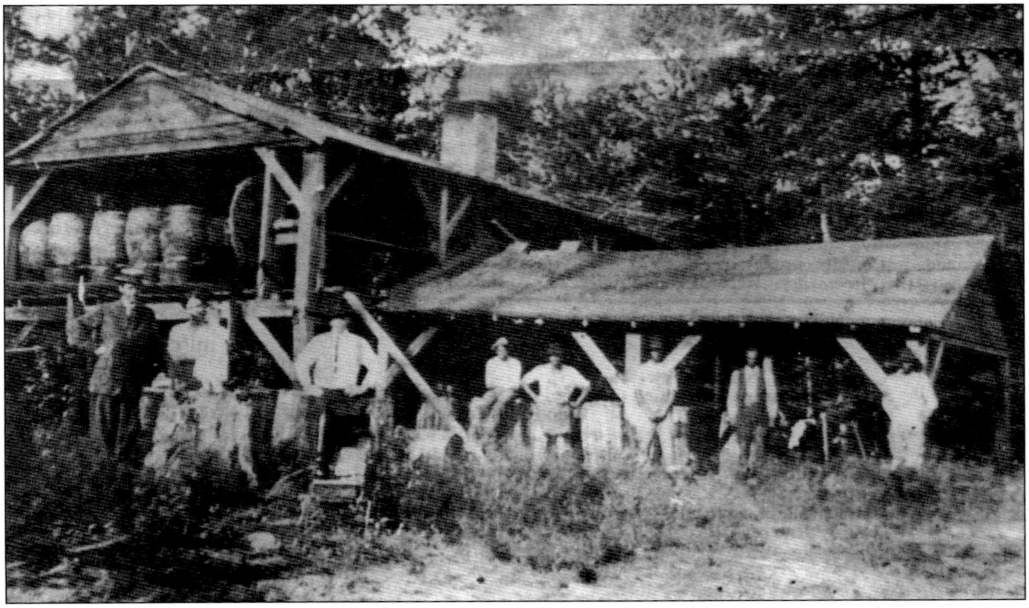

"Turpentine Jim" McFarley Brown migrated from Florida to Alabama, and finally, in 1914, to Spurger, Texas. The area's longleaf pine provided the pine sap that Brown distilled into marketable turpentine. His wife, Lilla Maud Davis Brown, sidetracked a small portion of the volatile product to use when nursing a community member back to health. Their grandson practices 21st-century family medicine in Woodville. (Courtesy of TW.)

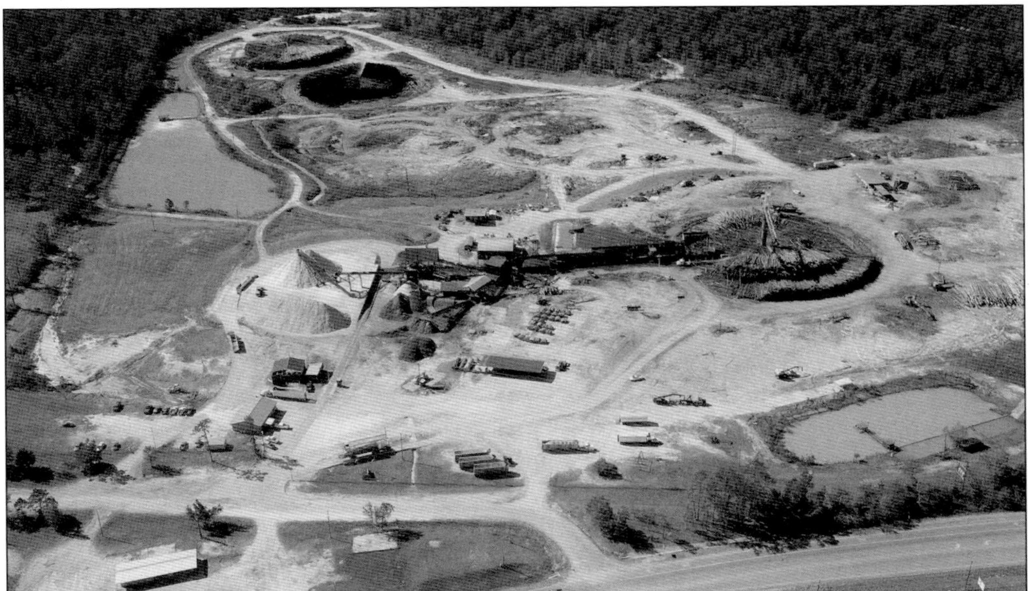

Through the years, Tyler County forests have provided resources for a wide variety of wood products. An aerial view of the North American Procurement Company (NAPCO) site brings to mind past and future products made there: first, board road made from hardwood trees; then, wood chips for fueling manufacturing plants; and coming soon, a biofuel plant to generate electricity. (Courtesy of Bob Boykin Photography.)

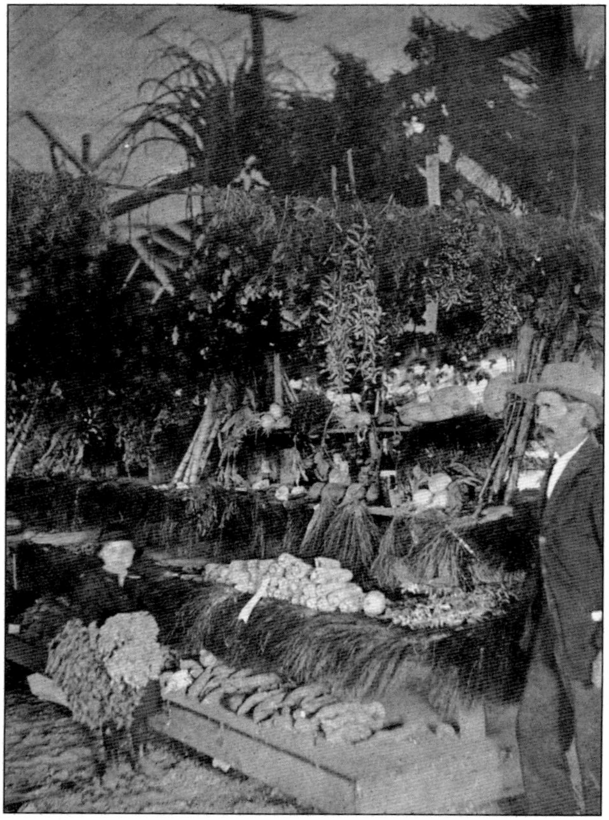

Participating at the 1914 Tyler County Fair, J.B. Riley and his daughter Mary admire their produce display. They celebrated success with many blue ribbons. Mary grew up to marry Lee Hudson, who operated a grade A commercial dairy. He shipped milk products by train to such far away destinations as Houston. The Hudsons also managed a very successful florist business. (Courtesy of TCHS.)

The 1857 cotton fields in Tyler County produced 2,017 bales of cotton. Some 462 slaves, valued at $197,524, contributed the labor to bring the cotton crop through the cycle from planting to market. The lands of the 83 cotton farmers generated a taxable value of $66,181. Twenty-seven of the farmers operated gins for processing their own cotton and that of their neighbors. Colmesneil farmers continued harvesting cotton into the 1920s. (Courtesy of CISD.)

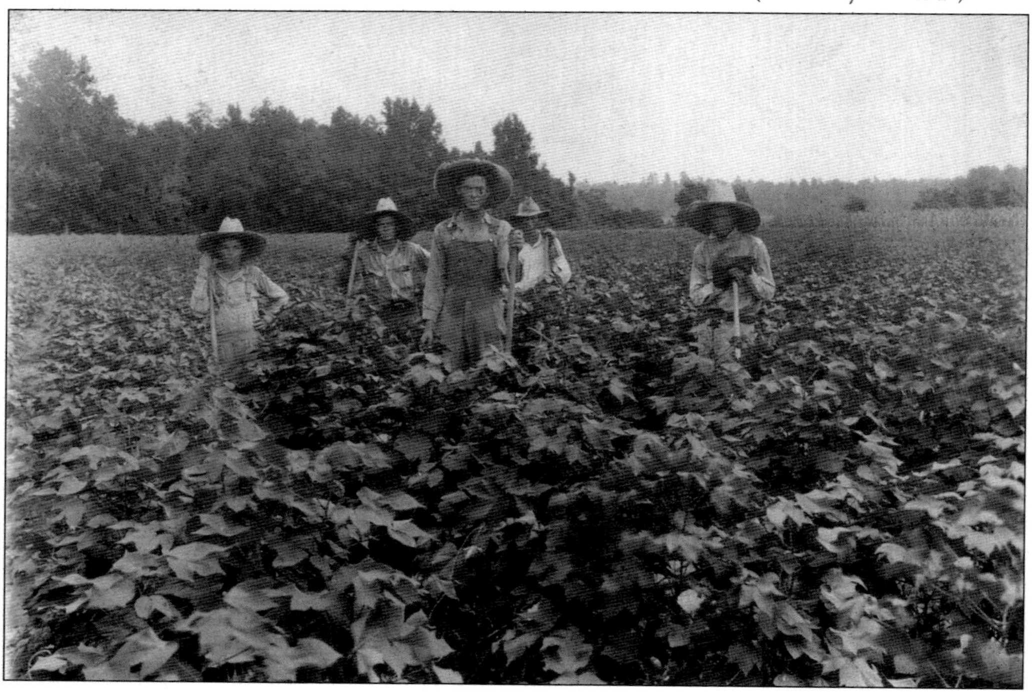

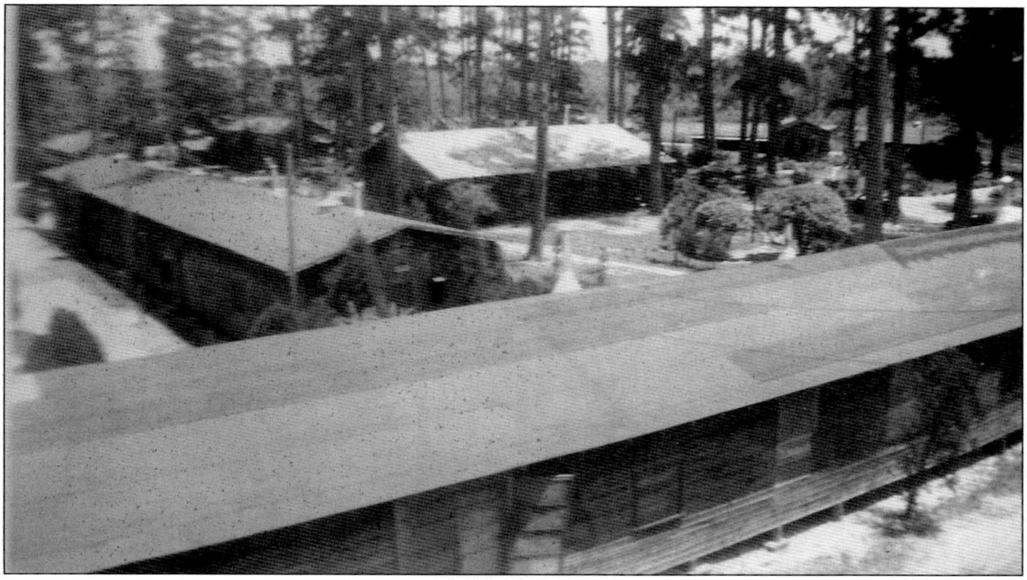

In 1932, the Civilian Conservation Corps (CCC) brought together two of America's most wasted resources: land and unemployed young men. Company 891, Camp Leonard Wood, located near today's Nutrition Center in Woodville, housed young men between the ages of 17 and 24 and put them to work in construction jobs for $30 per month. The work provided much needed income for workers and their families while it battled the destruction and erosion of natural resources. Workers used stones mined from nearby Rockland to construct schools at Chester, Warren, and Woodville. They also built a roadside park on US Highway 287 and a natural amphitheater in Woodville. Wade Best served as a cook for the unit until he went to work at Levingston Shipbuilding Company in Orange, finally joining the US Navy to serve in Japan during World War II. (Both, courtesy of Bertis Best.)

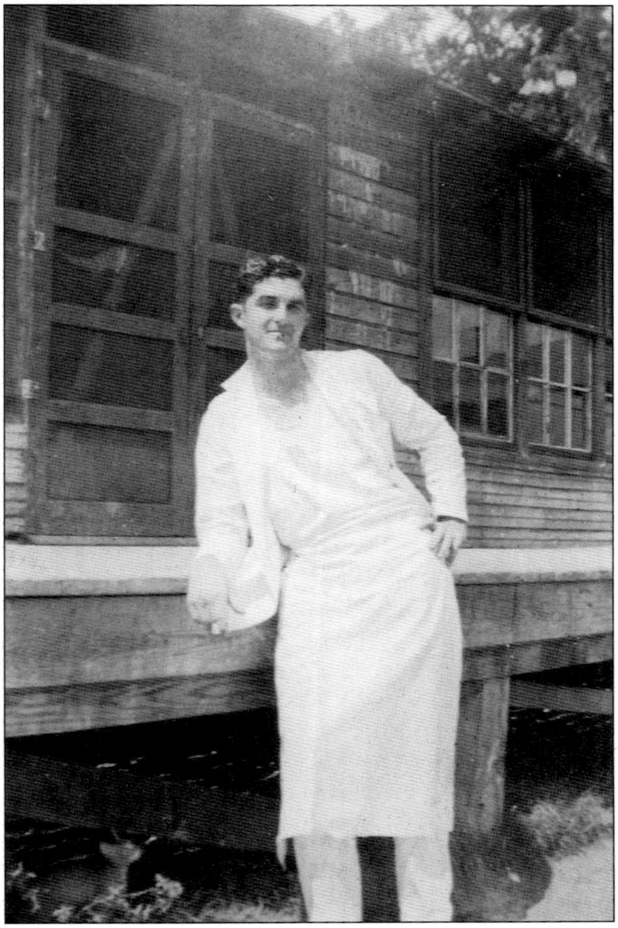

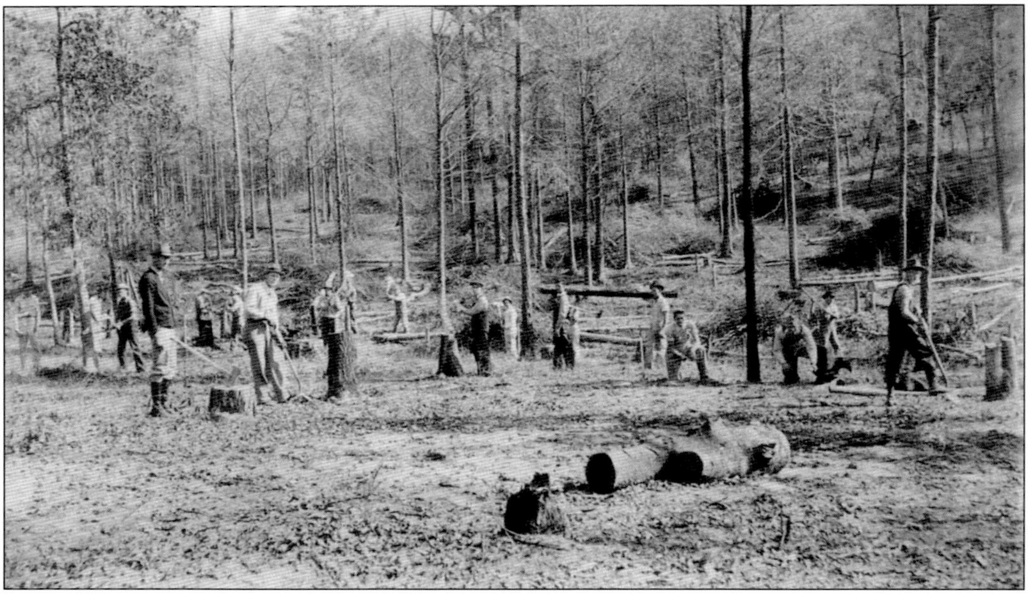

The Lake Tejas complex contains a 14-acre lake and 13 acres of parks and beaches on land donated to Colmesneil School by Lee Feagin, J.P. Mann, and D.P. Mann. The National Youth Administration (NYA) project began construction in 1939, and the dedication took place on July 24, 1940. Lee Taylor, CISD superintendent, oversaw the construction along with J.A. Kellum, state director for the NYA. Kellum commented at the dedication that, "Youth need three things: good health, good character, and good work habits." Applying those three qualities, young men cleared land and built a lake named for its shape and a large arrowhead found during excavation. The Indian name Tejas means "friendship." After 70 years of operation, an aerial view of the complex still reveals a lake whose shape resembles that of Texas's boundaries. Tejas still welcomes friends. (Both, courtesy of TCB.)

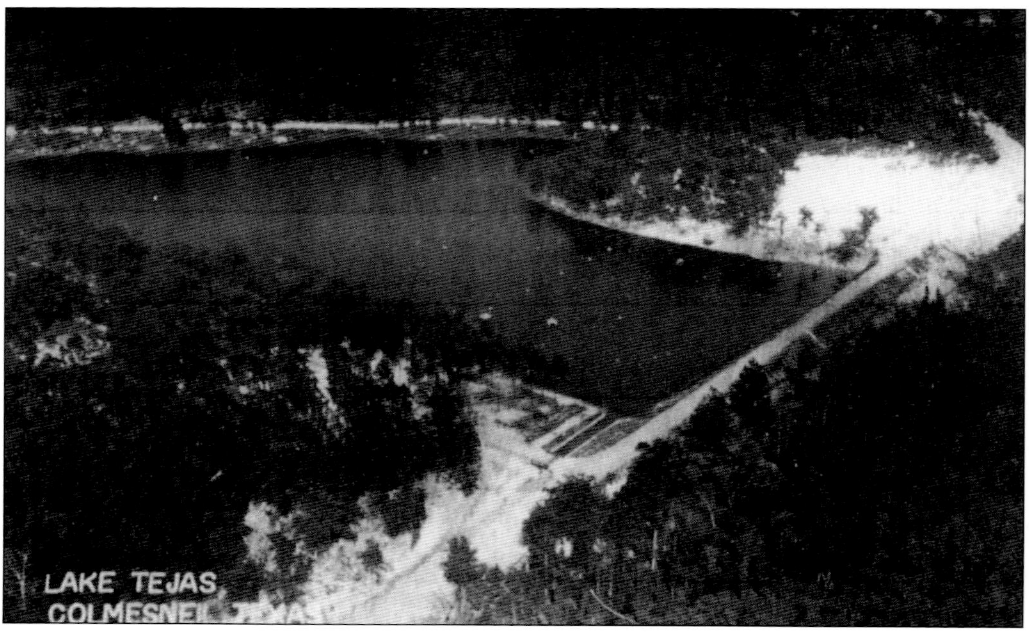

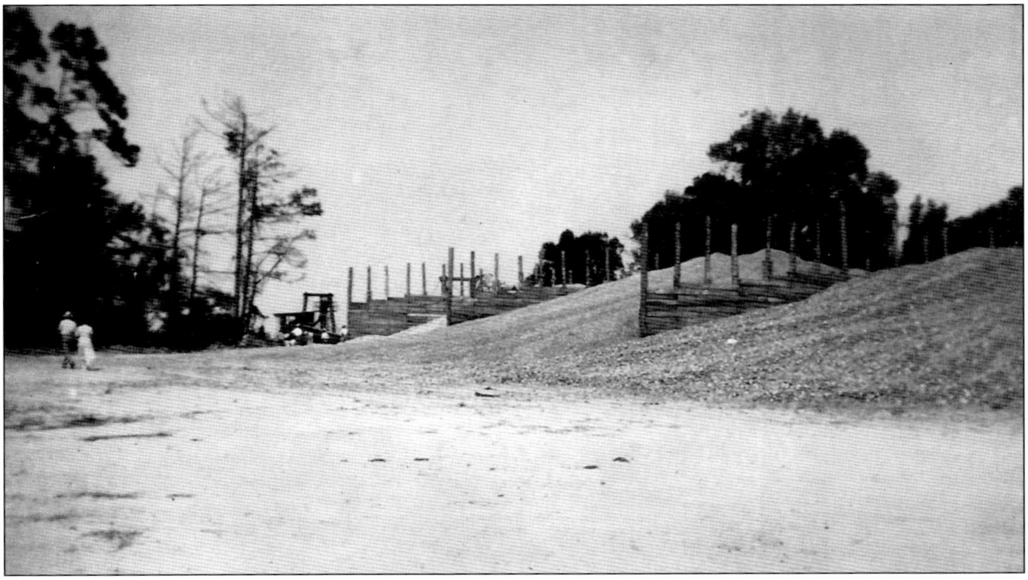

A few miles south of the confluence of the Angelina and Neches Rivers, near the original site of Town Bluff, Dam B regulates the flow of water to the Lower Neches Valley. Built in 1951 by the US Army Corps of Engineers, the project cost $7 million. Originally called the Town Bluff Dam by some (including Judge James E. Wheat, who described the project in a 1952 Tyler County Dogwood Festival publication), the working name for the project caught on with locals. The title, Dam B, extended beyond the concrete and steel edifice, and the dam applied its name to the surrounding community. Travelers on Highway 92 pass by an out-of-the-way granite monument that describes the original Town Bluff. Their attention is also directed to official green-and-white town signs as they drive into Dam B. (Both, courtesy of Johnny Dele Brown.)

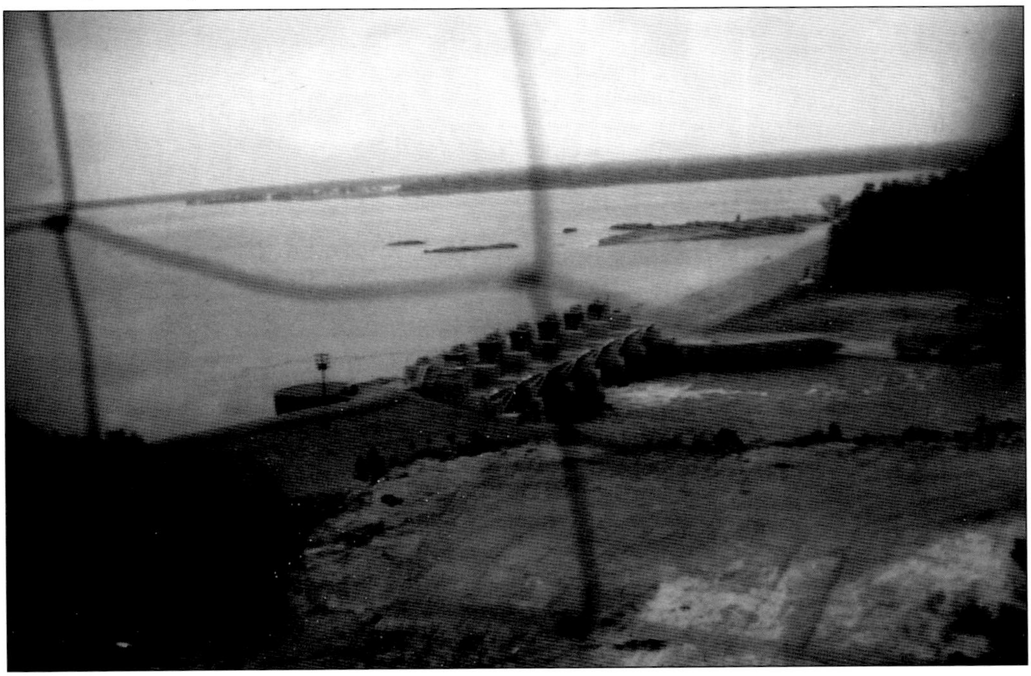

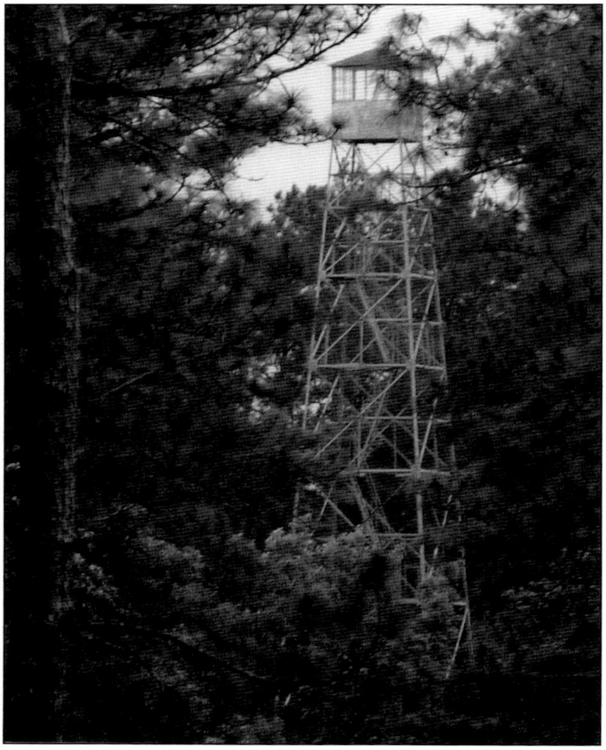

Before the age of aerial surveillance and satellite GPS maps, fire towers gave a vantage point for protecting the county's greatest natural resource: pine and hardwood forests. These towers dotted the landscape in strategic locations. They provided workstations for foresters and a challenge for teens seeking the excitement of a climb to the cab on top. (Courtesy of Warren Independent School District.)

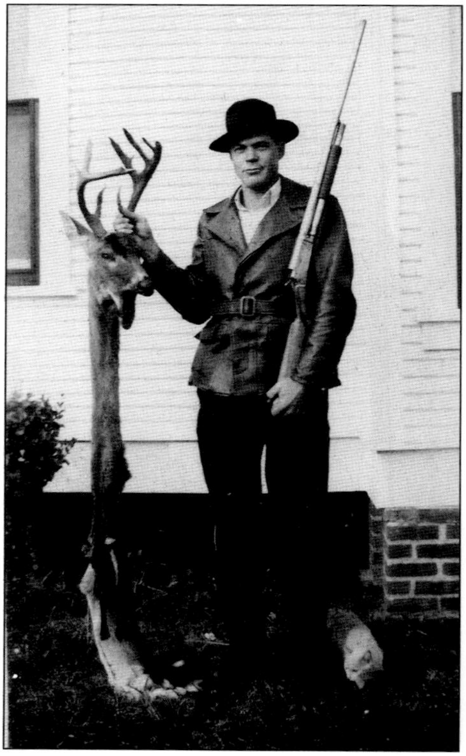

Jim Cawley, superintendent at Joe's Lake Refinery, might have shot this deer on the old Battle Axe hunting grounds east of Spurger. Since hunting with dogs had not been outlawed in 1942, he proudly declared the method used to track the wild game. A visit to the taxidermist would soon convert the sagging skin and drooping feet into a lifelike, full-mounted trophy. (Courtesy of Shirley Spurlock.)

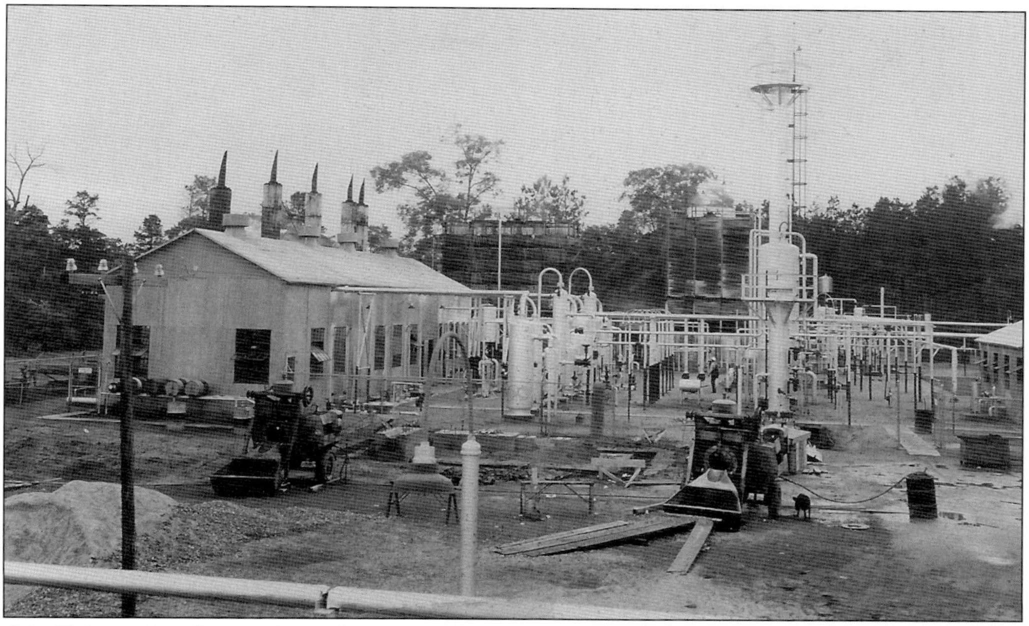

A half-dozen families made up the company town at Joe's Lake, just a few miles south of Spurger. Each family occupied a framed home that was provided by the company. The small neighborhood provided a safe and friendly environment for children's play. Three different companies operated the refinery over a span of three decades. American Republic Oil Company began the enterprise and later sold to Sinclair Oil and Refining Company. Atlantic Richfield Company (ARCO) owned the plant when it closed in 1964. In contrast to the small, local plant operation situated near the source of its raw material, 21st-century pipelines transmit Tyler County oil and gas to distant locations for refining. Thirty-six-inch pipes crisscross the county, collecting and moving millions of cubic feet of natural gas each month. (Above, courtesy of a friend; below, courtesy of Bob Boykin Photography.)

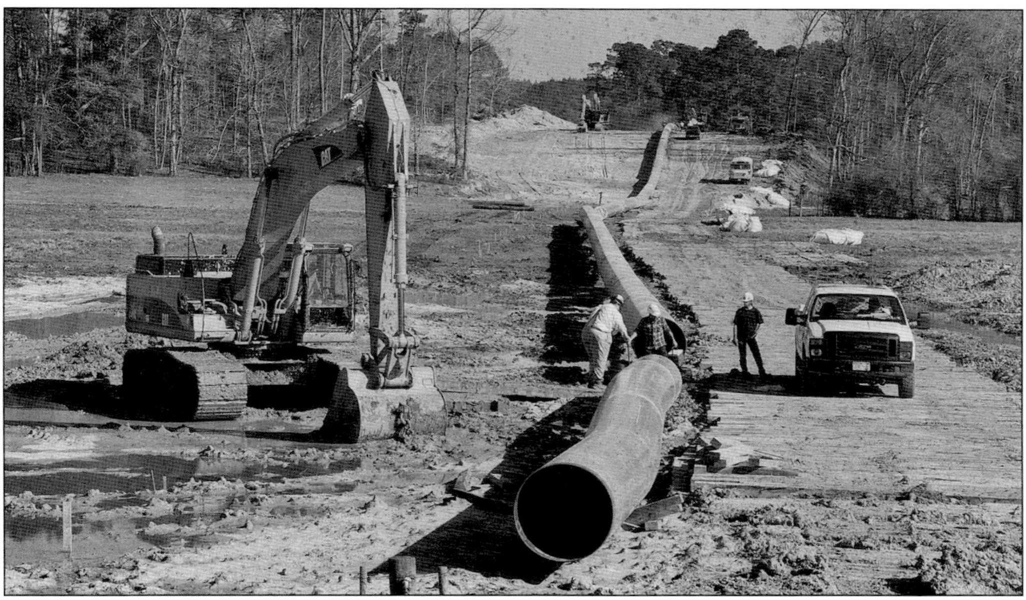

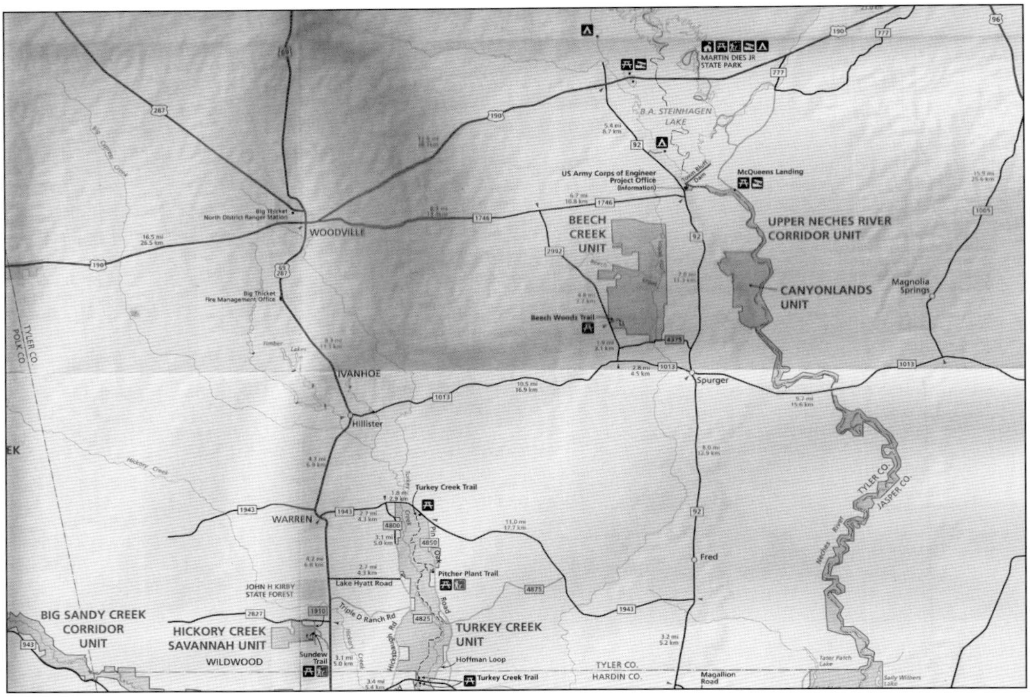

Of the Big Thicket National Preserve's 15 units, five have a presence in Tyler County. Visitors may float, hike, bird watch, ride bikes, picnic, and camp in this biological crossroads of North America. Four of our nation's five carnivorous plant species grow along the trails in the Preserve. Most notably, the pitcher plant makes a spectacular display in the Turkey Creek Unit during March and April each year. The Big Thicket Visitor Center, located on US Highway 69 just a short distance south of the Tyler County line, offers entertaining and informative displays. Many interactive exhibits introduce children to the rich heritage of the lower East Texas thicket where four ecosystems collided ages ago and survived peaceably side-by-side. (Above, courtesy of National Parks Service; below, courtesy of TCHC.)

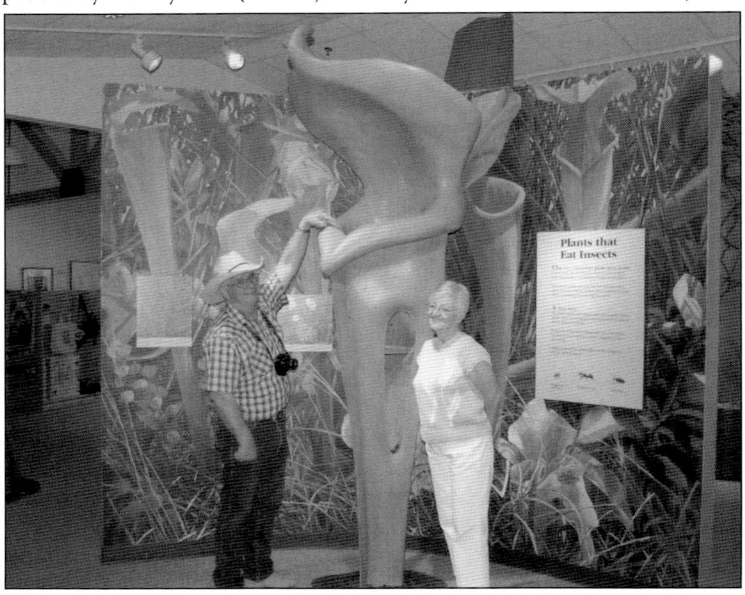

Three

Rivers, Rails, and Roads

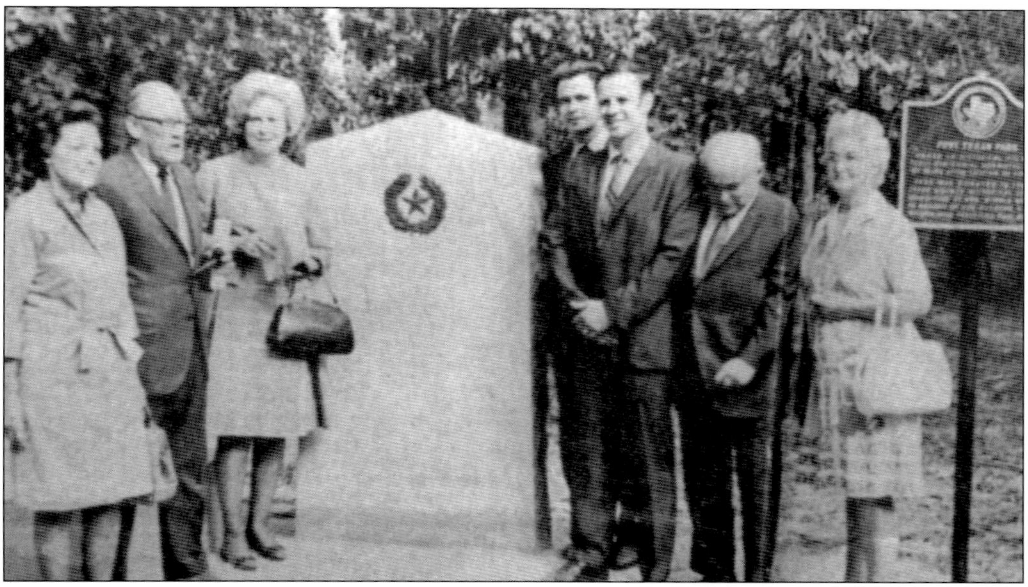

In 1968, a mere 132 years after Texas declared its independence from Mexico, the Tyler County Historical Survey Committee remarked the site of the county's first official river crossing. Commercial activities had ceased with the coming of railroads and the declining use of steamboats by farmers and travelers. Winnie H. Wilson of Houston donated the land for Fort Teran Park, honoring her husband who had tended the fort site. (Courtesy of TCB.)

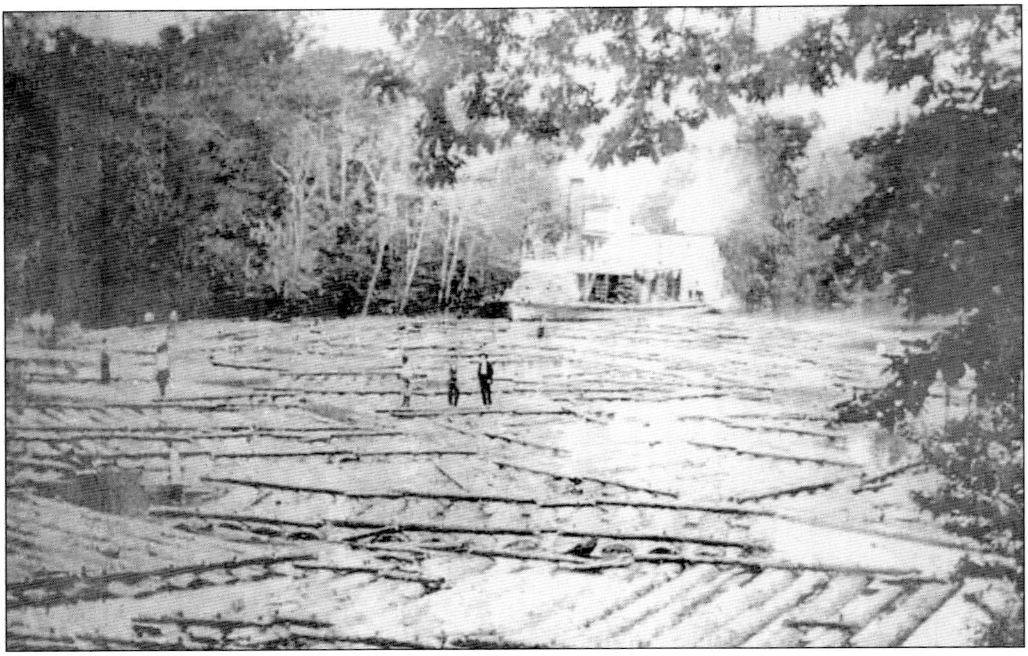

Rivers and rails provided the most efficient routes for connecting a farmer with his market before paved roads and diesel equipment came into the picture. Timbermen might spend an entire winter harvesting pine logs and binding them into rafts to be floated down the Neches River. Before cutting down the trees, crews would gird the trees with cuts near their bases to let sap drain out, thus deadening the logs, making them more buoyant and easier to manage in the river. While springtime meant woodsmen could deliver their timber to the market on the swollen river and its tributaries, children of those hardworking men could celebrate with May Day festivities. Miss Liberty and her court of school children paraded through the streets of Colmesneil to honor American freedoms. (Above, courtesy of CISD; below, courtesy of TCHC.)

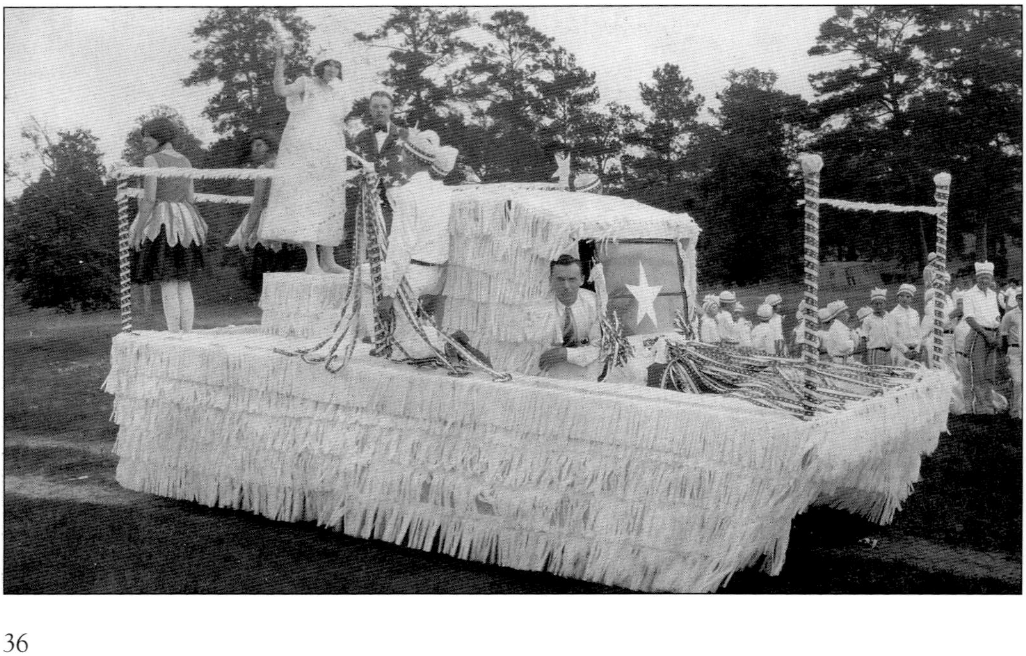

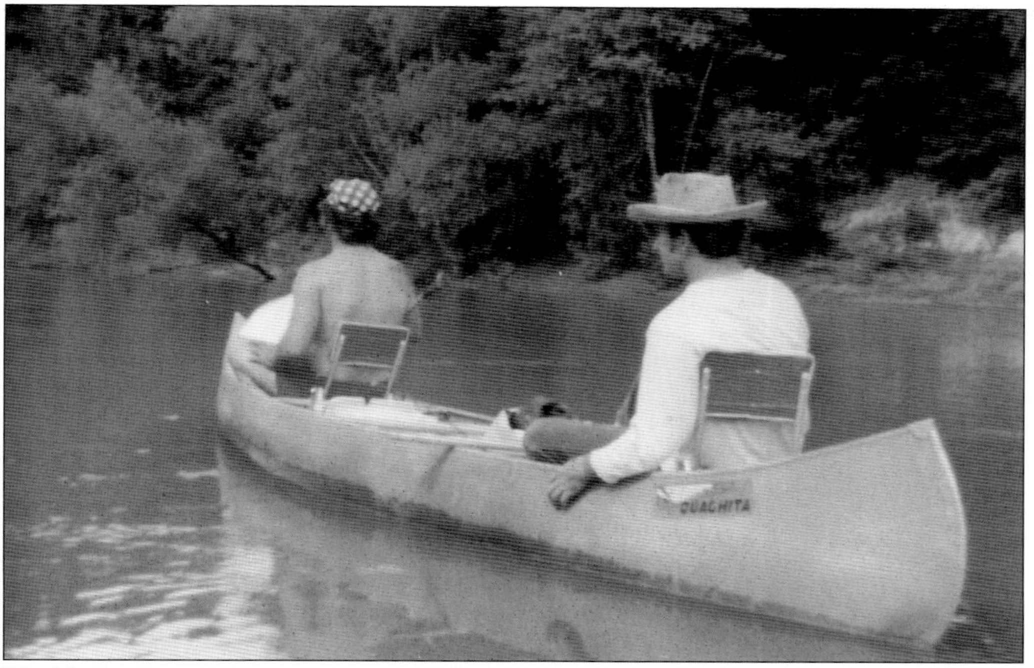

The Neches River attracts sportsmen of all types. Known for its sandy beaches and picturesque views, the river welcomes fishermen in boats and canoes in every season of the year. A popular sport in the 1970s included canoeing from US Highway 59, near Diboll, to US Highway 69, north of Rockland, camping overnight before continuing to Recreation Road 255, and finally to Martin Dies State Park on Lake Steinhagen. Local naturalist Jackie Blakney organized many such float trips, and only the river knows the true stories those adventures spawned. Campers enthusiastically shared the sand bars with alligators—ideally, not at the same time. (Both, courtesy of TCHC.)

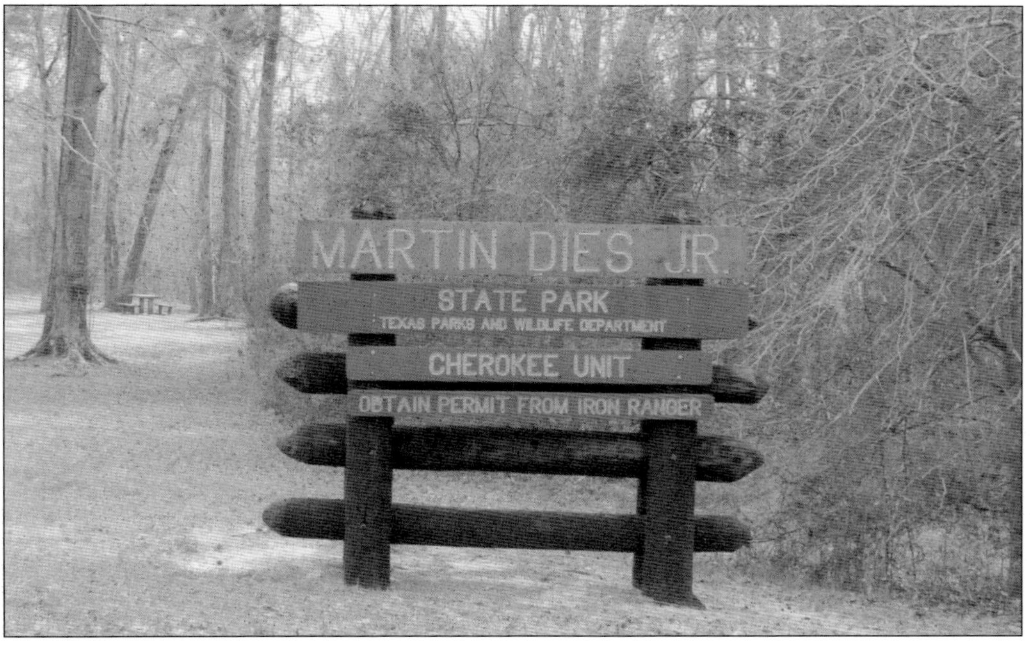

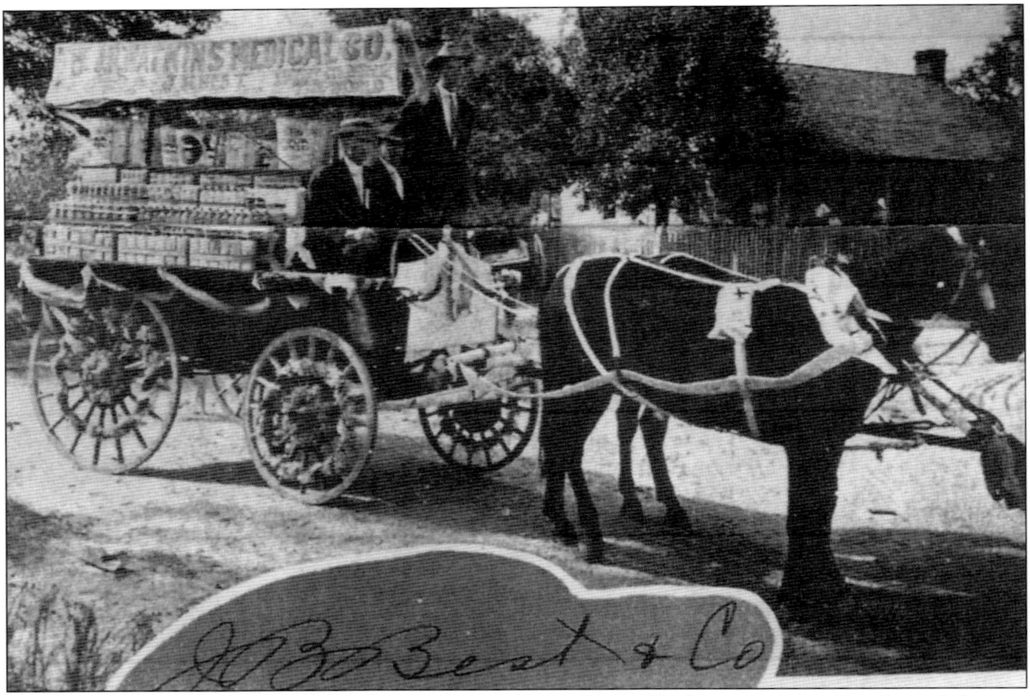

Julius Britton Best travelled throughout Tyler County, offering Watkins products for sale and sharing news among the communities. Occasionally, he ventured into such communities as Midway in neighboring Polk County. There he met the beautiful Alma McKee whom he later married. The couple settled in Woodville and established J.B. Best and Company—a general merchandise store offering such goods as feed, seed, coffee, tobacco, lace, and linens. (Courtesy of Huntley Kenesson.)

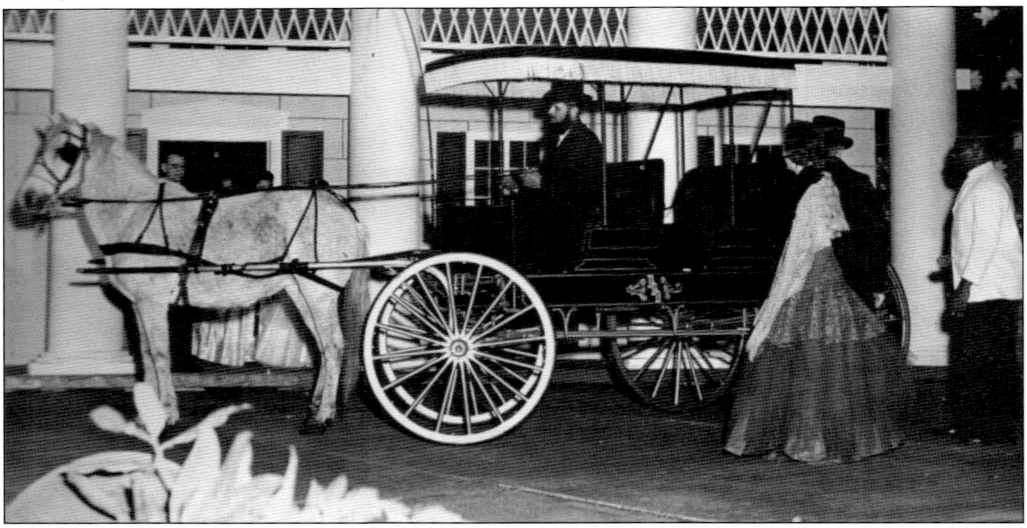

Tyler County Dogwood Festivals featured historical pageants to entertain the royal court beginning in the 1940s. Judge James E. Wheat, festival founder, conducted research and wrote about a different strand of county history each year. His 1956 writings reported on the "Era of Elegance" that had existed in Tyler County 100 years earlier. Live animals made regular appearances on the Dogwood Amphitheater stage, reenacting modes of travel in early days. (Courtesy of TCDF.)

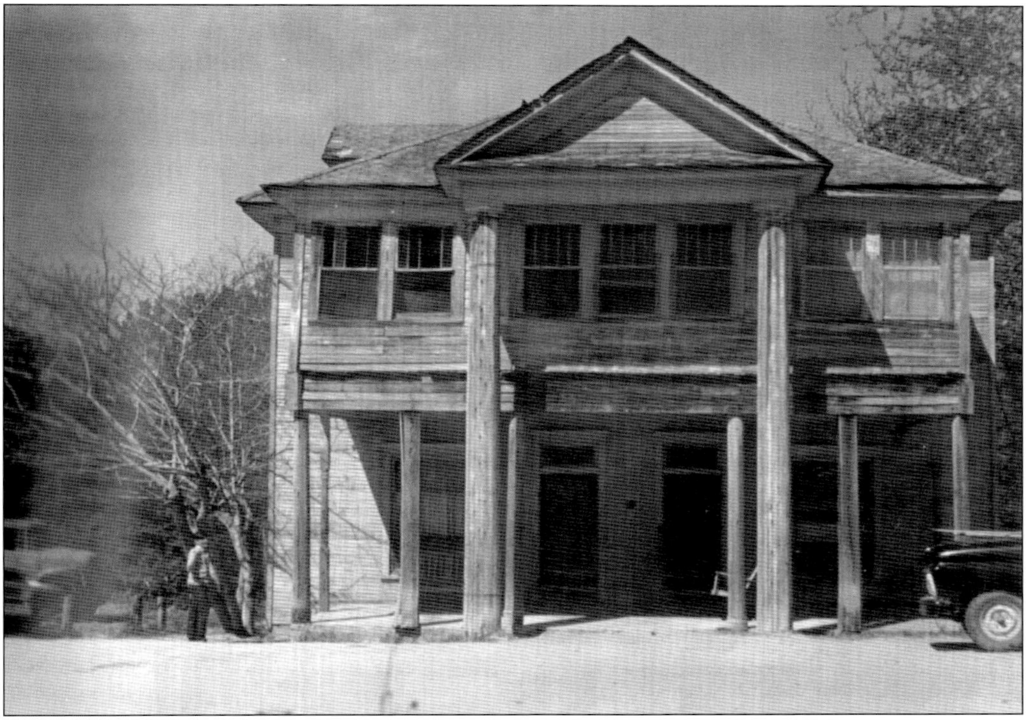

Mrs. Leggett ran the Commercial Hotel, which was originally named the Collier Hotel. When she married Dave Russell (a business associate of T.H. Neyland), Jim Milliner bought the hotel. He sold it to John Mann Sr. Other proprietors of the impressive hotel included Issac Hayes and Tom Abbott. (Courtesy of CISD.)

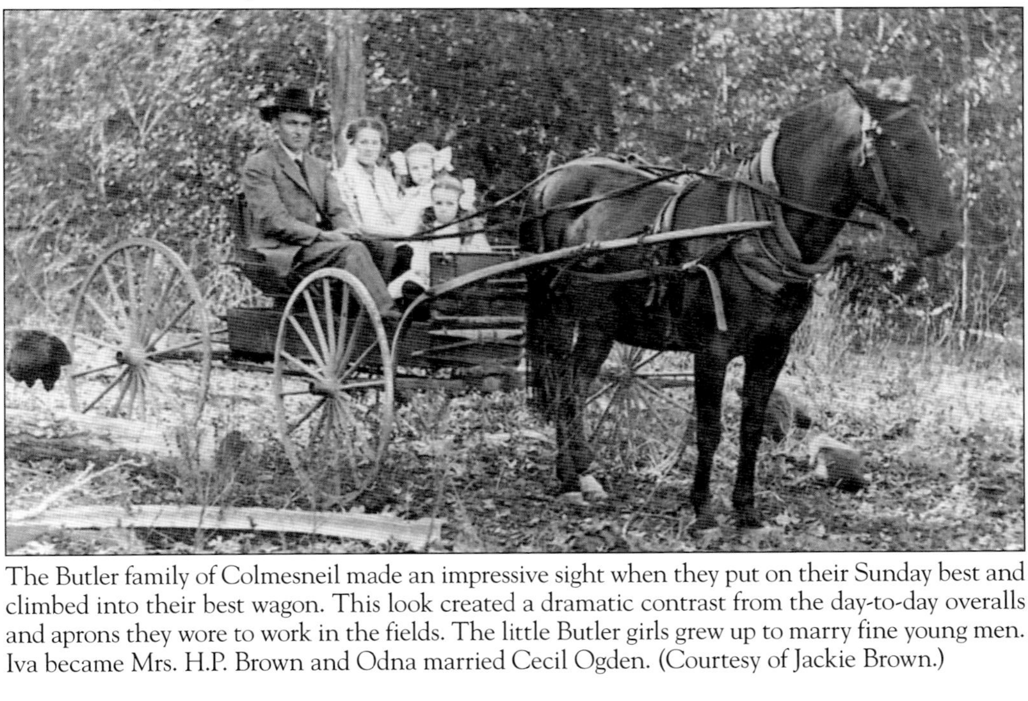

The Butler family of Colmesneil made an impressive sight when they put on their Sunday best and climbed into their best wagon. This look created a dramatic contrast from the day-to-day overalls and aprons they wore to work in the fields. The little Butler girls grew up to marry fine young men. Iva became Mrs. H.P. Brown and Odna married Cecil Ogden. (Courtesy of Jackie Brown.)

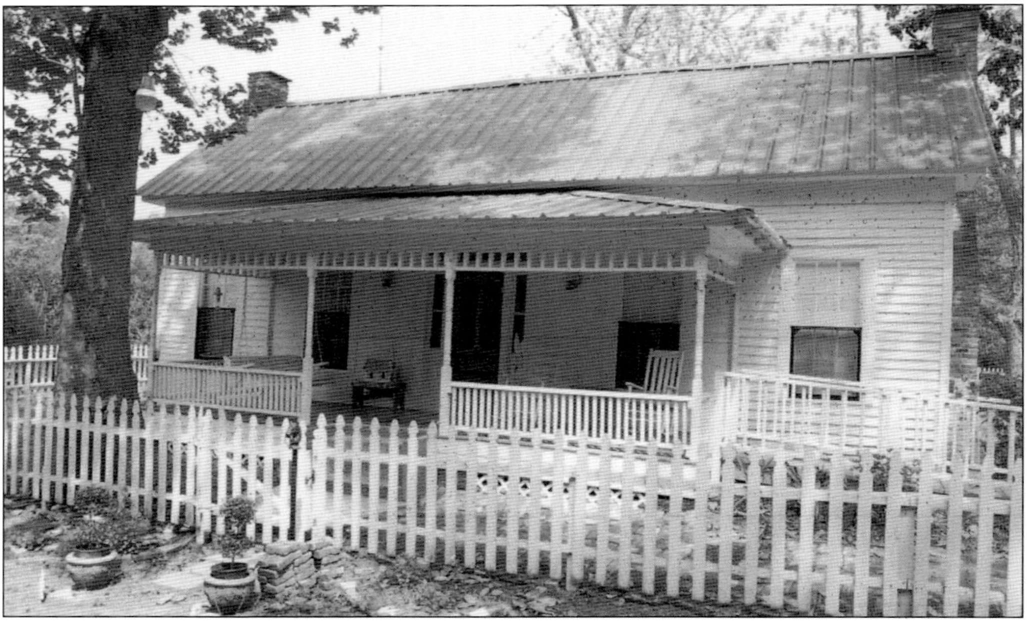

William Neyland gave Colmesneil its name, honoring the conductor of the first passenger train that came into the area. Neyland divided property he owned to create a town where the north-south T&NO railroad met with the east-west T&S (called the Katy) railroad. Conductor W.T. Colmesneil acquired a lot and built his home facing the railroad tracks so he could watch the trains pass by. Lying just north of the Katy line was the community of Ogden, whose population when added to Colmesneil's exceeded 3,000 people. The Yellow Pine Tram and Lumber Company gave employment to hundreds of workers in both the logging woods and a sawmill. Hotels such as the East Texas (below) and the Fortenberry provided lodging for workers and traveling businessmen. Passengers rested between trains at these hotels, perhaps enjoying such fancy foods as chicken and dumplings. (Above, courtesy of TCHC; below, courtesy of CISD.)

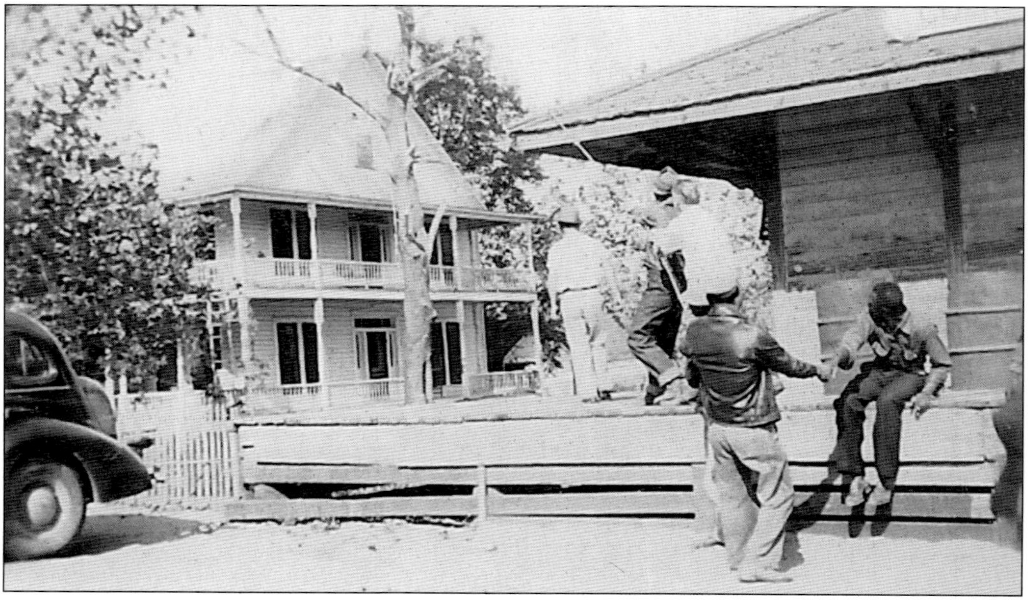

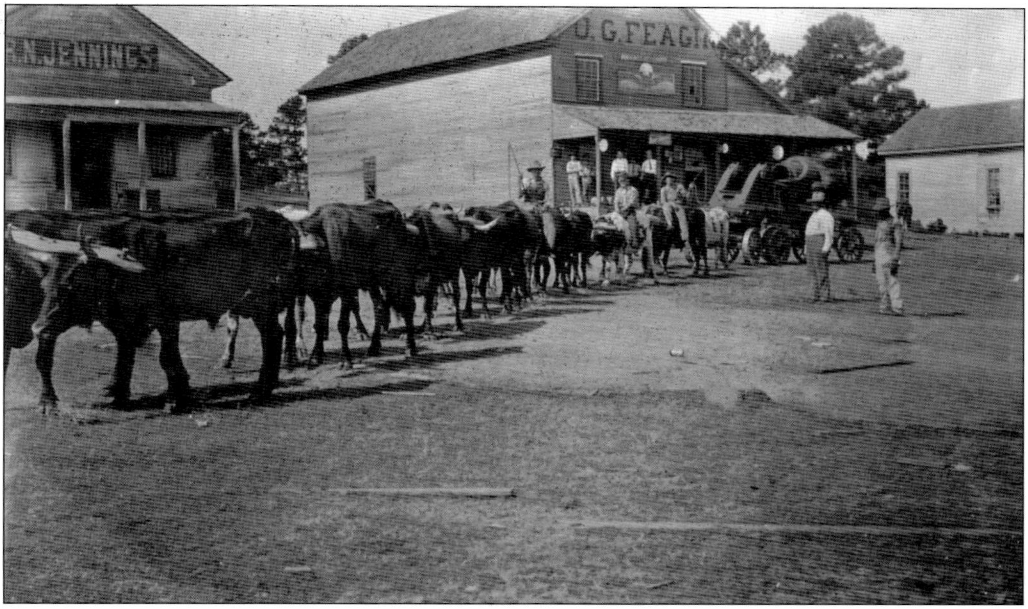

When the pump station was built near Chester, these oxen brought some of the heavy machinery from Corpus Christi. Uncle Tom Seaman oversaw the 330-mile trip. Having walked more than 100 miles to return home from the Civil War, Seaman did not hesitate to face the longer adventure from the coast. The hope of a pump station, which he thought would bring economic growth to Tyler County, made the expedition worthwhile. (Courtesy of TCHS.)

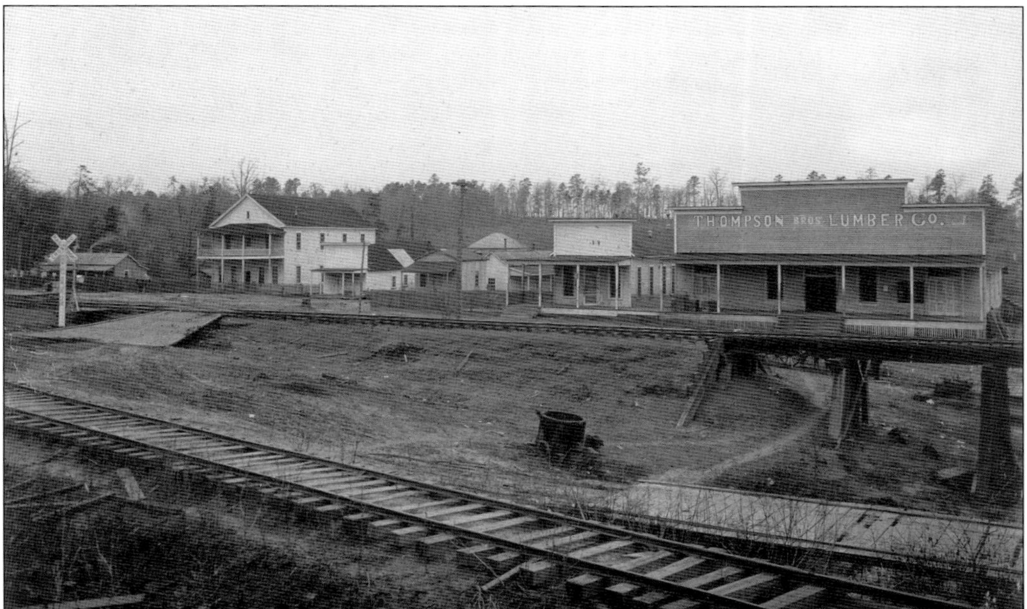

The Thompson brothers operated numerous sawmills in lower East Texas. Their Doucette operation, one of the largest and most prosperous mills in the area, took advantage of the Texas and New Orleans rail line that ran from Beaumont to Dallas. The Thompsons also used tram road spurs to bring logs in from logging sites. (Courtesy of TFM.)

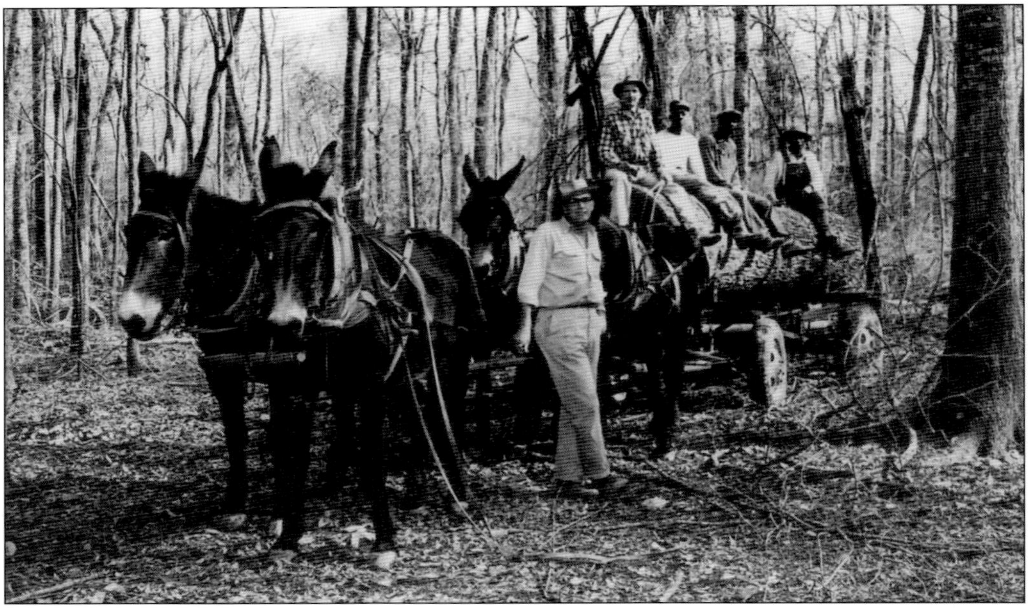

Although longleaf pine dominated Tyler County forests, hardwood trees also contributed to the landscape. Most noted for the beauty of their colorful leaves, hardwoods also met an economic need. This majestic red oak tree might have been on its way to a flooring mill, or perhaps it would become furniture. (Courtesy of Warren Independent School District.)

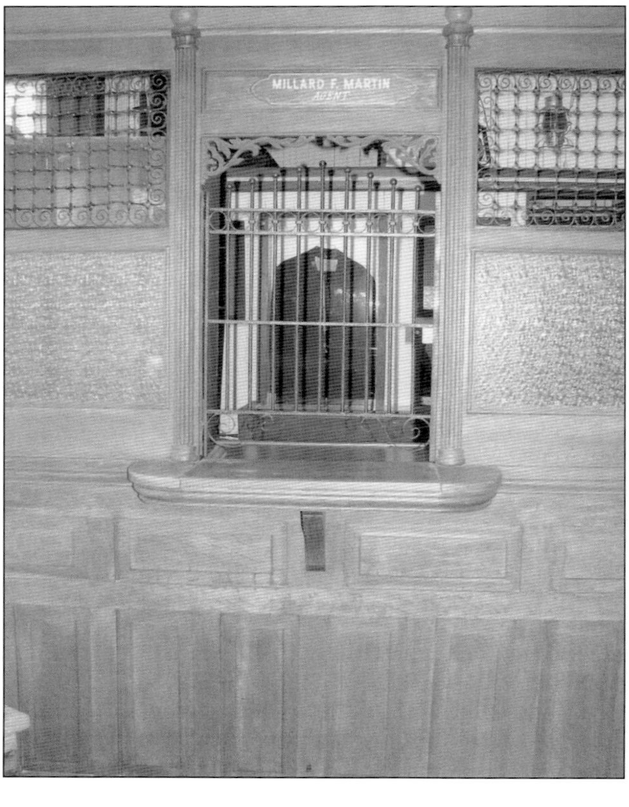

Hearty 19th-century pioneers arriving by train in Hillister could expect first-class service from agent Millard F. Martin. They found their ride to be far superior to the stagecoach and wagon treks reported by their predecessors. Baggage cars made room for personal items and furnishings brought from "back home" in Mississippi, Georgia, or Alabama. Wagons waited to deliver their belongings the last few miles to home. (Courtesy of TCHC.)

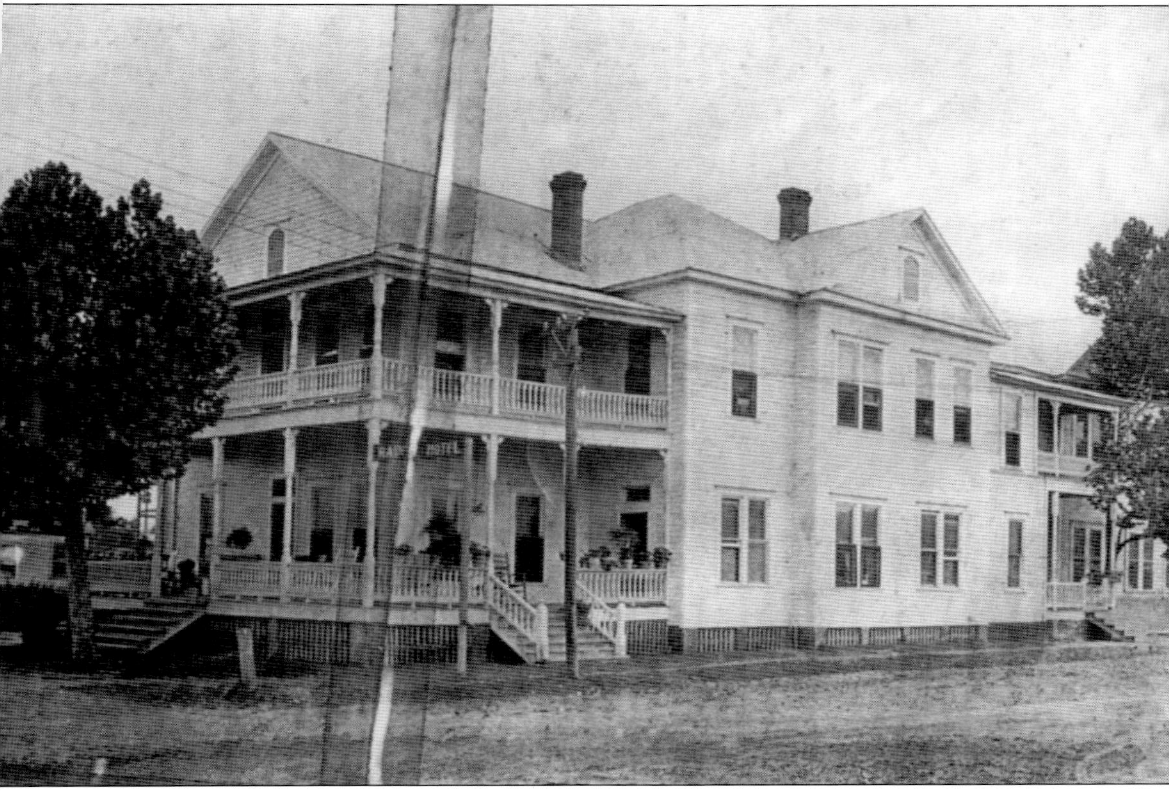

The Rainey Hotel, earlier known as the Stewart Hotel, was located in Woodville at the corner of Bluff and Beaver Streets. On January 14, 1925, a deed conveyed the hotel's title from Mollie Stewart to S.L. Rainey. Located diagonally across from the depot and facing the railroad tracks, the hotel had 27 bedrooms, a large lobby, dining room, kitchen, and two wraparound porches. L.M. Feagin, Dave Mann, Joe Shillings, and others roomed there, sleeping on an upstairs, screened porch in the summertime. During court sessions, judges, lawyers, and others involved in court proceedings crowded the hotel. Traveling salesmen, called drummers, arrived on passenger trains and stayed at the hotel. Ettle Rainey drove them all around the county in a Model T jitney, so they could peddle their wares. Delicious meals, served boardinghouse style, drew customers from across the region—especially for Sunday dinner after church. (Courtesy of Rainey Family.)

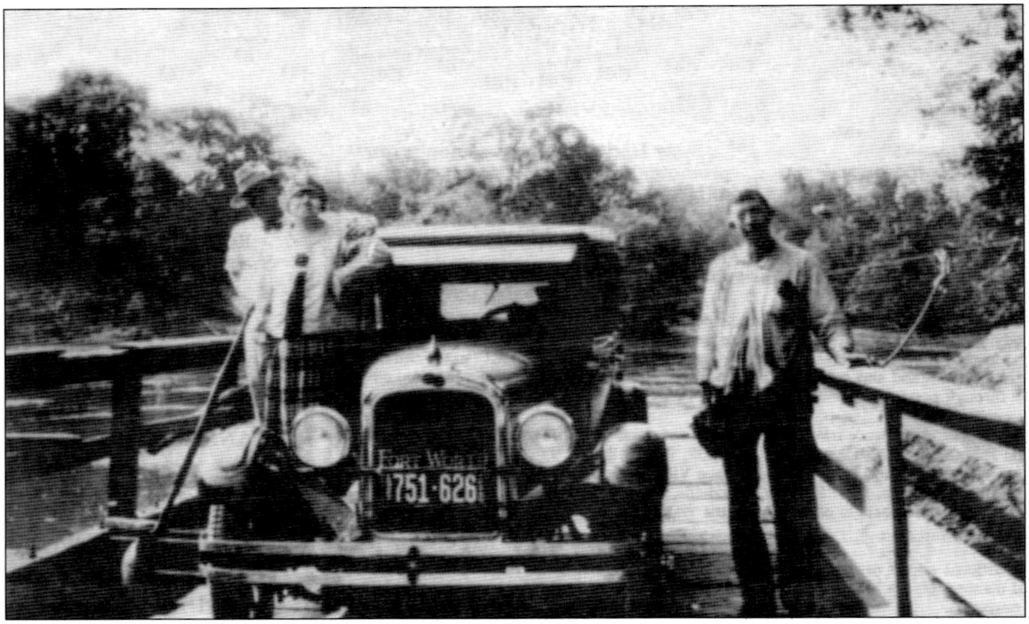

Infamous bank robbers Bonnie Parker and Clyde Barrow (pictured at left) sparked local interest when they appeared at the Neches River wanting to cross on the Rockland Ferry. Legend has it that once on the south side of the river, the couple continued to Colmesneil and enjoyed a malt at Bendy Drug Store. (Courtesy of *Cracker Barrel Journal.*)

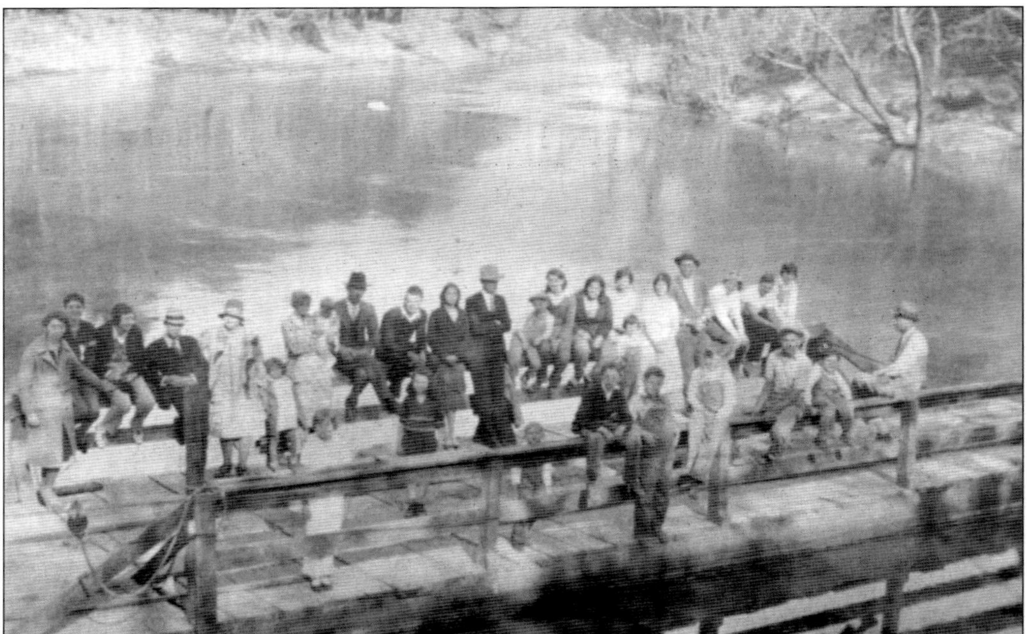

A more common occurrence at the Rockland Ferry was the regular traffic of families going across the river for a picnic. The Saturday, May 8, 1920, edition of the *Tyler County Messenger* recorded such a trip. Picnic baskets must have been loaded into a car or pickup truck that would follow the party-goers. (Courtesy of ASLM.)

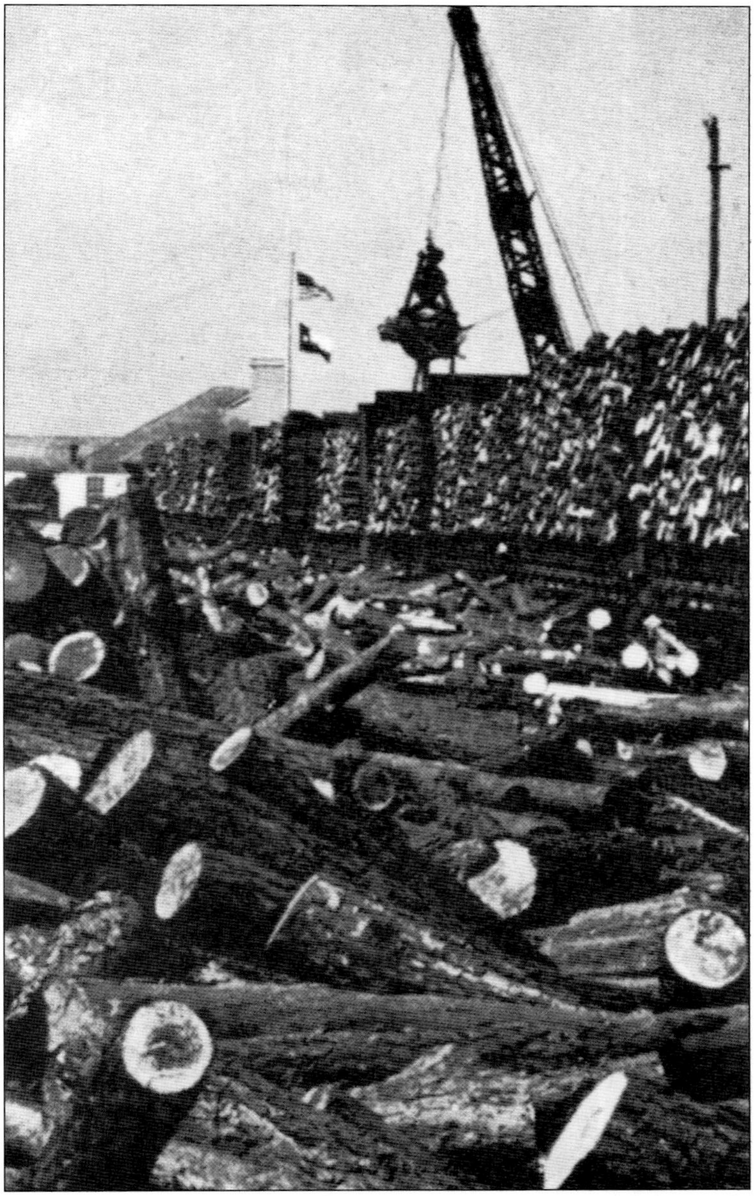

Through the years, East Texas paper mills have generated a continual demand for pulpwood chips. At the same time, timber growers needed to manage their forests by thinning out the smaller trees so that larger trees would grow faster. The smaller trees provided pulpwood and played a vital role in the cycle of transforming trees into paper. Pulpwood haulers loaded and delivered the small trees to chipping mills, where they would be weighed, unloaded in the yard, transferred to the debarker, and finally fed into the chipper. Trucks weighed in with full loads, dumped their logs, and then returned to the scales for final weighing so that the tonnage of their loads could be calculated. When railroads still provided a good network throughout the county, pulpwood often arrived at the chipping mill loaded onto train cars. The process of unloading those logs became safer and less labor intensive as the industry moved from mule teams to steam engines and then finally to diesel-powered cranes. (Courtesy of TFM.)

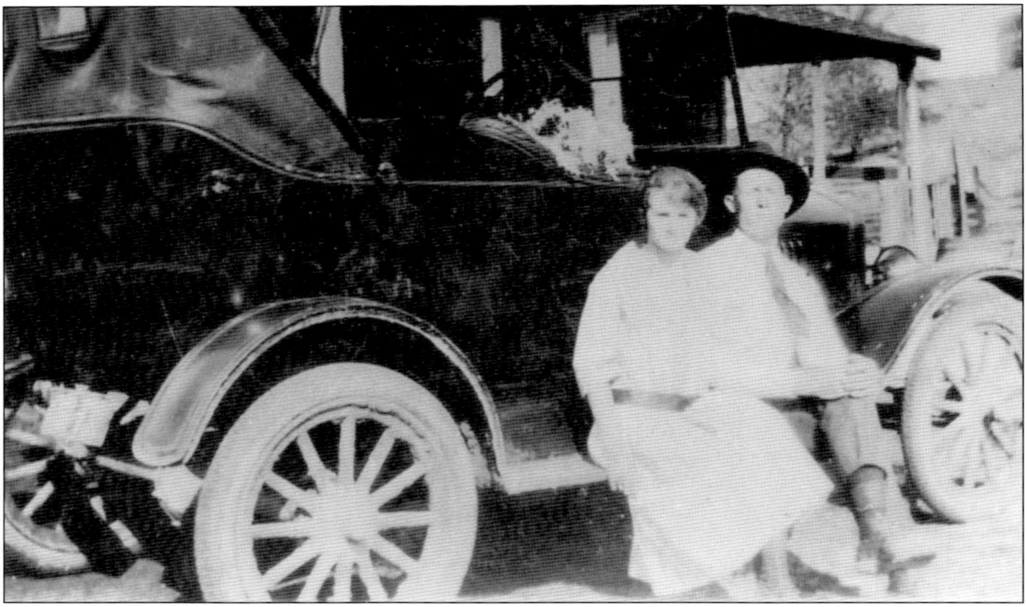

H.P. and Iva Brown celebrated their newlywed status by posing for a photograph on the running board of their new Ford Touring Car. Although Ogden had lost some of its population with the burning of the Yellow Pine Tram and Lumber Company in 1893, the sister town of Colmesneil continued to prosper. The Browns settled there and raised a fine family of sons: James Harold, Travis, and Kenneth. (Courtesy of Jackie Brown.)

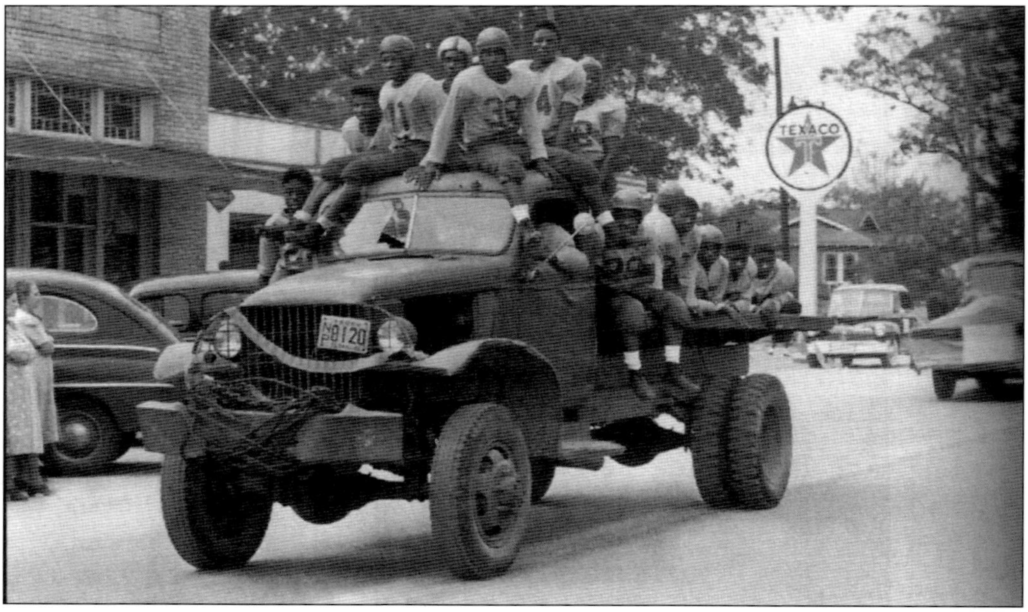

Henry T. Scott High School in Woodville celebrated its 1947 homecoming with a parade on Saturday and a spirited football game that was played on the shared Kirby High School field. The Scott High Panthers showed their enthusiasm for the occasion as they passed in front of Adams' Texaco station and Roy Pate's Store on their float—a vehicle used the previous day to haul loads of lumber to some unknown destination. (Courtesy of Mayme Canada Brown.)

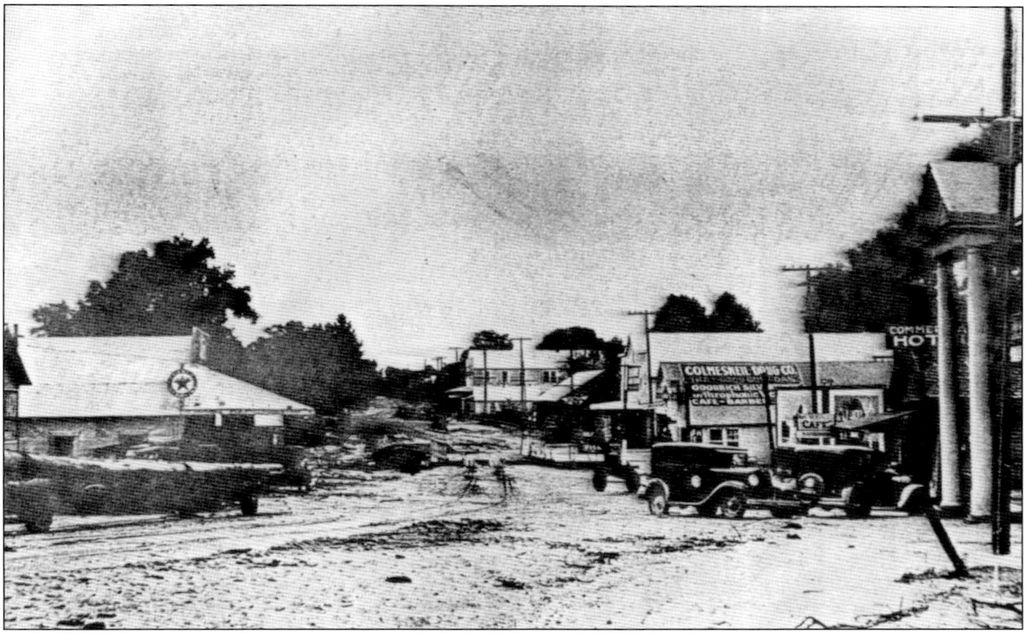

Paved streets began to appear in Tyler County in the early 1940s. Prior to that time, Colmesneil pedestrians counted themselves lucky to find boardwalks for crossing muddy streets. Mud was only one hazard. Stock laws did not exist, meaning hogs and other livestock often roamed at will, causing streets to sometimes resemble stock pens and chicken yards. (Courtesy of CISD.)

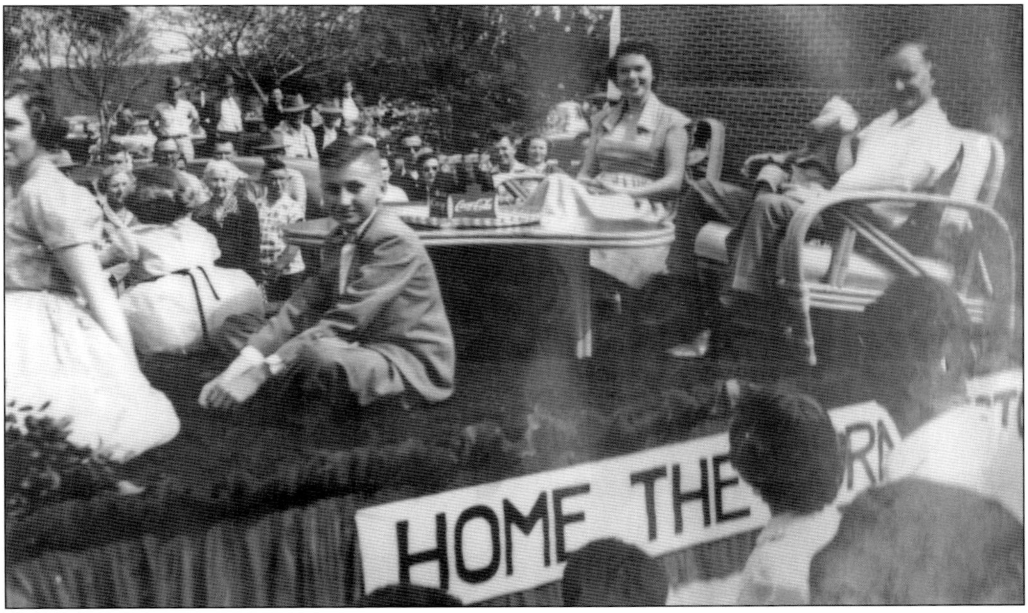

The Beech Creek Home Demonstration Club received its charter in March 1941 and became the first such club located in Tyler County. Club members took training in a wide range of home improvement techniques and appliances. In addition to raising, preserving, and preparing nutritious foods, the club also promoted community improvements. It mounted a successful campaign to bring telephones into Spurger homes in 1953. (Courtesy of Beech Creek Home Demonstration Club.)

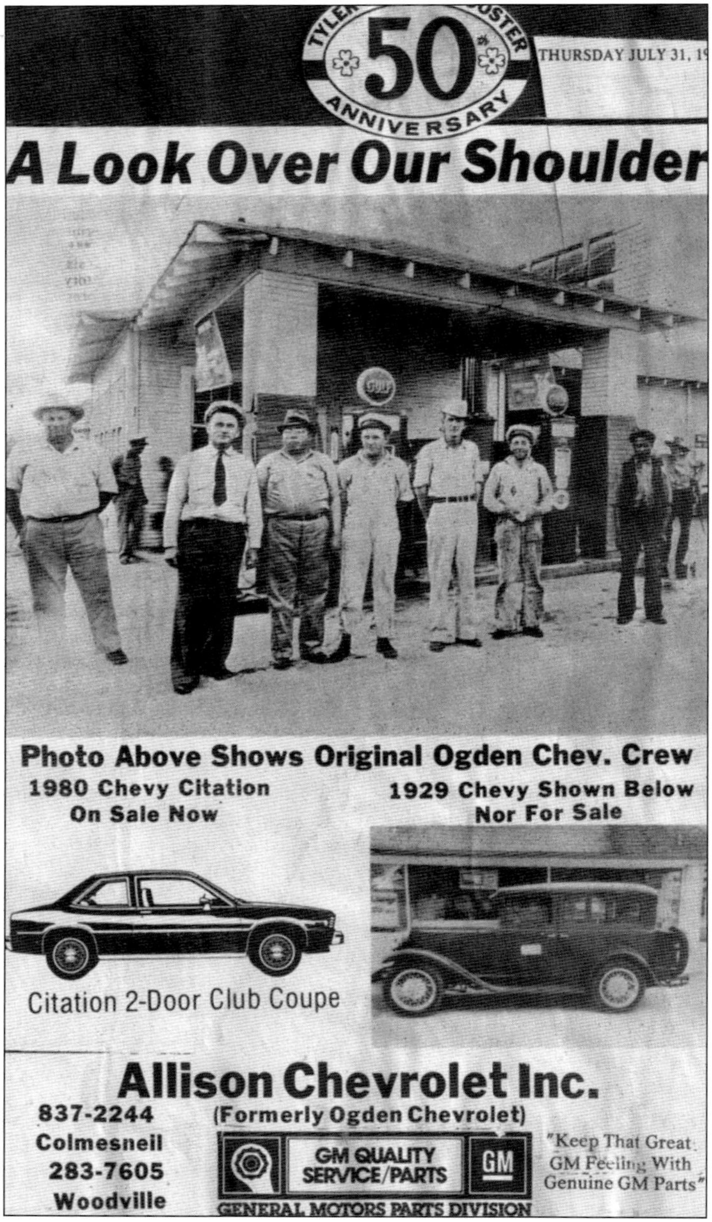

Cecil and Odna Ogden operated their Chevrolet dealership in Colmesneil for almost 50 years before they sold it to Robert Allison in March 1980. Selling cars and trucks gave the business its official purpose, but the heart of the business was all about relationships. The Ogdens took a personal interest in the people of their community, and they did whatever it took to see the businesses, churches, and schools of the county prosper. Many repeat customers came from hundreds of miles away to do business with their friends in Colmesneil. New owners Robert and Earlene Allison continued the tradition of giving personal attention to their customers and providing support for activities and projects in their home county. Loyal employees first hired by the Ogdens continued with the Allisons as they expanded the business to include dealerships in Woodville and Jasper. (Courtesy of TCB.)

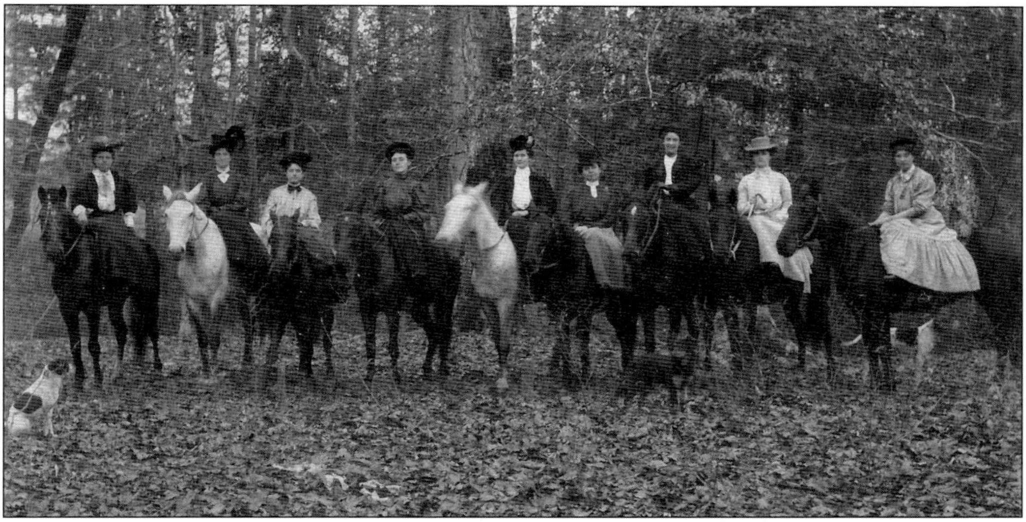

An inscription on the reverse of this image names all but two of the ladies, who were setting out for an entertaining ride. From left to right, the first and eighth riders remain unknown. Others are Lila Pennington, Mrs. George W. Collier, Lula Collier Wickline, Odessa Murphy Lowe, Kate Billingsley Rock, Monique Doucette Minter, and Lucille Rock Daily. (Courtesy of TCHS.)

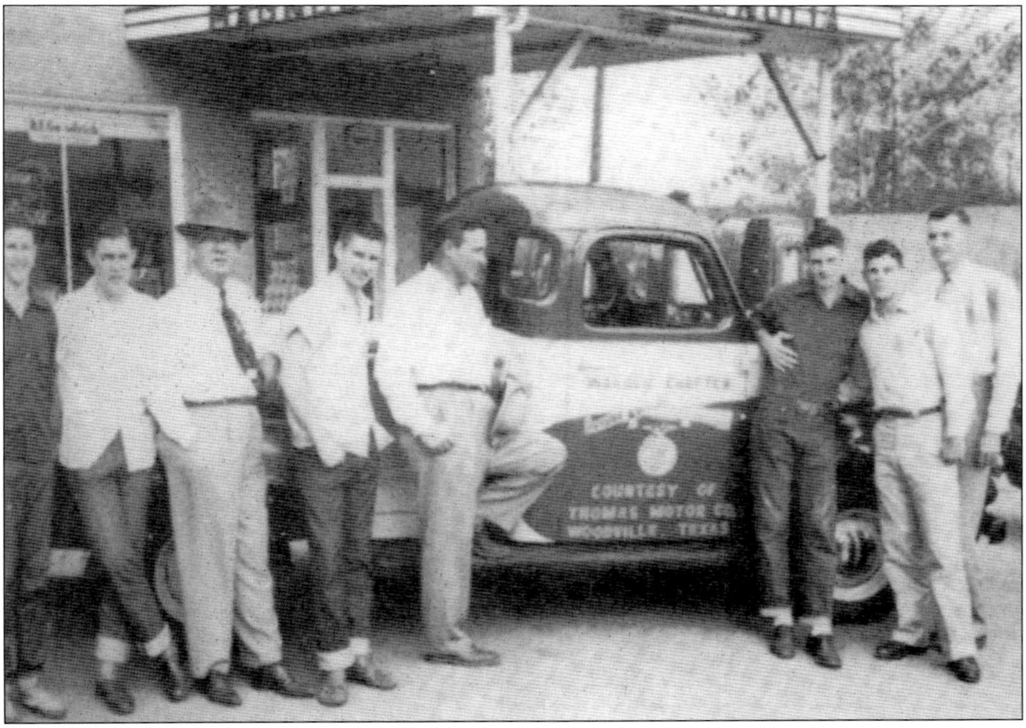

The Warren High School Chapter of the Future Farmers of America enjoys a long history of prize-winning members. The community has always encouraged students to apply what they learn at school to their jobs in local businesses, farms, and ranches. As a reward for hard work, Thomas Motor Company presented the chapter members with a truck for use in their school projects. (Courtesy of Warren Independent School District.)

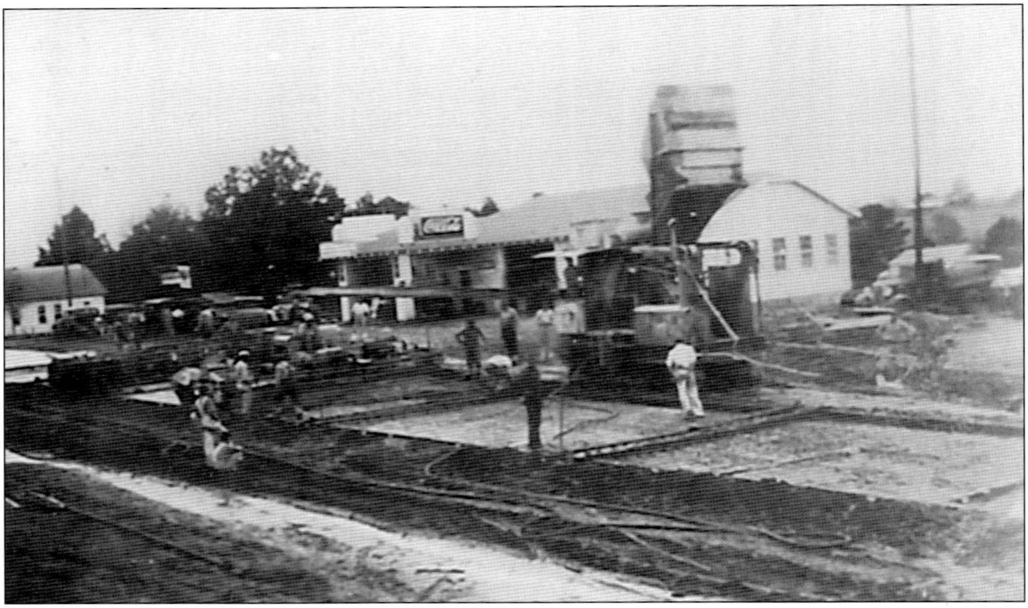

Highway 40 (now US Highway 69) revolutionized transportation in Tyler County when it arrived with two lanes of paved roads in 1938–1939. Travel between towns no longer relied on train schedules. Now, those with automobiles did not need to wait for dry weather before planning a trip to visit family or friends in Colmesneil, Doucette, Woodville, Hillister, or Warren. (Courtesy of CISD.)

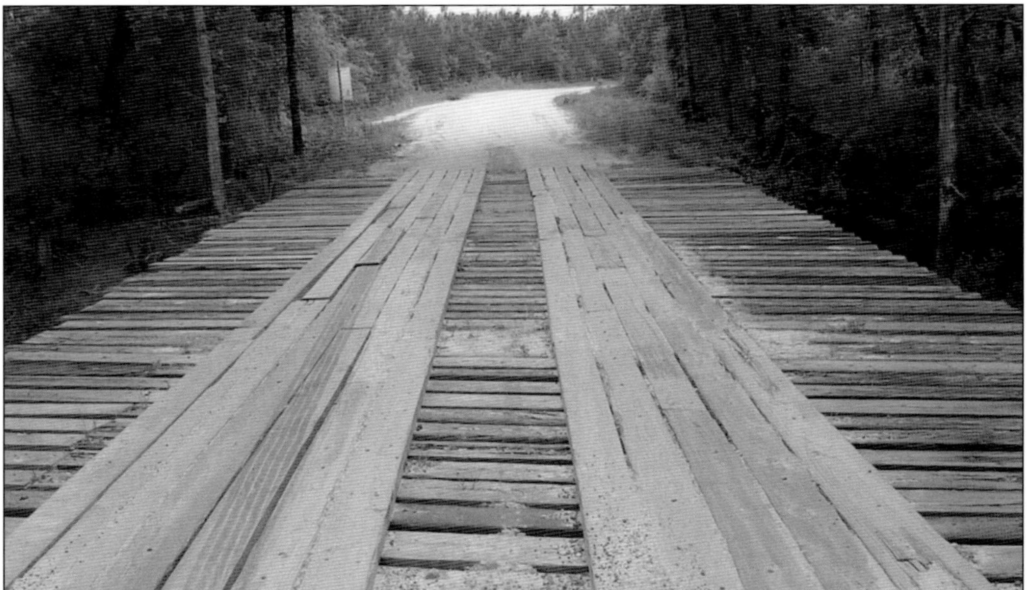

Sometimes highway traveling is important; other times, a leisurely drive through the countryside is "just what the doctor ordered." When dogwoods bloom or autumn leaves spread waves of color across hardwood forests, that is the time to enjoy the simple life and beautiful scenery found on country roads. Teens loved the challenge of learning to drive across creeks on bridges (like Hicksbaugh) with board runners and open sides. (Courtesy of Warren Independent School District.)

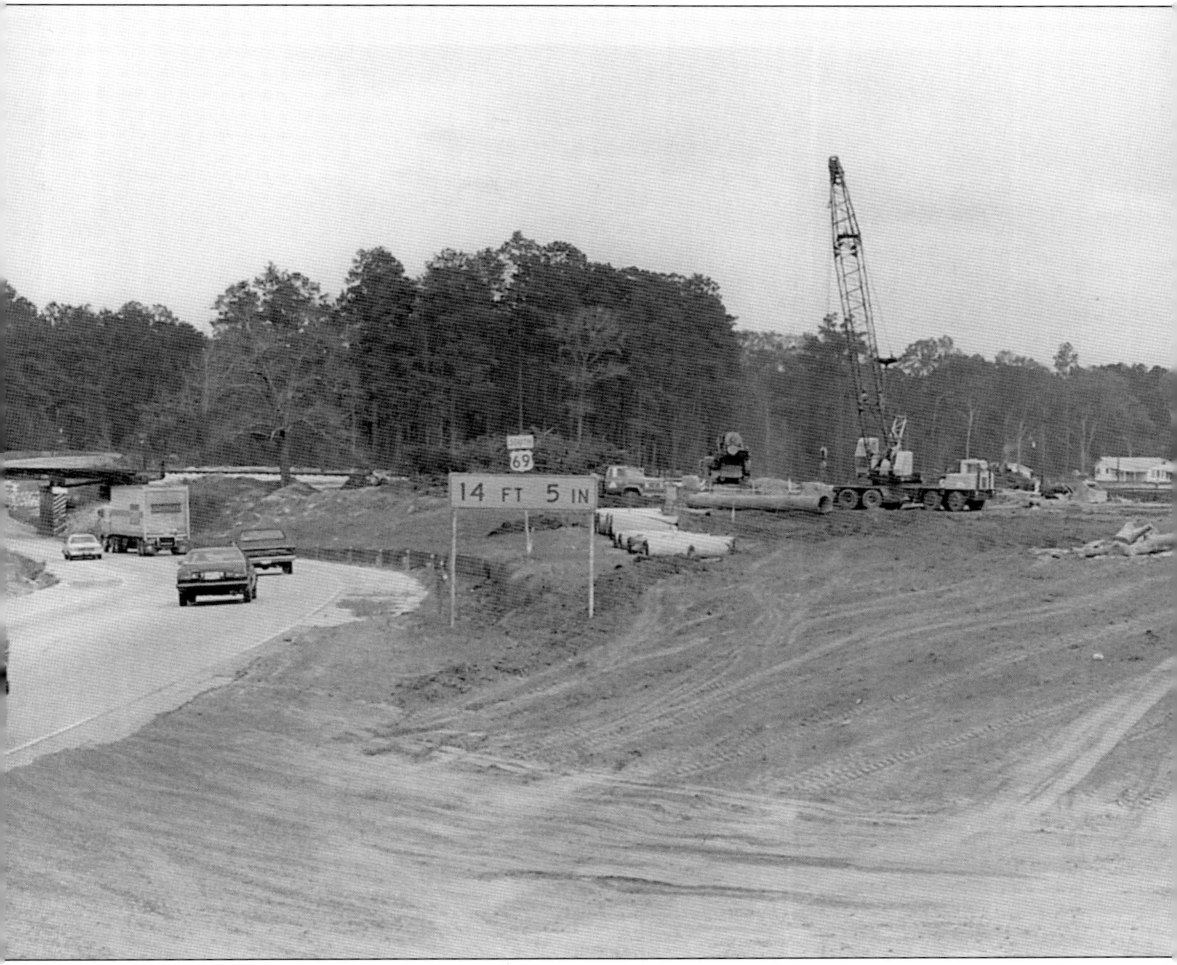

The underpass on US Highway 69 at Warren created treacherous driving conditions from the time it was built in the 1940s until it was replaced with an extra-wide overpass two decades later. Ironically, contractors completed the overpass at almost the same time that Southern Pacific (owner of the T&NO company) discontinued its rail service through Tyler County. Only road beds remain where rails and ties once laced their way through the piney woods. Other changes, such as the end of the age of independently owned sawmills, forced many communities like Warren to reevaluate their approach to economic development. A quick pass through town today will convince any skeptic that Warrenites still believe in their community. Two banks, a newly restored general store, a modern convenience store, two new discount stores, and new school buildings with sports facilities all send the same message: "We are proud of our community and we are here to stay." (Courtesy of TxDOT.)

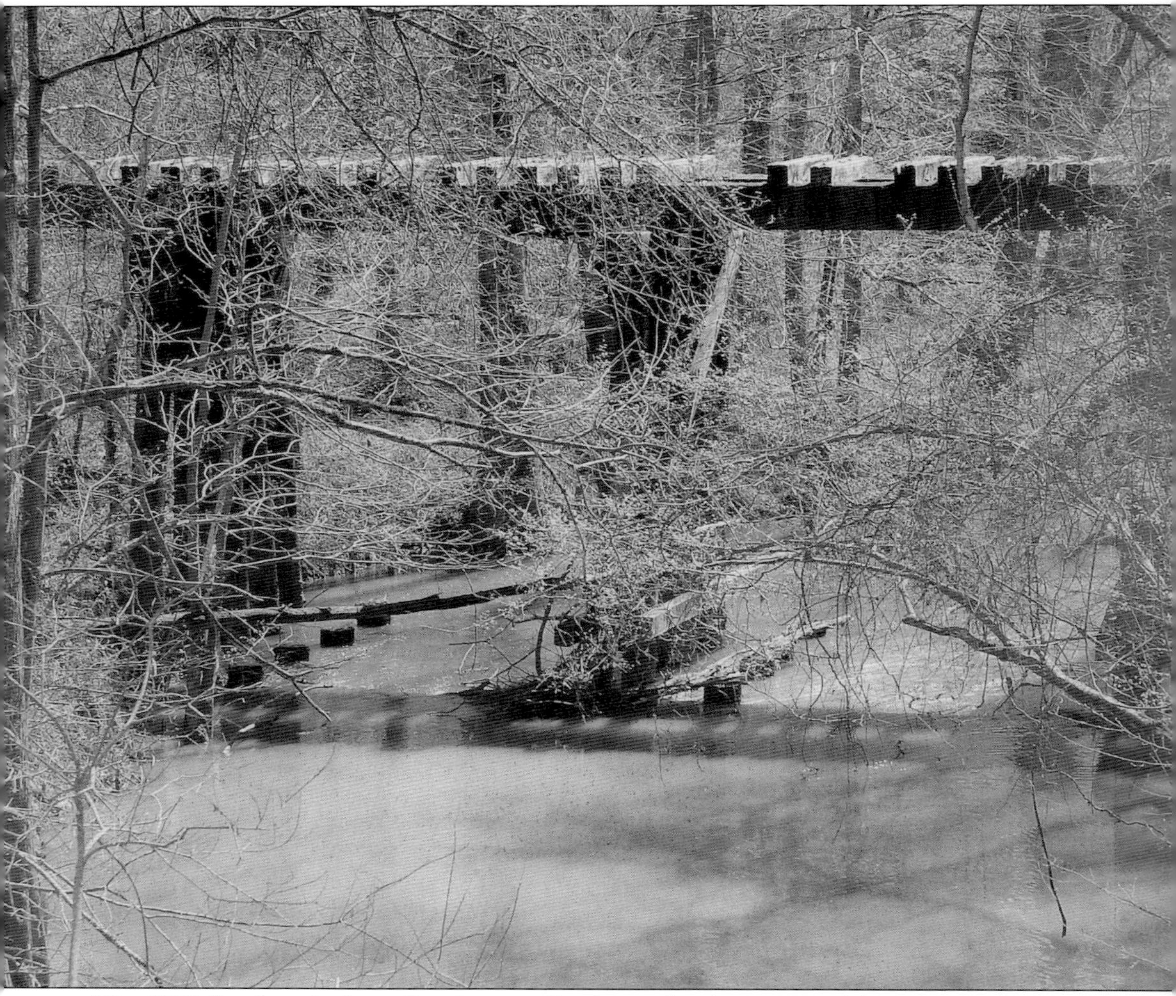

The 1929 flood washed out Big Cypress Creek trestles, leaving southbound train passengers waiting while another train backed from Beaumont to the creek's south side. While waiting, some boys walked to the nearby Norton home to get milk for a baby on the train. Mr. Norton and his obliging cow averted the pending crisis. Eventually, passengers crossed the flooded creek on a handcar or by walking on the rails. In Woodville, Ezra Eaves called Beaumont to ask for yeast to be delivered to his bakery. A young pilot took the challenge and tied a case of yeast packets and a bundle of newspapers under his plane's wings. Once over Woodville, he cut the ropes, releasing his cargo and frightening the unsuspecting family who thought their home was being bombed when the crates hit the roof. Yeast and newspapers littered their yard. (Courtesy of Warren Independent School District.)

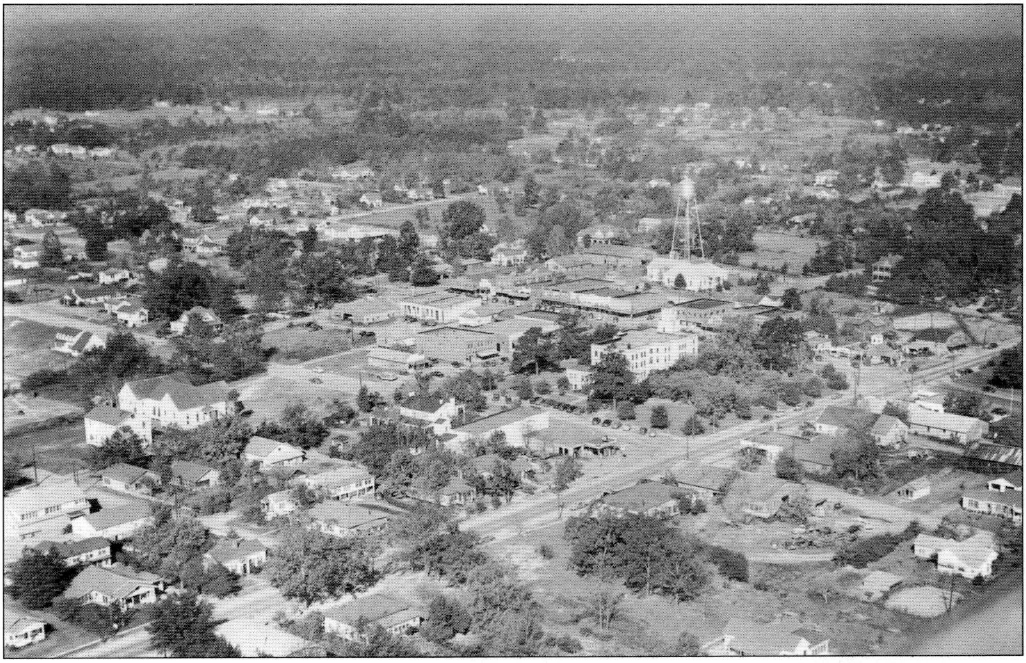

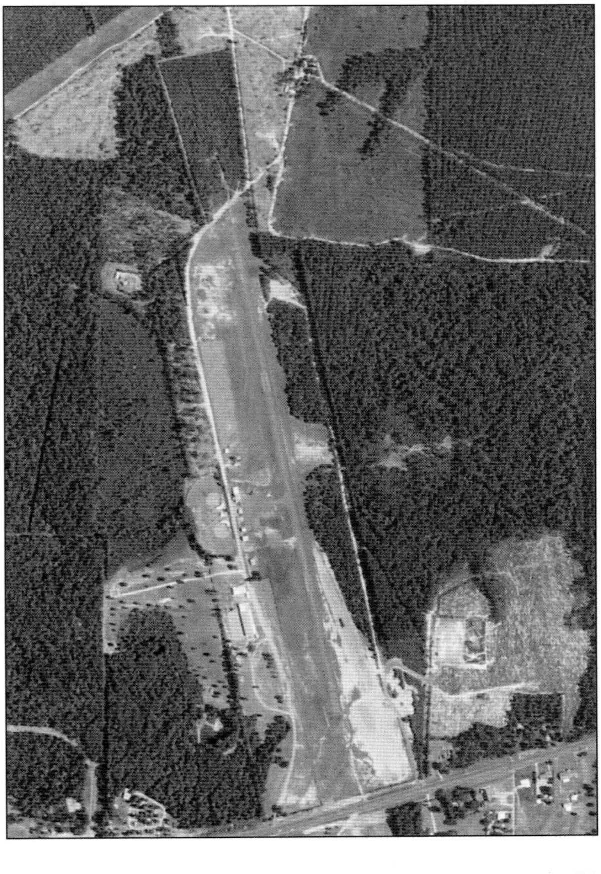

Above, an aerial view of Woodville in 1950 shows the old icehouse, some backyard clothes lines, and the newly built United Methodist Church. Missing from the picture are current buildings for Citizens State Bank and First Baptist Church. During the 1950s, local citizens, governments, and the International Paper Company (IP) cooperated to develop the Tyler County Airport and 4H Fairgrounds and Rodeo Complex west of Woodville. Deke O'Brien and Morris Clemmons led the efforts to acquire 187 acres of land from IP and grants from the Federal Aviation Agency and Texas Aeronautics Commission. Clinton Currie, county agent, led students and parents in clearing land for the fairgrounds and arena (right). Volunteers constructed facilities for animals and spectators. In the 1980s, additional volunteers developed a series of girls' softball fields to complete the complex. (Above, courtesy of Woodville Independent School District; right, courtesy of Tyler County Appraisal District.)

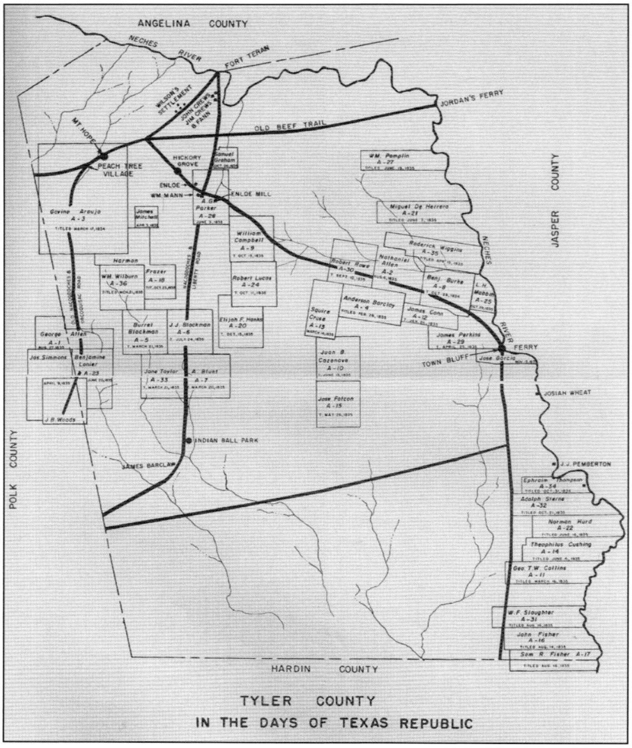

When Texas declared independence on March 2, 1836, the area that became Tyler County contained three dozen surveys of land granted by the Mexican government. The few roads took advantage of existing Indian traces. In the next 60 years, the Republic of Texas and the State of Texas granted land to other visionary and industrious pioneers. Many of them had earned land certificates through their participation in the Texas War for Independence. The pioneers' task was simply to locate some unallocated land that suited them, have it surveyed according to the number of acres they had earned, and then settle and cultivate the land. With that, the land was free to them. (Both, courtesy of TGLO.)

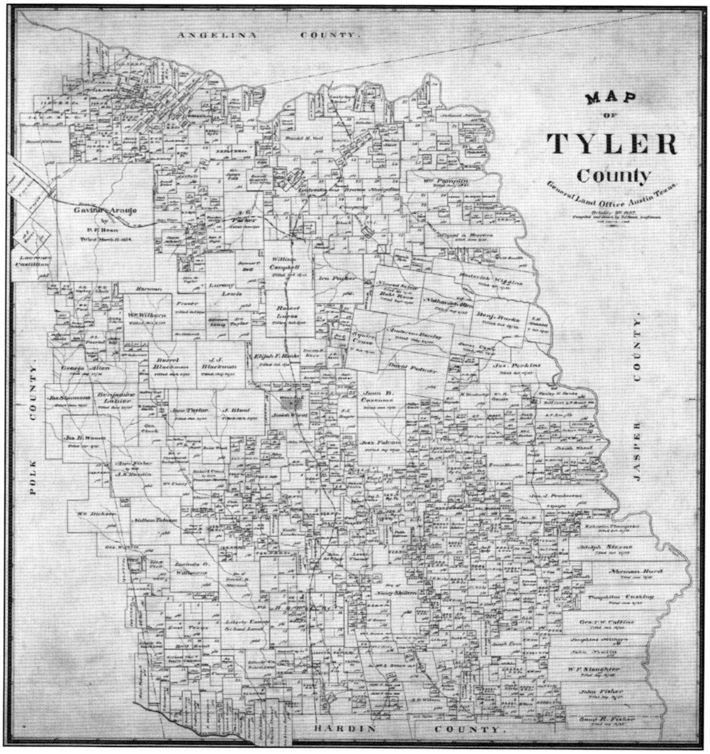

Four

The Marketplace

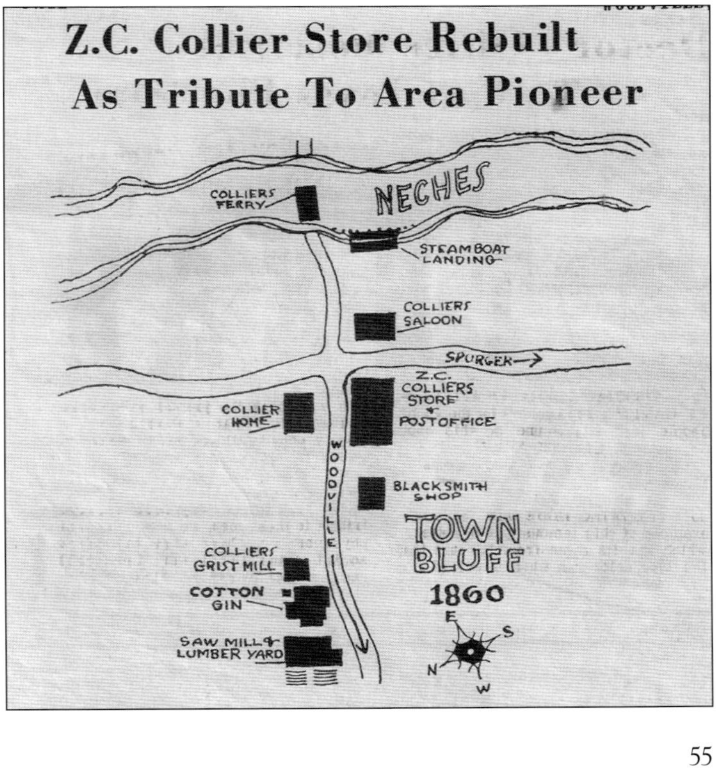

The Colliers played a prominent part in bringing prosperity to Town Bluff. Though disappointed about the decision to establish Tyler County's new seat of government in the forks of Turkey Creek, Capt. James G. Collier conducted the survey laying out the new road between Town Bluff and the chosen location. That road became the main east-west thoroughfare in the new town, Woodville, and was called Bluff Street. (Courtesy of Woodville Independent School District.)

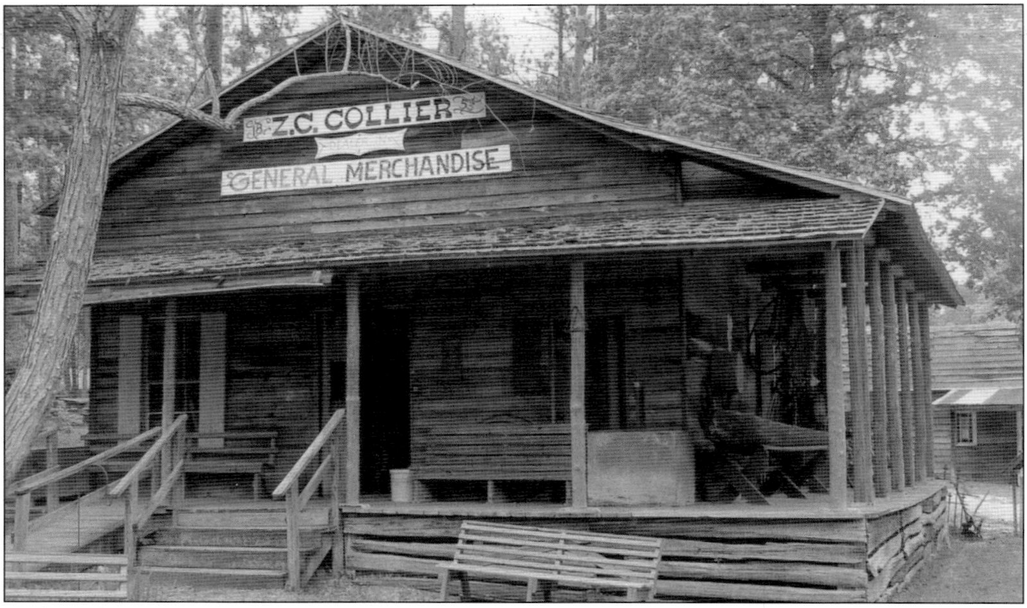

Zachariah Cowart Collier built a general merchandise store as part of the Town Bluff complex in 1863. He and his family served the needs of overland and river travelers until the late 1920s when they sold the business to the Barlow family. Ultimately, the Barlow family donated the building and many artifacts to Heritage Village, where they would be maintained as a permanent display of early commerce in Tyler County. (Courtesy of TCHS.)

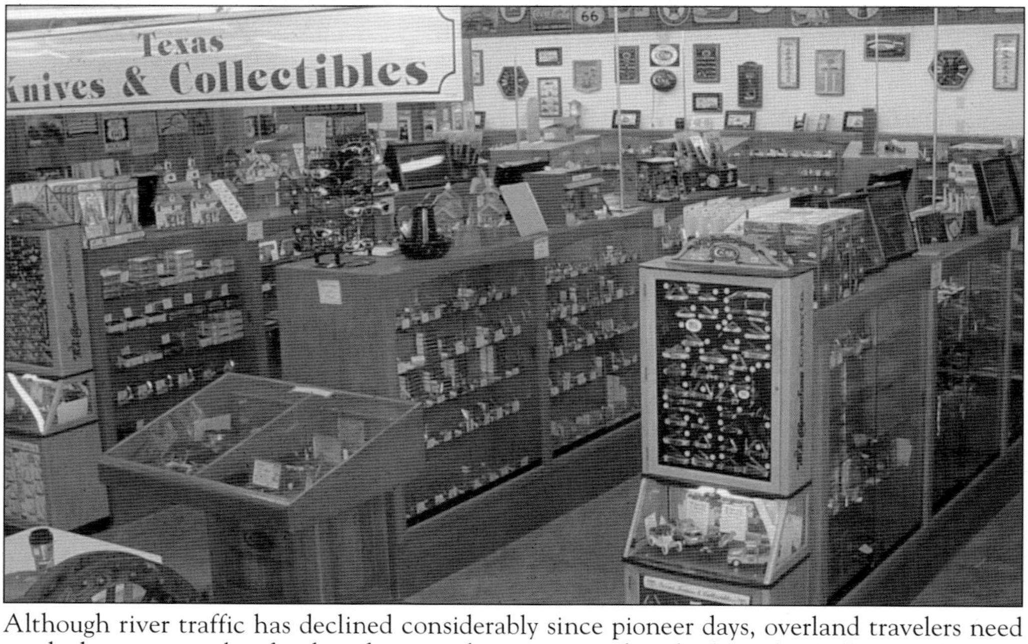

Although river traffic has declined considerably since pioneer days, overland travelers need much the same supplies for their farms as their ancestors bought from the Colliers in the 19th century. A few miles south of the original Town Bluff marketplace, Mott Wholesale, Inc., meets those 21st-century needs with hardware, feed, and one of the largest Case knife dealerships in the South. (Courtesy of Marvin Mott.)

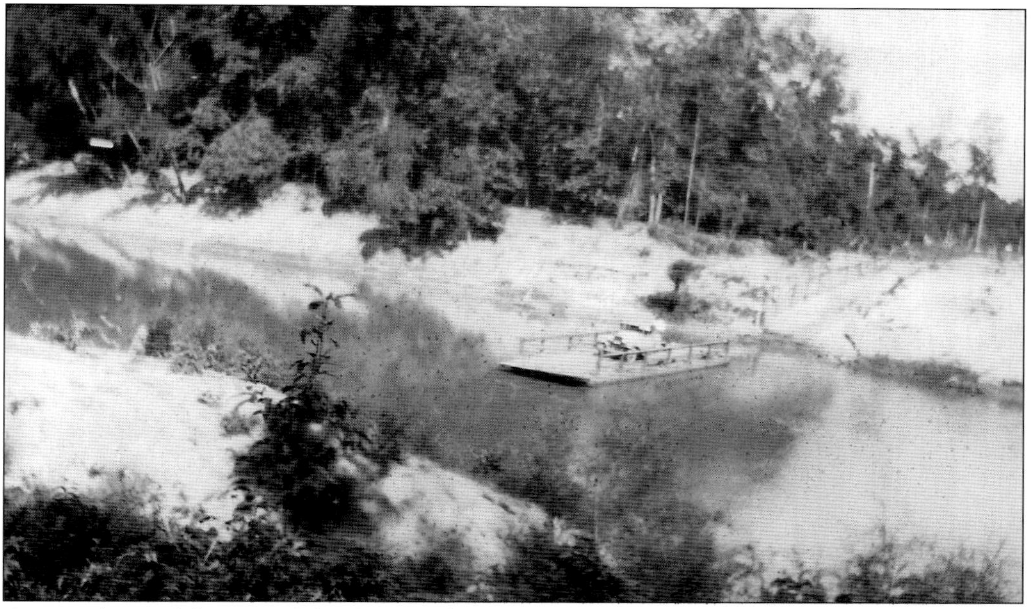

At any of several ferries in Tyler County, drivers merely needed to show up and honk for service. Once loaded, operators used a notched axe handle inserted into a system of pulleys and ropes or steel cables to crank their way across the waterway. It was the summer of 1959 when the last ferry, Sheffield's, gave way to a concrete and steel bridge connecting FM 1013 from Hillister to Kirbyville. (Courtesy of Ivy Jo Cook.)

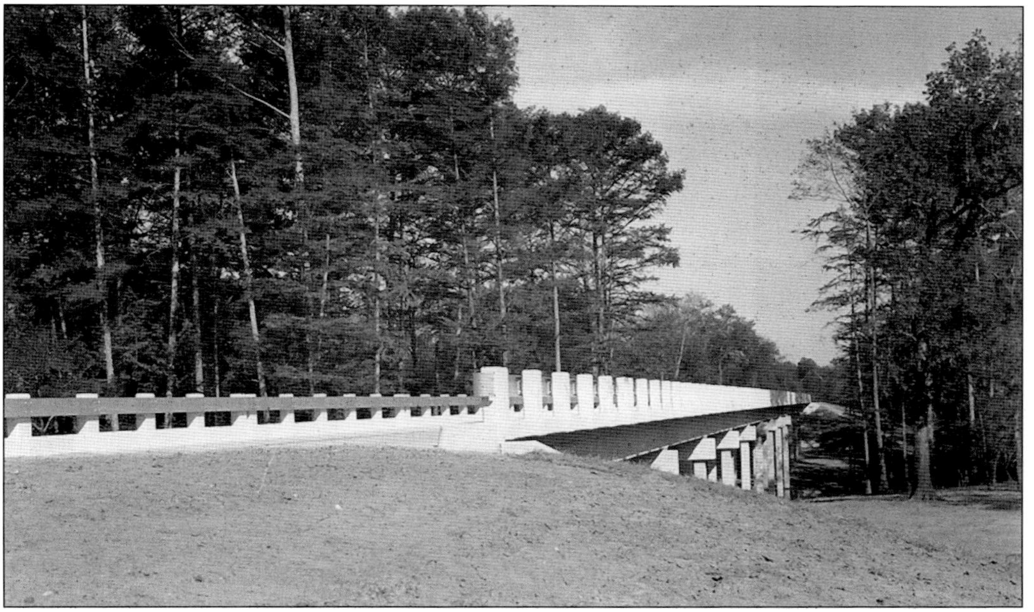

In 1935, Highway 45 consisted of an unpaved strip of road crossing the Trinity, Neches, and Sabine Rivers, continuing into Louisiana. Town leaders along that highway formed the Sam Houston Highway Association to help acquire federal funds for paving the road and building the three expensive bridges. By 1938, the bridges (including this one over the Neches) had been completed, and in another year US Highway 190 was paved. (Courtesy of TxDOT.)

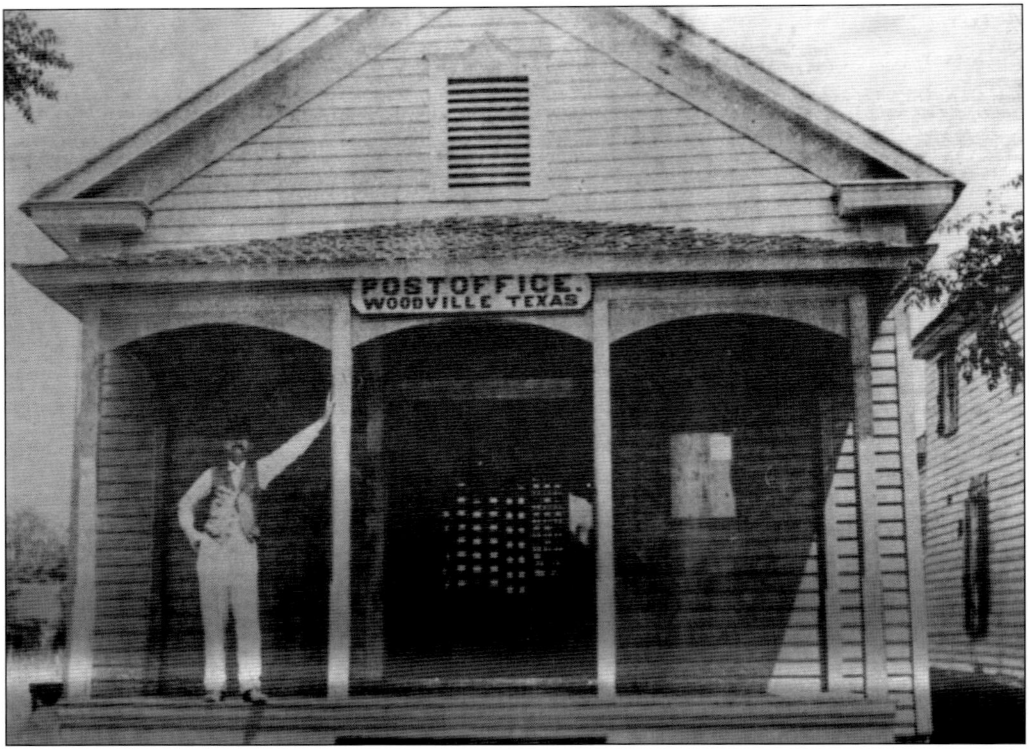

After an interesting career as a state surveyor, John McBride took up the job of postmaster in Woodville at the new post office that was built in 1909. It was not until 1912 that Pres. William Taft and Congress mandated the closing of US post offices on Sunday. A courtyard next to the Emporium for the Arts now occupies the old postal site. Just one block east of the post office, the Star Café had gained a reputation for serving delicious, daily Blue Plate Specials to downtown merchants, bankers, barbers, and folk having business across the street in the Tyler County courthouse. The Star Café site, though vacant today, hosts vendors' booths during seasonal events. (Both, courtesy of TCHS.)

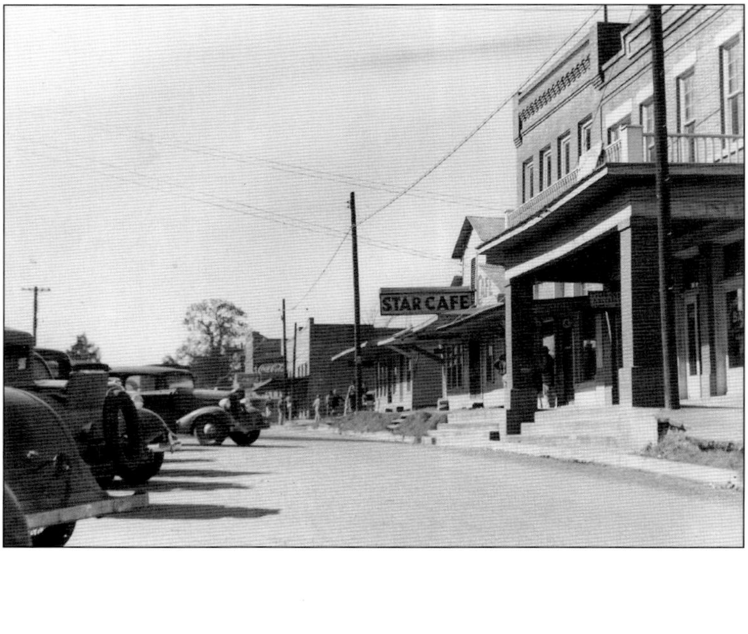

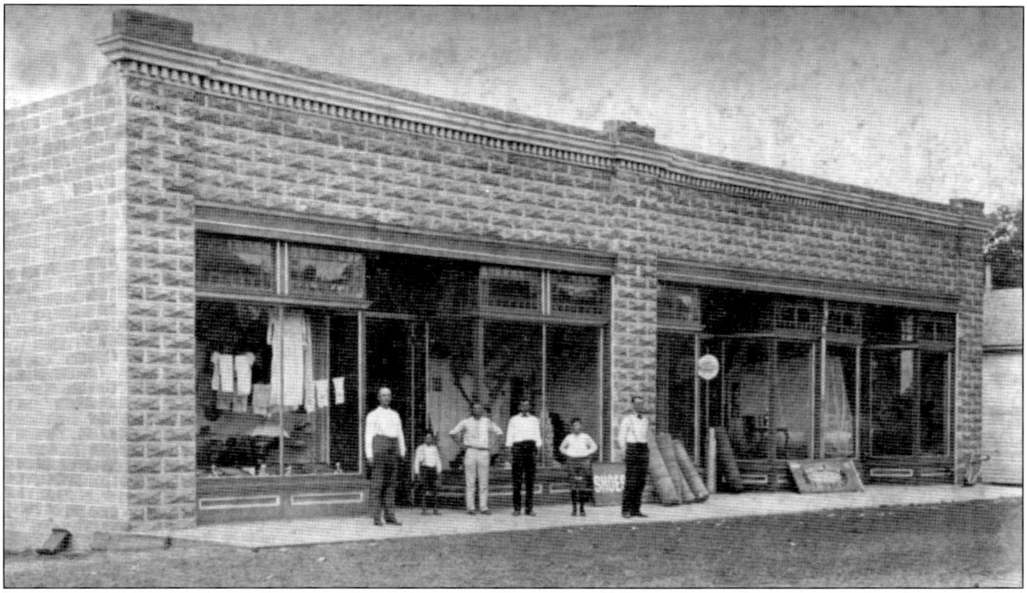

S.H. Reid offered a complete stock of household and farming supplies on West Bluff Street in Woodville. Ready-made clothing items hung in the display windows, while rolls of wire rested on the sidewalk. Later, Roy Pate operated a grocery store at this location and maintained a pen of live chickens for sale to the ladies who did not wish to raise their own chicks. (Courtesy of TCDF.)

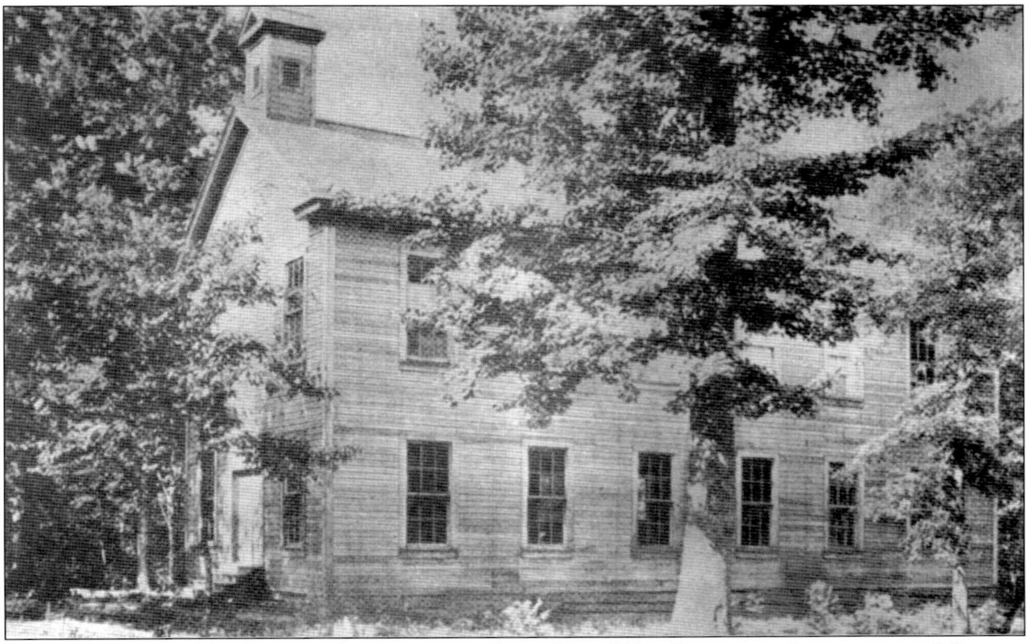

Doucette citizens, like their rural counterparts throughout Tyler County, took community life quite seriously from the earliest times. Thus, one of their first efforts was to construct a two-story frame building that would serve as a school, church, and lodge meeting hall. The structure remained in use through the first half of the 20th century. (Courtesy ASLM.)

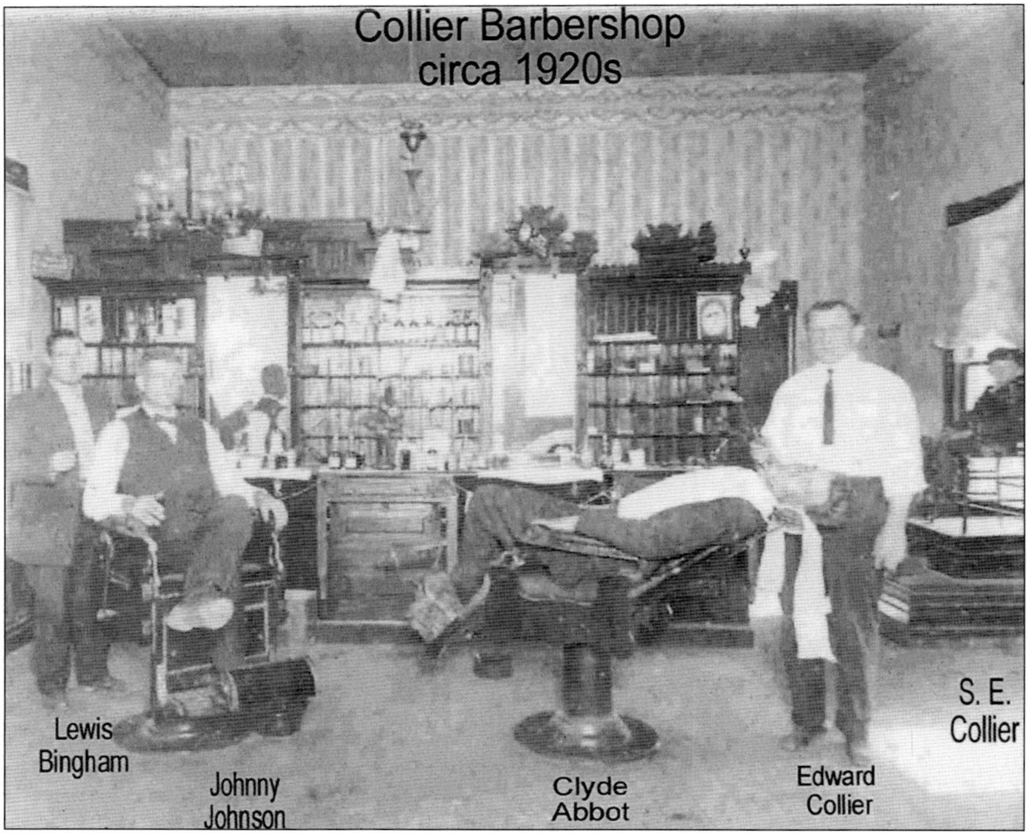

Early-20th-century gentlemen who visited the Collier Barbershop in Colmesneil could expect to receive refreshing shaves and stylish haircuts. Shoe shines performed by owner Edward's son added the extra luxury touch. Young S.E. Collier performed other duties at the shop, such as bringing in wood on cold winter days. (Courtesy Brenda Goode.)

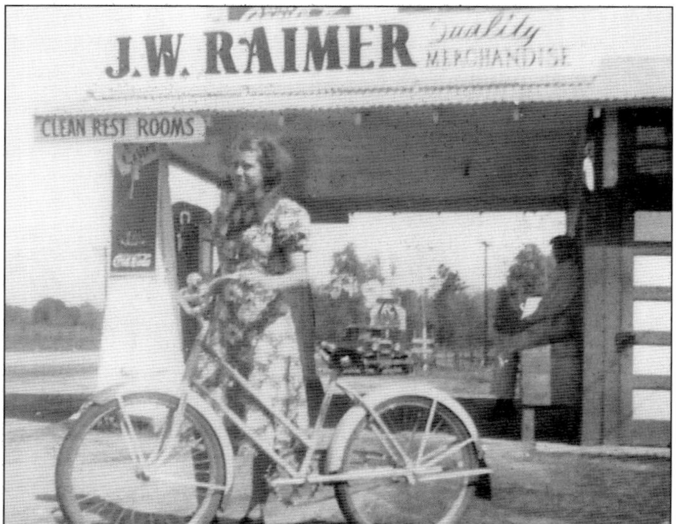

Johnnie Ruth Raimer Wilson enjoyed riding her bicycle all around Warren, especially to basketball practice. After graduating from Warren High School, she was allowed to keep taking courses so she could continue playing basketball. In tournaments against rivals at Kirby High School in Woodville, she guarded one of her best friends, Vera Dean Benthall. (Courtesy of Warren Independent School District.)

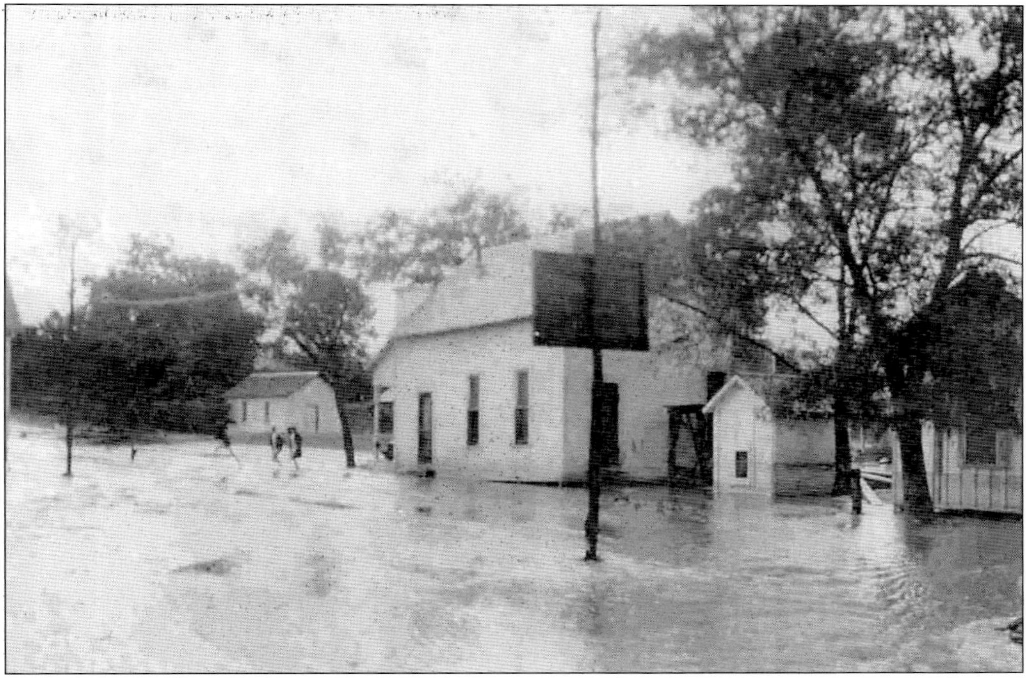

Tyler County and all of Southeast Texas saw heavy rains for the month of May 1929. The Neches and all its tributaries flooded outside their banks and isolated people from urgently needed assistance. In Warren, Clara Busselle needed surgery to prevent gangrene from taking her life. Her daughters convinced two doctors to make the trip from Beaumont to Warren, where they conducted the surgery in the ladies' home and left Mrs. Busselle resting comfortably in ICU (the back bedroom). She lived for another 26 years. On a farm near the Old Town Bluff Road, Mr. Watson died. His burial needed to take place at Mount Pisgah Cemetery. The family was forced to "hold him over" for four days until someone could get to town for a casket on a wagon that could make the trip to the cemetery. (Above, courtesy of CISD; below, courtesy of Warren Independent School District.)

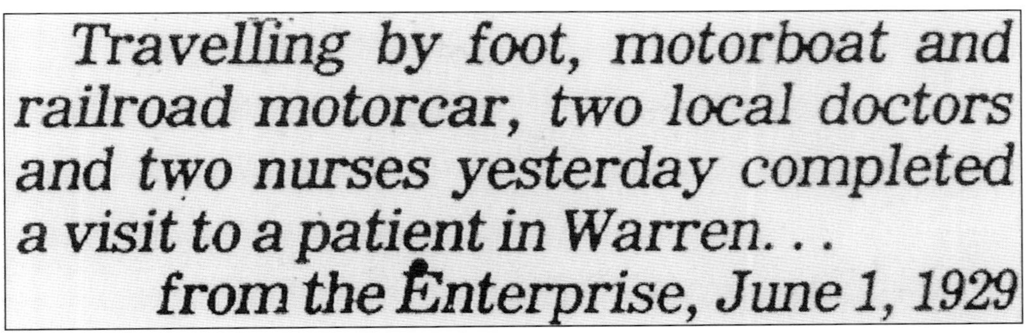

Travelling by foot, motorboat and railroad motorcar, two local doctors and two nurses yesterday completed a visit to a patient in Warren. . .
from the Enterprise, June 1, 1929

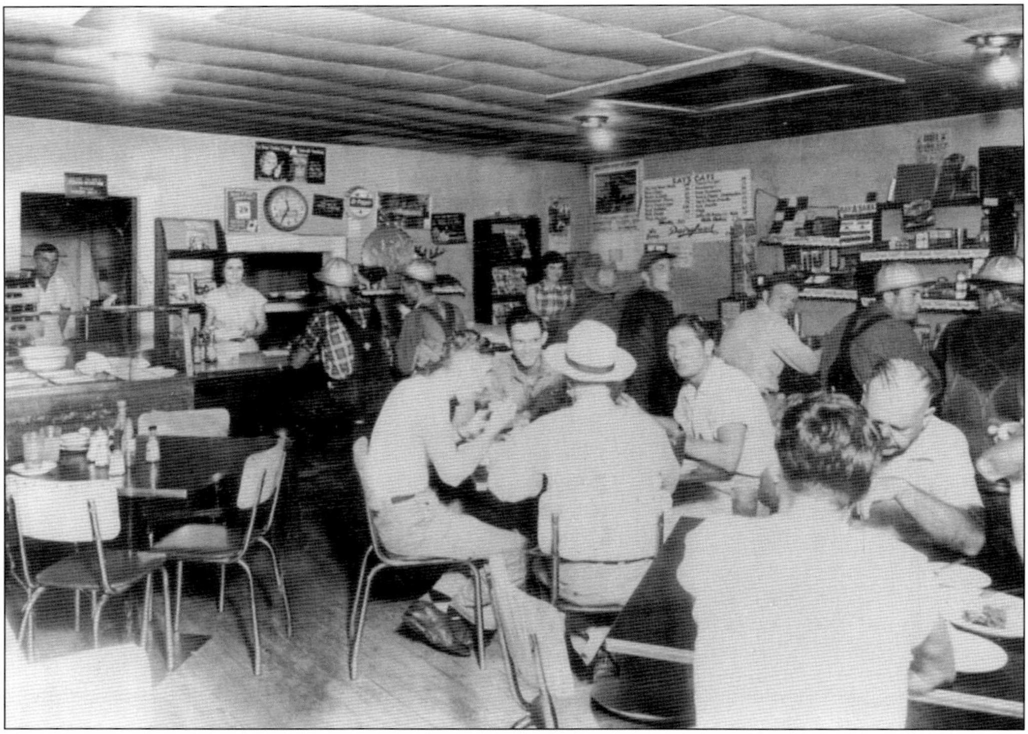

In addition to offering tantalizing menu items, cafés, restaurants, and drive-ins provided sites for social gatherings all across Tyler County in the 1950s. Ray's Café (above) in Warren served meals to local workers and also featured Dairyland ice cream. Buddy Spurlock recalls his personal favorite flavor being orange-pineapple. Red and Mabel Pitts operated a popular hangout for teens in Woodville, the Magnolia Drive-in and Restaurant (below). Mabel's pies took the grand prize with her customers. Her chicken and dumplings and crispy fried chicken tied for second. Named for the historic magnolia tree on the property, the business was located at the site now occupied by Pizza Hut. (Above, courtesy of Warren Independent School District; below, courtesy of Gladys Best.)

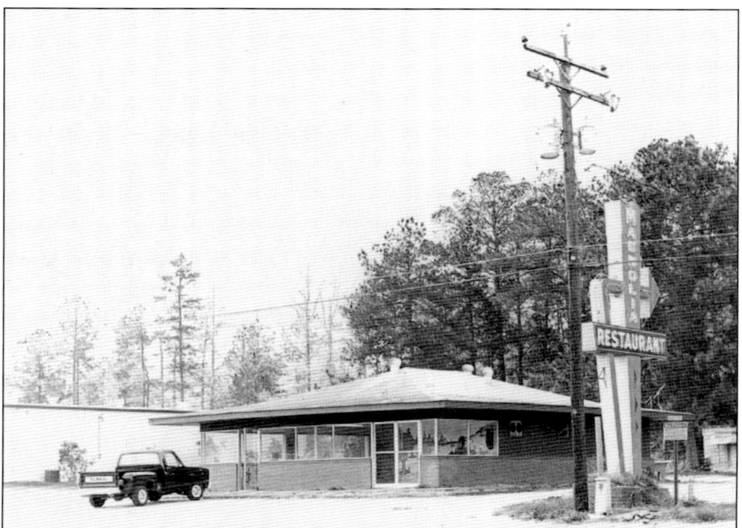

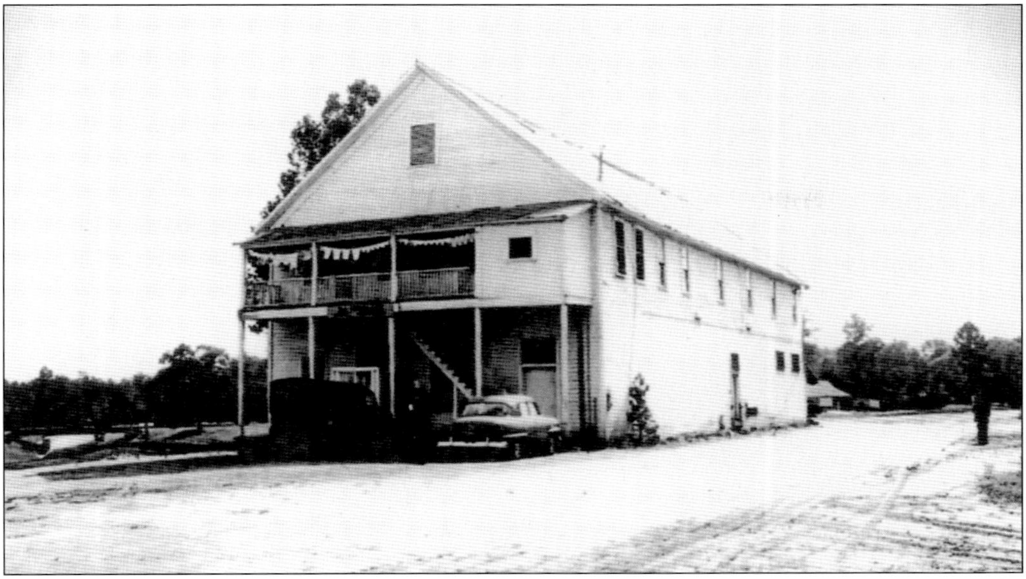

Carl Goolsbee, together with his wife, the former Ella Pedigo, and his brother Tom operated the Goolsbee Store in Warren from the time Goolsbee bought the Warren Lumber Company until he sold the stock to Archie Spurlock in 1954. Spurlock built a new store at the old Ace Hardware location and moved there just days after the snow of December 1954. Annie Raimer joined her husband in operating J.W. Raimer General Merchandise Store, also in Warren. In 1955, and shortly before the rerouting of US Highway 69 to replace the underpass with an overpass, Goolsbee tore down his store building, which also included an upstairs apartment. (Both, courtesy of Warren Independent School District.)

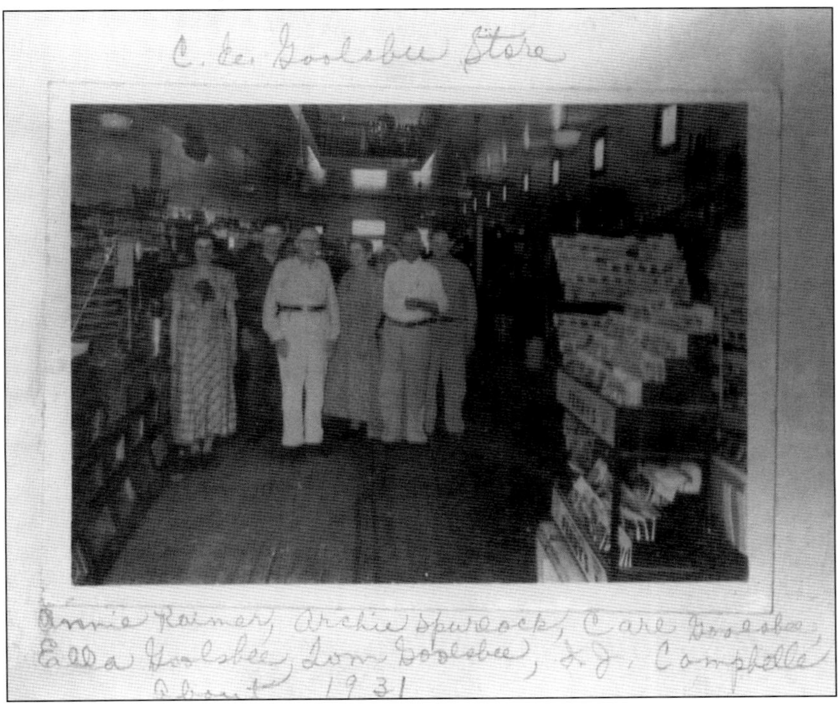

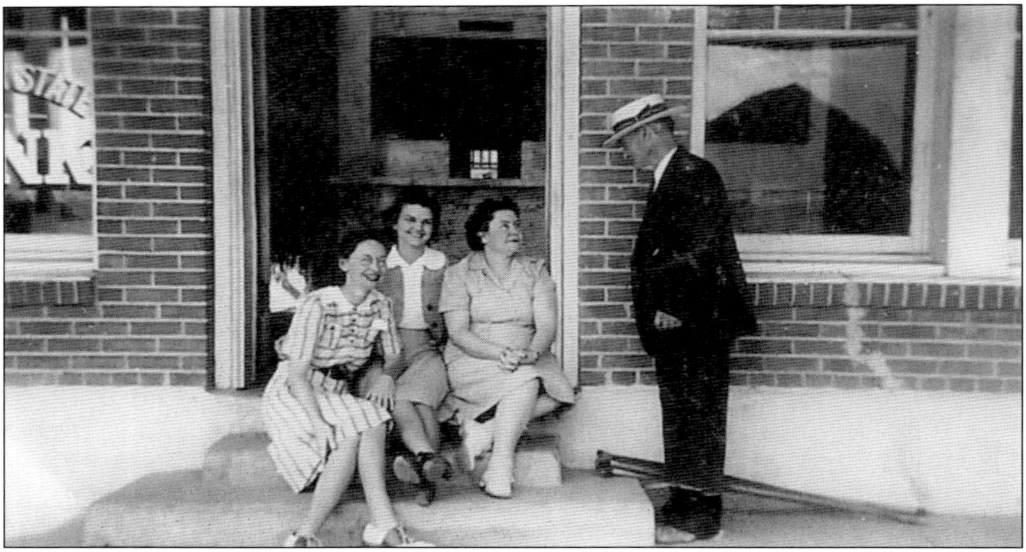

A beautiful 1940s spring day in Chester brought bank employees outdoors for fresh air. Pictured from left to right, Alice Powell Lakey, Henry Ella Willson David, and Angie Feagin Veal are greeted by Mr. Boardman. Having been chartered in the early 1920s, Chester State Bank continued into the 1980s as a family enterprise. Beginning with Lee Feagin, its founder, and continuing with his sister Angie and his son David, the bank served as a hub for a strong rural community. The town of Chester came into existence when the railroad connecting Trinity, Groveton, Corrigan, and Colmesneil established a depot between Peace Tree Village and Mount Hope. (Above, courtesy of Josh David; below, courtesy of Gladys Best.)

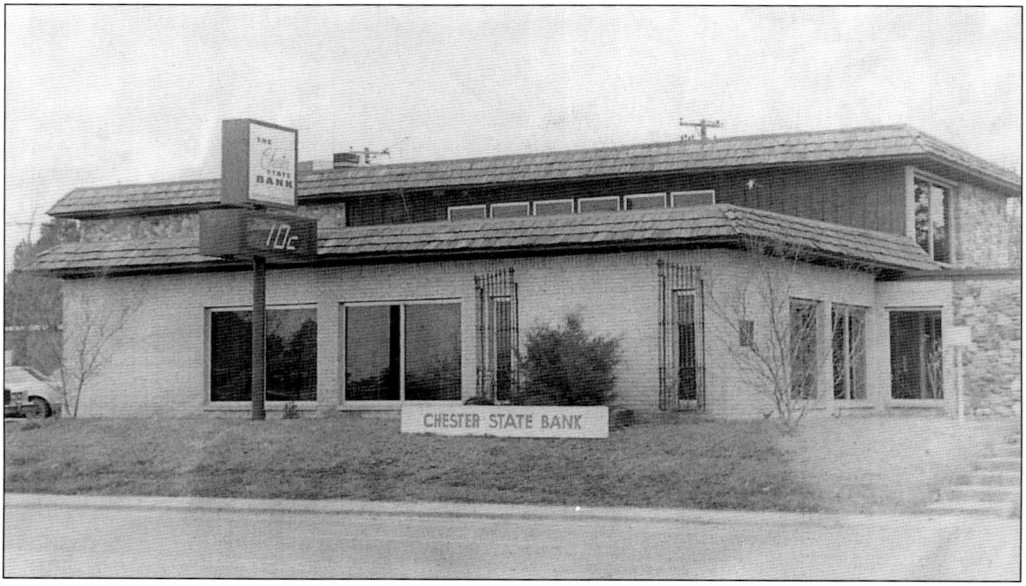

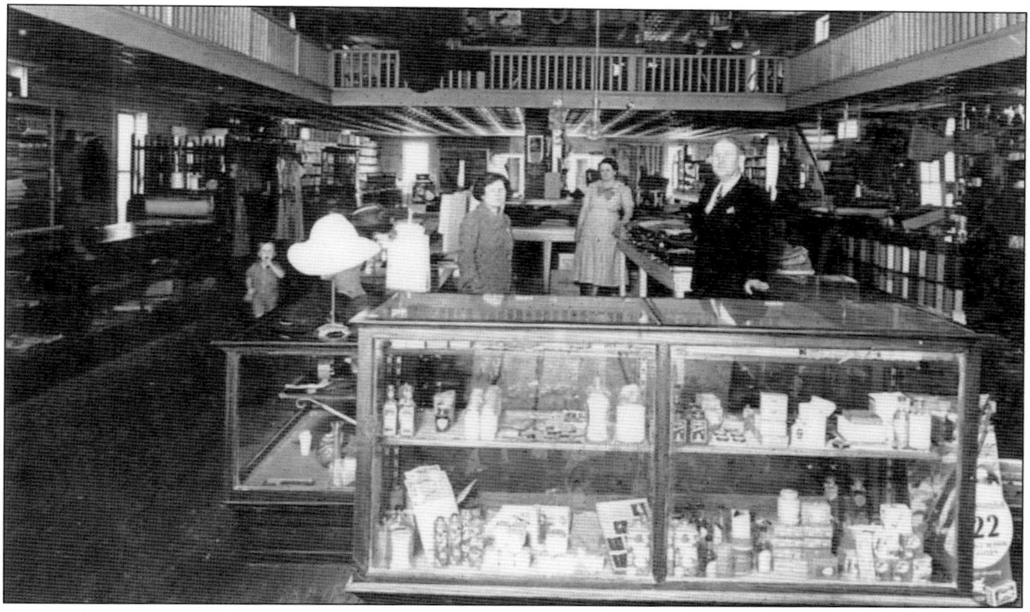

According to a *Beaumont Enterprise-Journal* writer, Colmesneil felt "empty" when Pomp Meadows (pictured), owner of Meadows General Merchandise, passed away in 1976. Like his father before him, Meadows had offered a full line of general merchandise plus an inviting atmosphere for visiting around the wood stove, where men loved to chew the fat and tobacco as well. (Courtesy of CISD.)

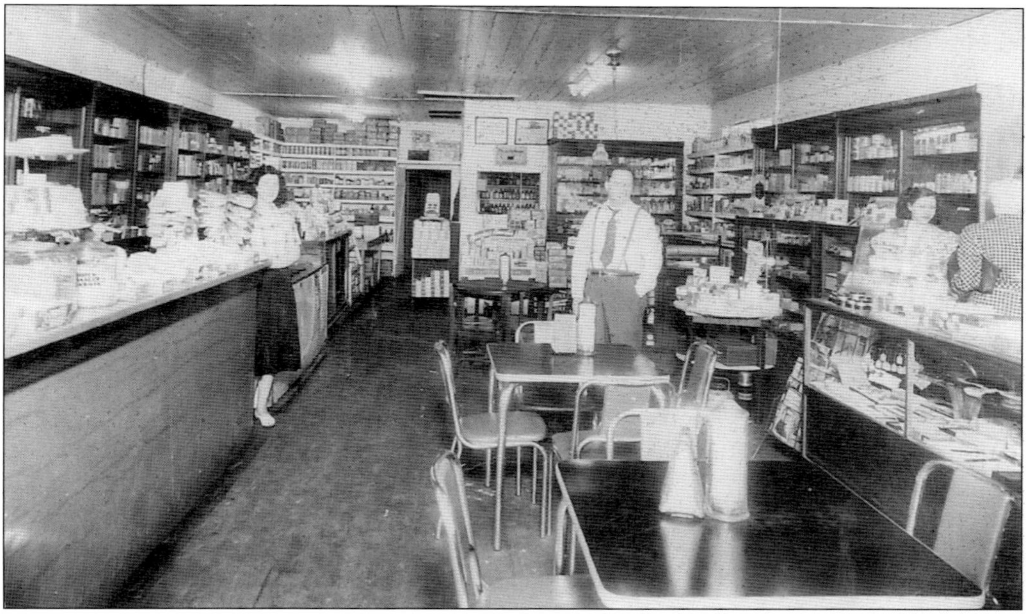

Richard Best moved his pharmacy from Colmesneil to Woodville around 1943. Before moving into the brick building between Ramsey's store and J.B. Best and Company, he occupied Ezra Eaves's frame building across the street from First Baptist Church (now Lindsey Whisenhant's office location). Eaves had previously run a combination grocery store and bakery at the site. (Courtesy of Gladys Best.)

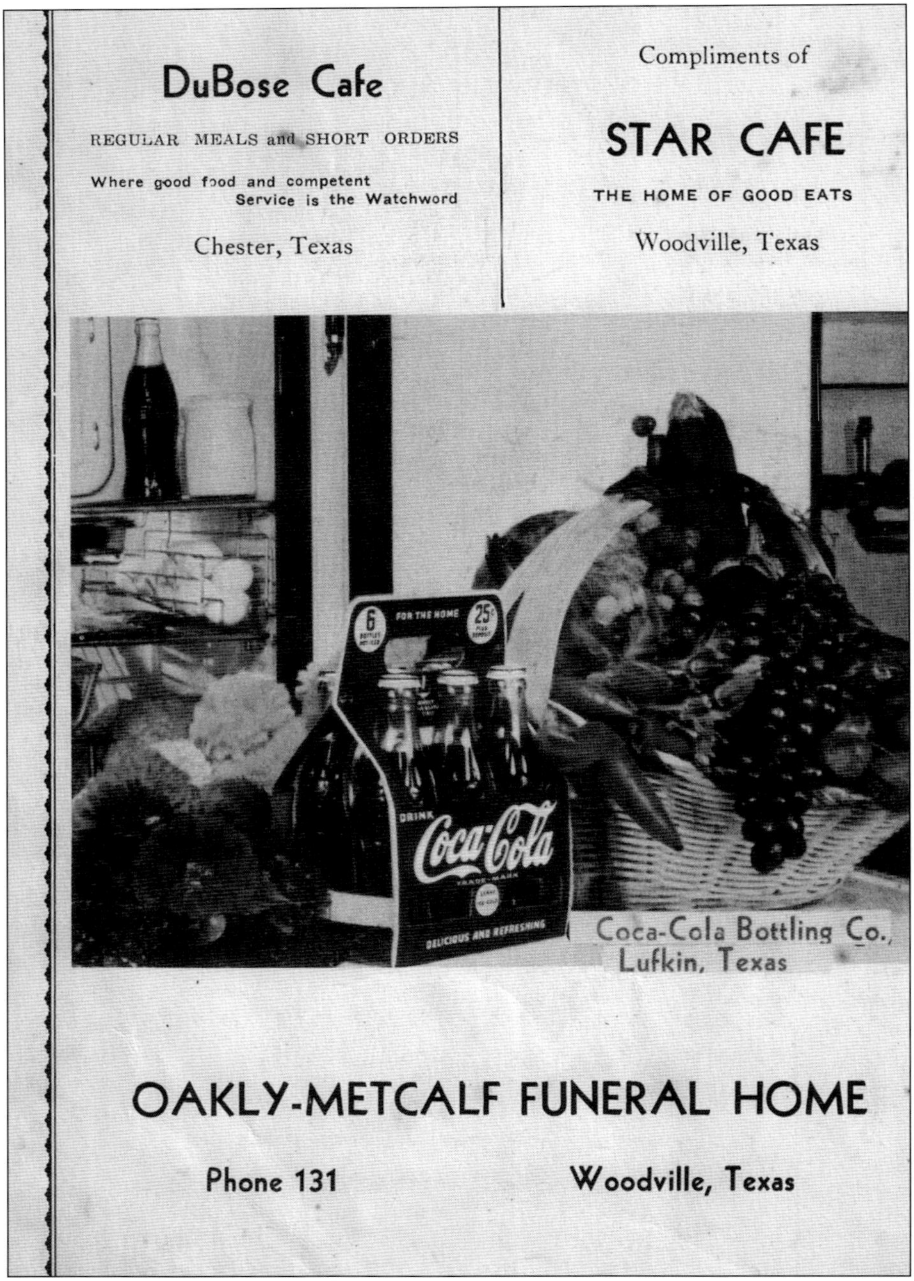

In 1942, the *Chester Echo* (school yearbook) featured advertisements from businesses in Chester, Lufkin, and Woodville. Chester residents of that day could reach one another by telephone using three-digit phone numbers. If they had a phone, or at least access to a phone, it was probably connected to a party line, which meant taking turns with neighbors to use it and always being able to listen in on the conversations of others or vice versa. Shoppers could purchase a six-pack of Cokes for a quarter. Oakly-Metcalf Funeral Home had bought out Mr. Lee's funeral home in Woodville. The business later sold to Joe Edwards, who was followed briefly by George Stanley and presently by Stringer-Griffen. (Courtesy of Chester Independent School District.)

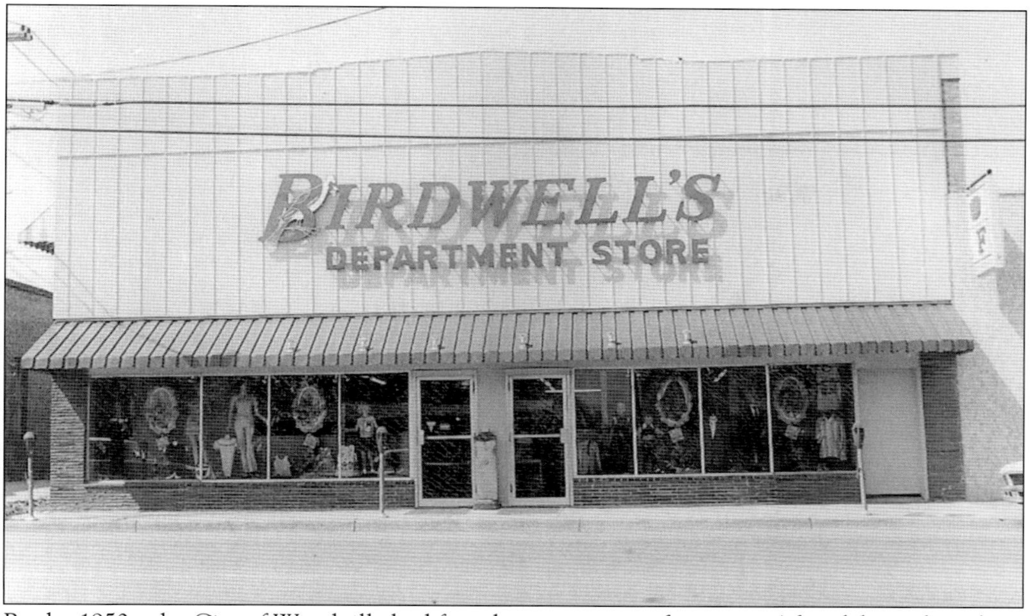

By the 1950s, the City of Woodville had found a new source of revenue. After debate about how to reserve downtown parking spaces for retail customers rather than workers in and visitors to the courthouse, the city installed parking meters. John Grammer faithfully administered the law to citizens needing a reminder to pay up or move on. The parking issue eventually settled down and the city removed the meters. Currently, the J.B. Best Building houses the Tyler County Clerk's Office and provides spacious surroundings for researchers and county workers. The recently remodeled Birdwell's Building contains office space on the ground floor and loft apartments above. (Both, courtesy of Gladys Best.)

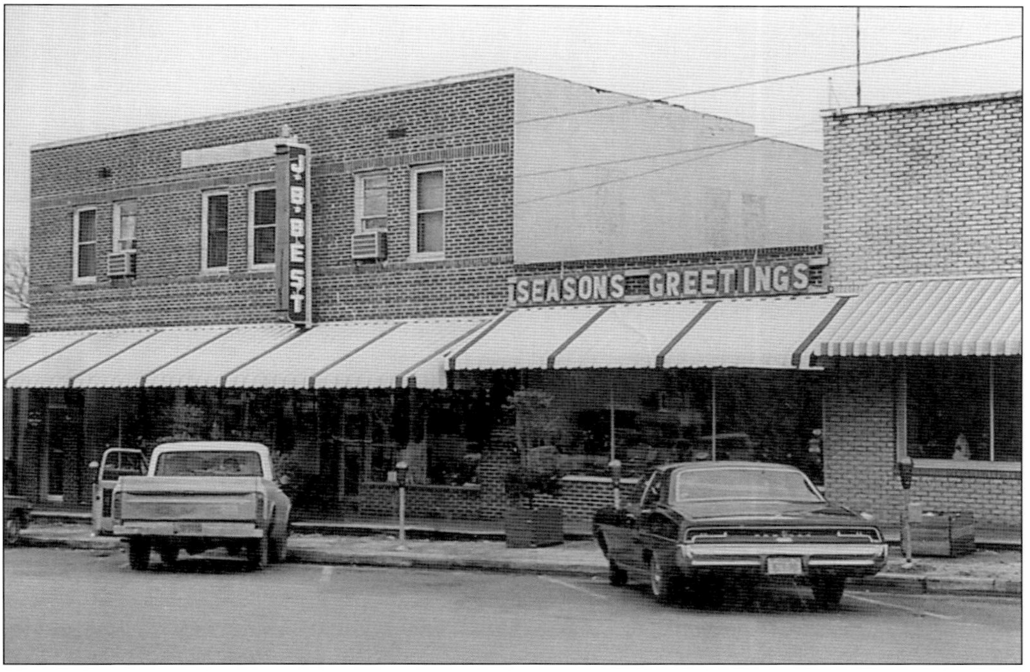

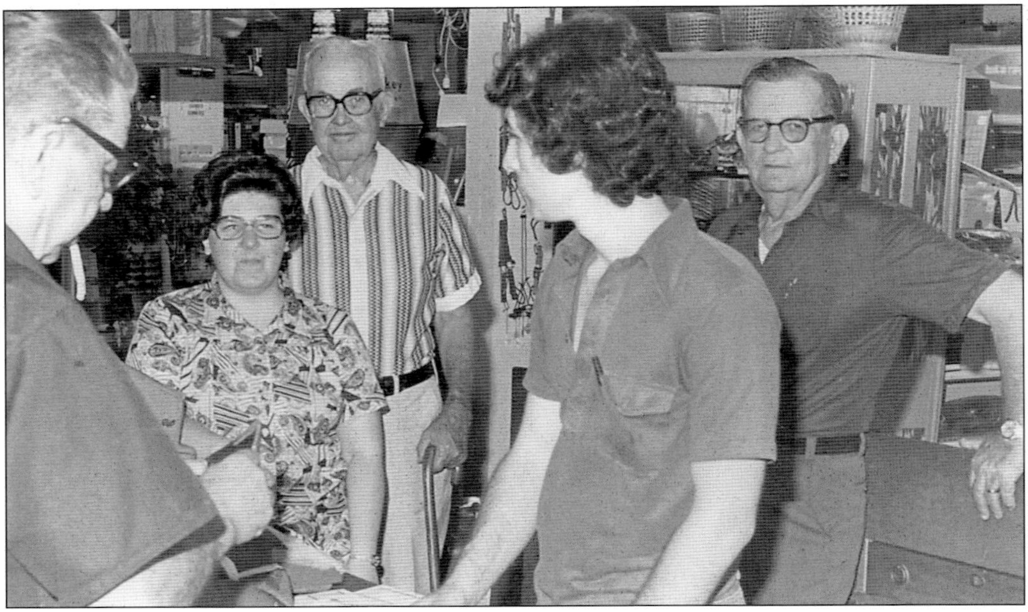

Sam Sullivan (center, with walking cane) began his early career as an agricultural science teacher in the 1930s. Judge Wheat, president of the Woodville School Board, hired Sullivan at a salary slightly higher than the school superintendent's. In 1944, Sullivan opened his hardware store (pictured) and began meeting the needs of households, farms, and ranches county-wide. Almost seven decades later, his son Fred continues the family business with an expansion of gifts and home decor items. (Courtesy Gladys Best.)

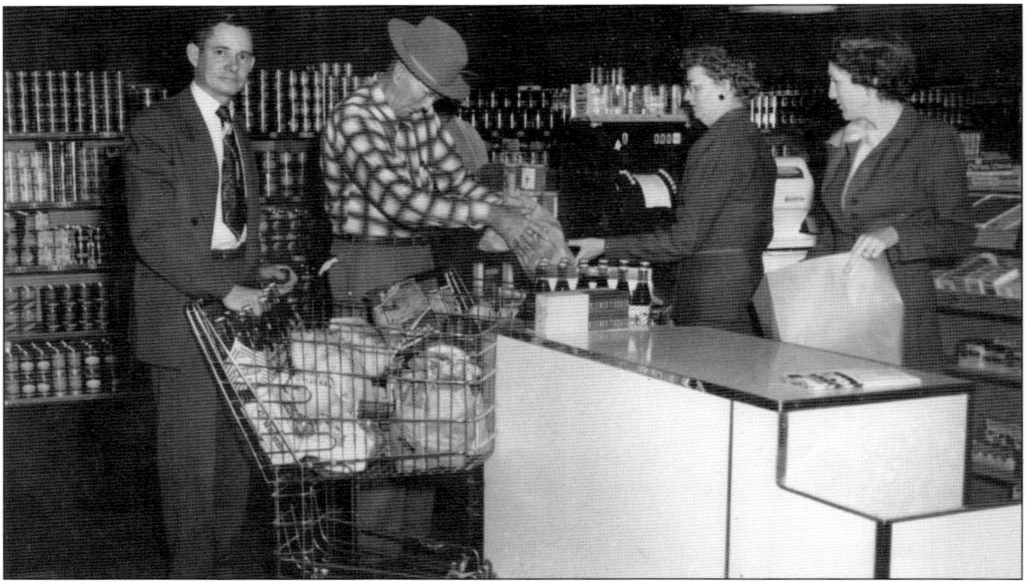

Horton-McCombs Minimax opened in 1952 as Tyler County's first supermarket. Featuring "minimum prices and maximum quality," the store sold frozen food, self-service meat, and Farmer Brown's fresh produce, which was delivered straight from the garden, in addition to regular grocery items. Unusual for the time, Minimax operated as a cash-and-carry store with no credit accounts. After 15 years of building a loyal clientele, Minimax sold to Brookshire Bros. (Courtesy TCHC.)

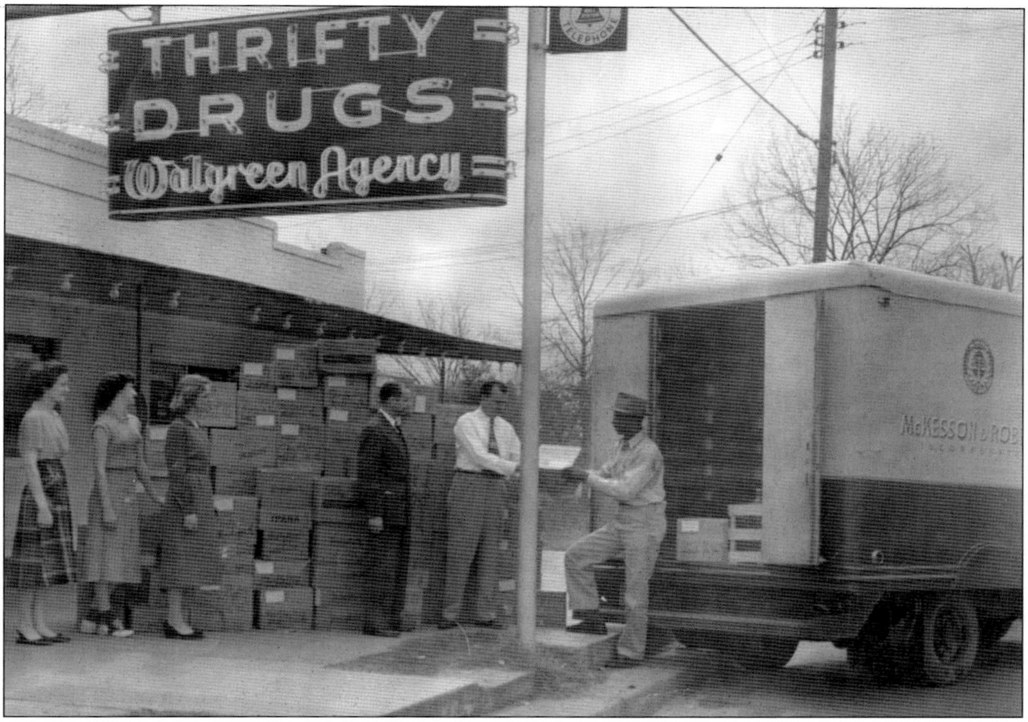

Bill and Floy Jarrott began their pharmacy in May 1952 and continued at the same location in Woodville until his death in 1982. Their son George and his wife, Dixie, joined the family operation in 1971 and continued the traditional hometown service, including the old-fashioned soda fountain and an extensive line of gifts. For some families in Tyler County, as many as six generations of their family members have shopped at Jarrott's pharmacy. (Courtesy of George Jarrott.)

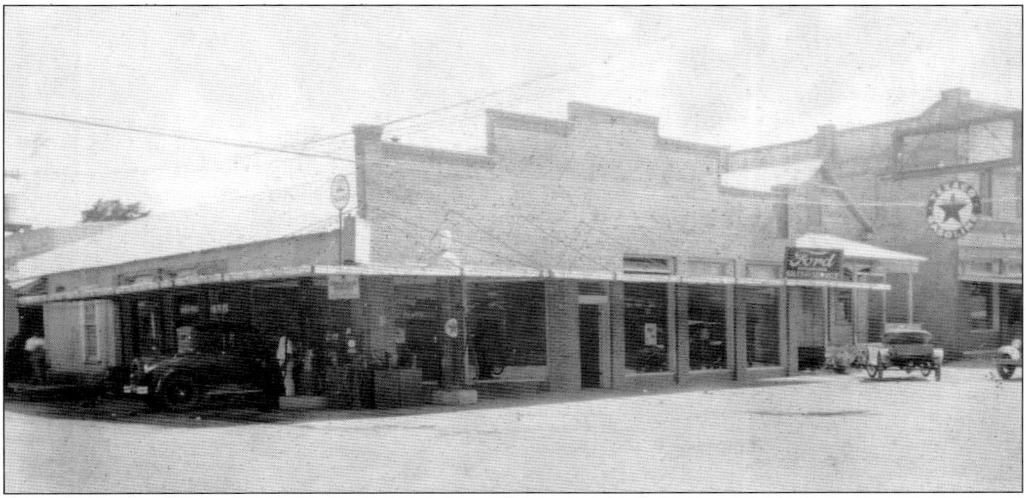

The northeast corner of Bluff and Village Streets in Woodville has provided a home for retail businesses of many kinds. Beginning with a Ford dealership and Texaco service station in the 1920s, then housing a Western Auto dealership in the 1940s to 1980s, and later a glass company, the sturdy brick building continues its landmark status as host to its 21st-century occupant, a music studio. (Courtesy of TCHS.)

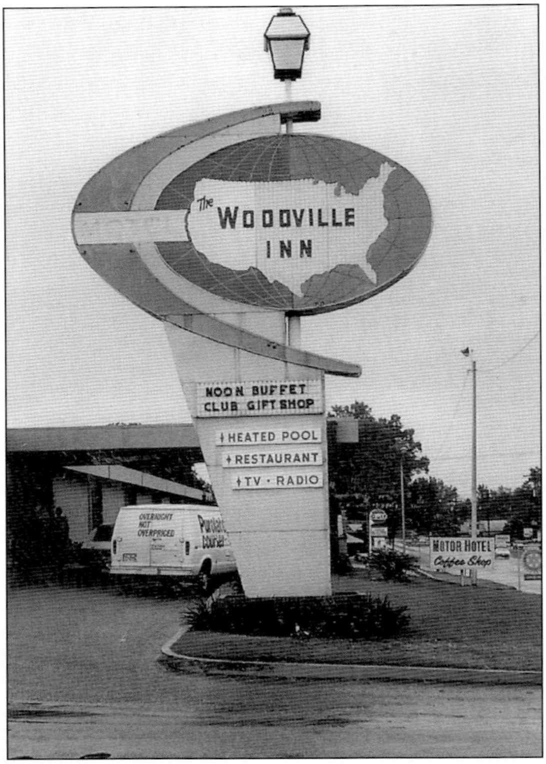

Civic-minded individuals joined in the 1960s to bring the Community Inn, later named the Woodville Inn, into being. The inn brought a whole new level of luxury to Tyler County. Besides the customary motel rooms, it featured a restaurant, banquet room, swimming pool, and club. The chamber of commerce, a gift shop, and an insurance company leased office space there. Hotel-motel taxes generated funds to support tourism in the area. (Courtesy of Gladys Best.)

Pat Brown (front row, left) charmed all those he met, whether at a school function (as pictured) or when making his regular Saturday rounds in Woodville with his barbecue sandwich bucket. Exactly what had been barbecued didn't really matter, everyone just wanted to pay their 50¢ and enjoy their sandwich. As Brown so eloquently said, "They're juicy and sweet. You don't have to chew 'em, just waller-and-swaller 'em." (Courtesy of Mayme Canada Brown.)

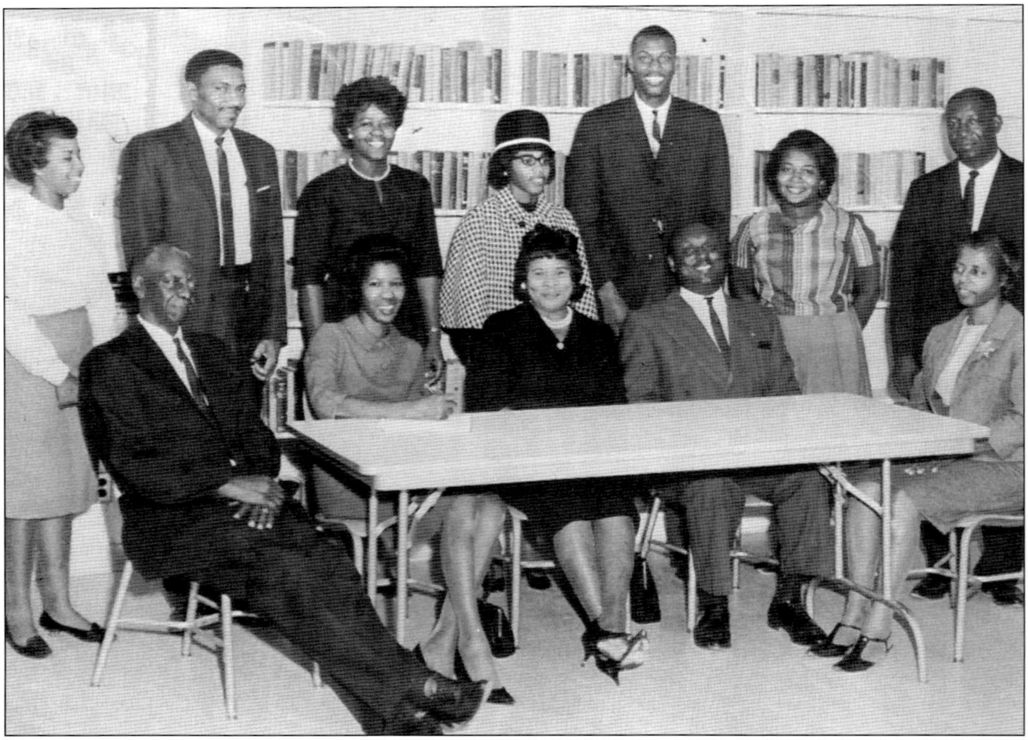

Ribbon cane syrup and buttermilk biscuits made mealtime special in Tyler County as far back as memory serves. D.T. Shepherd and his wife, Goldie Mae Hanks, cornered the market for the sweet delicacy at their sugar cane mill near Doucette. Friends from near and far made their way to the Shepherds' place when syrup-making time came each year. Heritage Village acquired the mill through generous donations. (Courtesy of Shirley Rawls.)

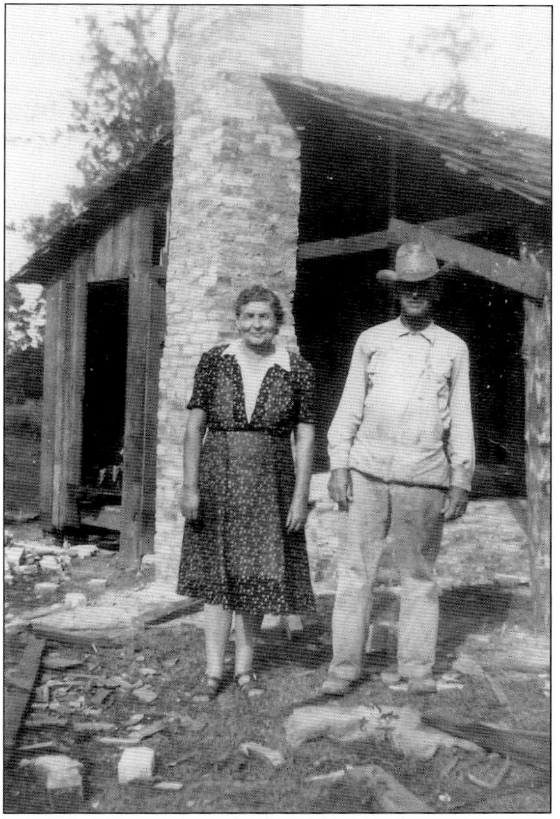

Auctions took center stage on Tuesdays in the 1940s through the 1980s. Originally located near the railroad tracks and later on US Highway 287, stock pens filled up on Mondays in preparation for the sales. Cattle, sheep, goats, and hogs made up the primary stock. Horse sales took place occasionally on Saturday. Dee Fortenberry's sons Rod and Jeff continued the family auction business for many years. (Courtesy of Gladys Best.)

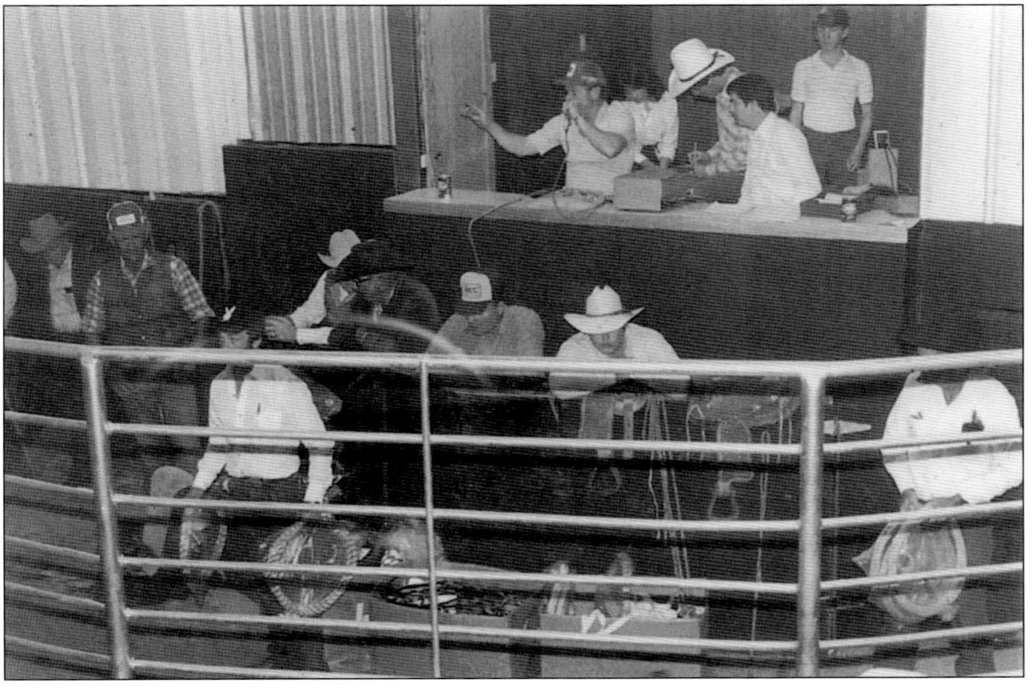

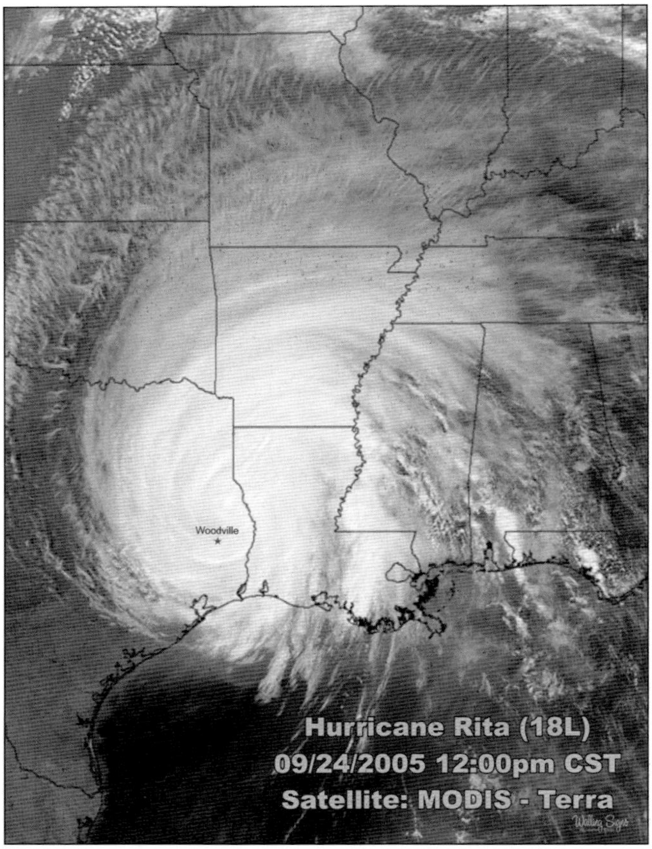

On September 24, 2005, the face of Tyler County changed forever. Hurricane Rita took a ferocious swipe through forests and towns, tossing hardwood trees on their sides and snapping pines in half. In the wake of the storm, blue tarps covered damaged rooftops, generators hummed for weeks, Red Cross and Baptist Men from California fed thousands daily, and the National Guard doled out ice, water, and MREs. Emergency teams camped throughout the county working day and night to clear roads and restore power. All county citizens came together to share resources and to meet each other's needs. The term "community" took on a whole new meaning. (Left, courtesy of NASA; below, courtesy of TCHC.)

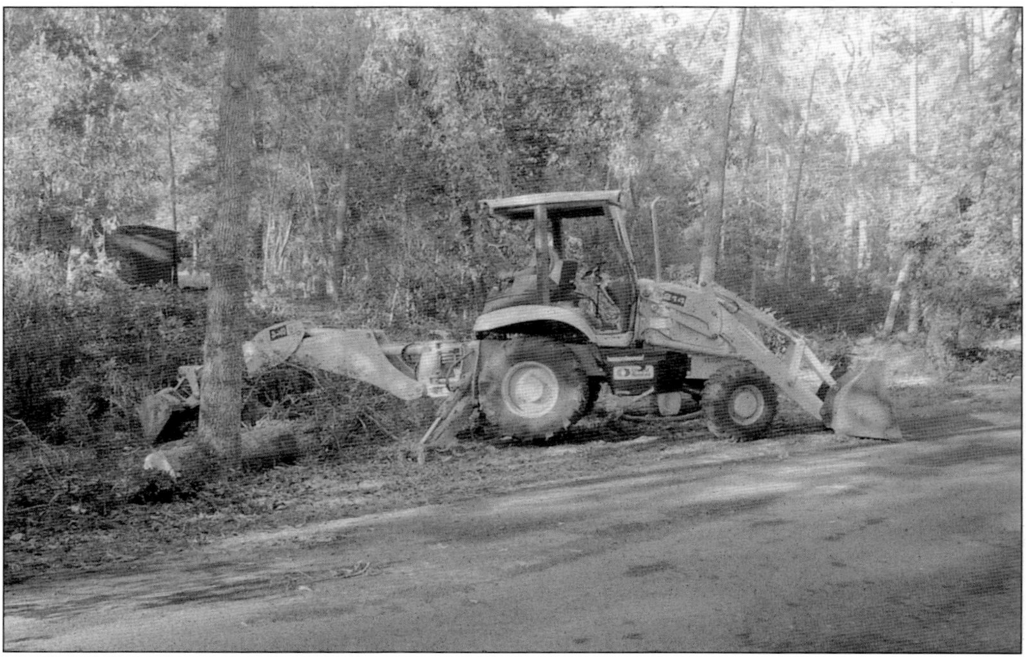

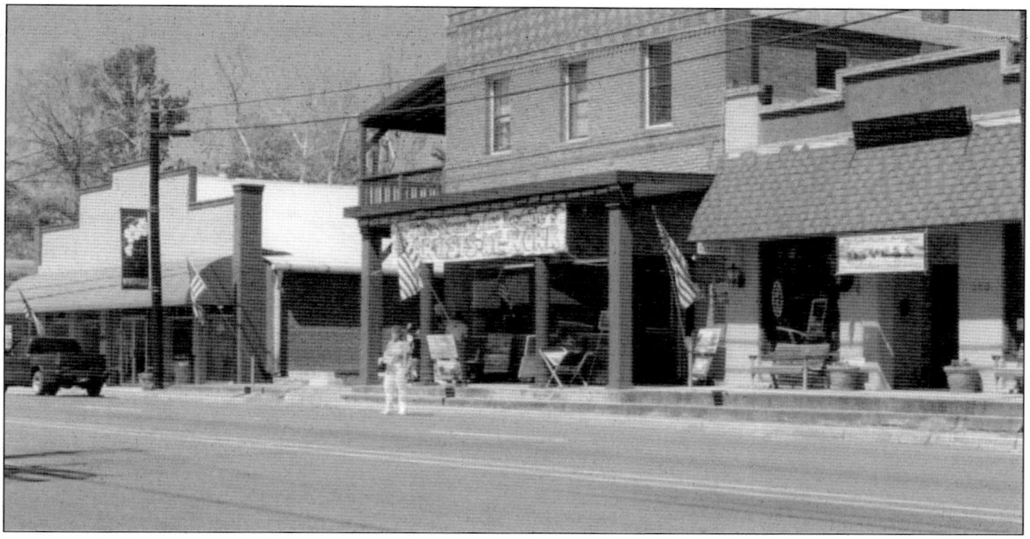

Under the leadership of Sam and Judith Haney, the Tyler County Art League grew from a vision to a full-scale arts district. It began with a simply furnished art gallery that has expanded into a museum-quality array of artwork, including paintings, photography, glass and wood works, and even jewelry. Additionally, the project includes an Emporium for the Arts (a theater) and a studio featuring art and music lessons. A storytelling circle presents historical and whimsical tales. Monthly gatherings of Tyler County Art League members showcase works of talented local and visiting artists. The Haneys also make the venues available for community meetings and social events. (Both, courtesy of TCHC.)

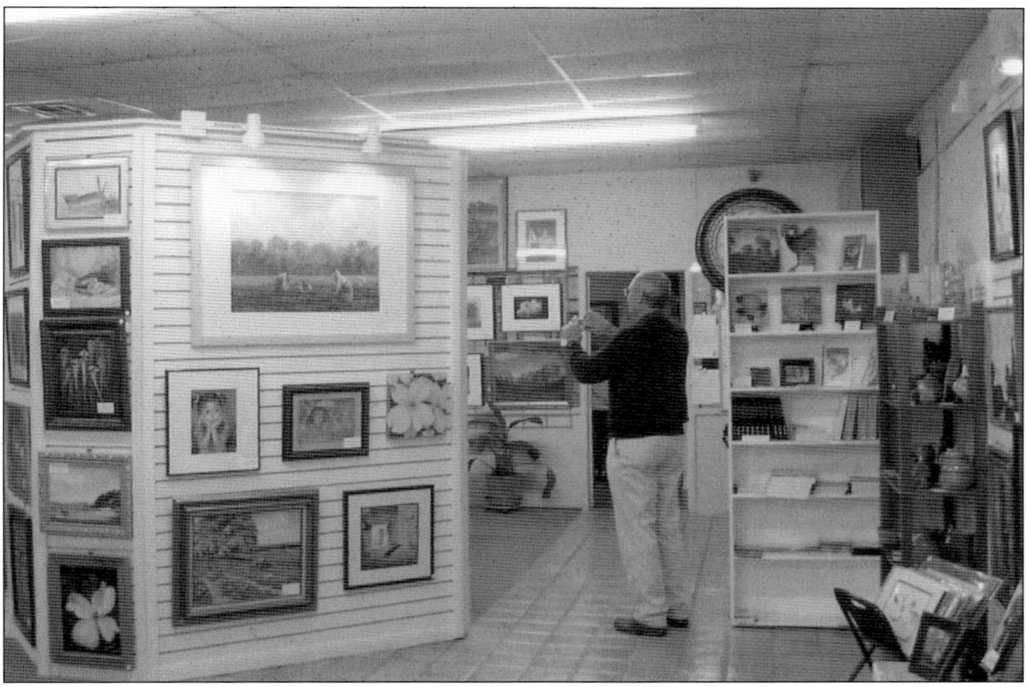

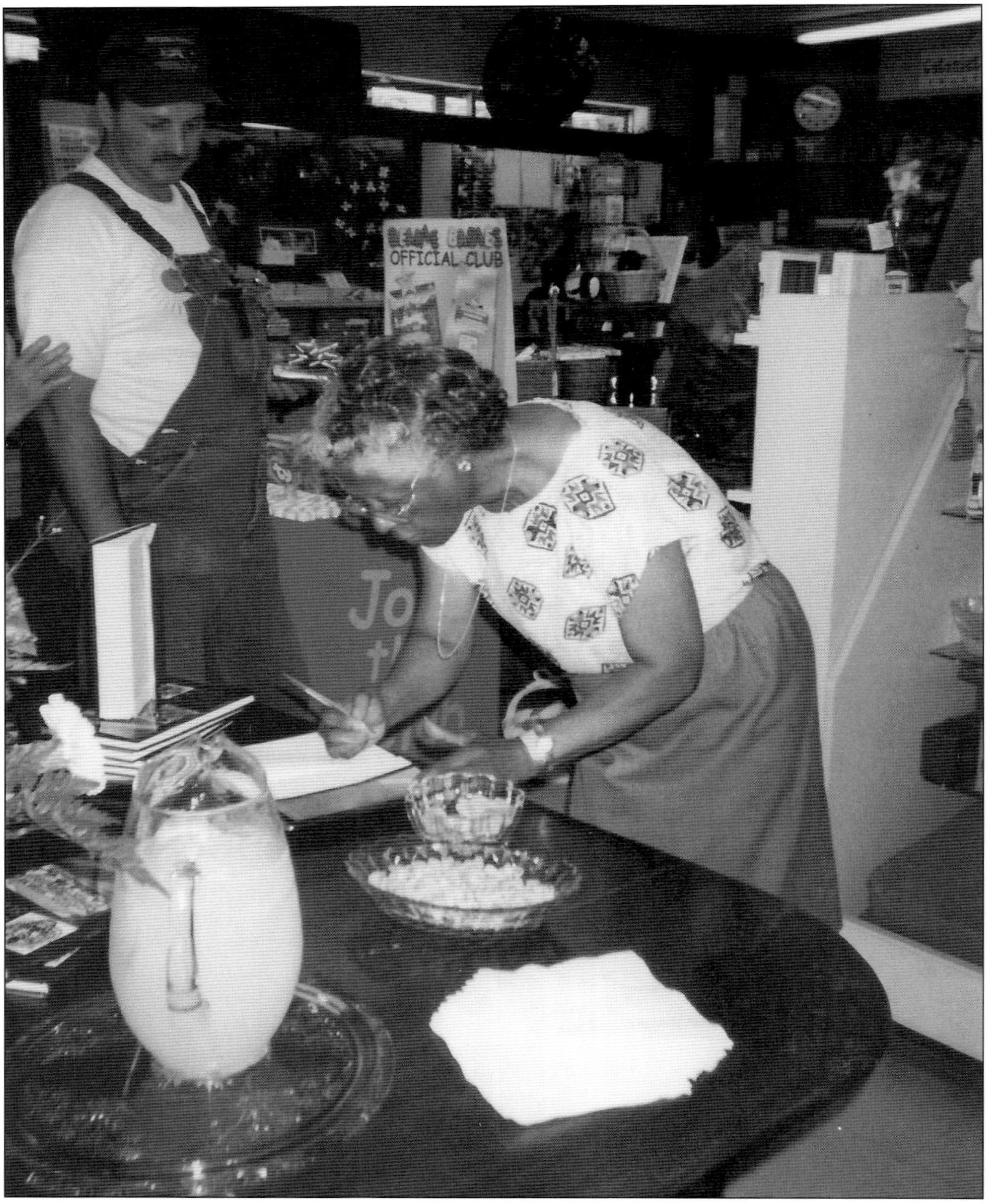

Mayme Canada Brown stands gracefully and humbly among the many talented Tyler County writers. Acting upon the encouragement of former students, Brown took on the daunting task of researching and recording the history of African American schools in Woodville. Her efforts produced a treasured outcome: a roughly 100-page volume, bound in the traditional Scott High School purple trimmed with gold. *A Historical Documentary of the Henry T. Scott School* contains more than 120 historical photographs and countless reports of scholastic, athletic, social, and community events. Additionally, Brown led the efforts to establish an annual Martin Luther King Jr. parade and day of celebration. At age 90, she continues as a productive member of the Tyler County Historical Commission and Heritage Society. (Courtesy of Mayme Canada Brown.)

Five

Faith and Fellowship

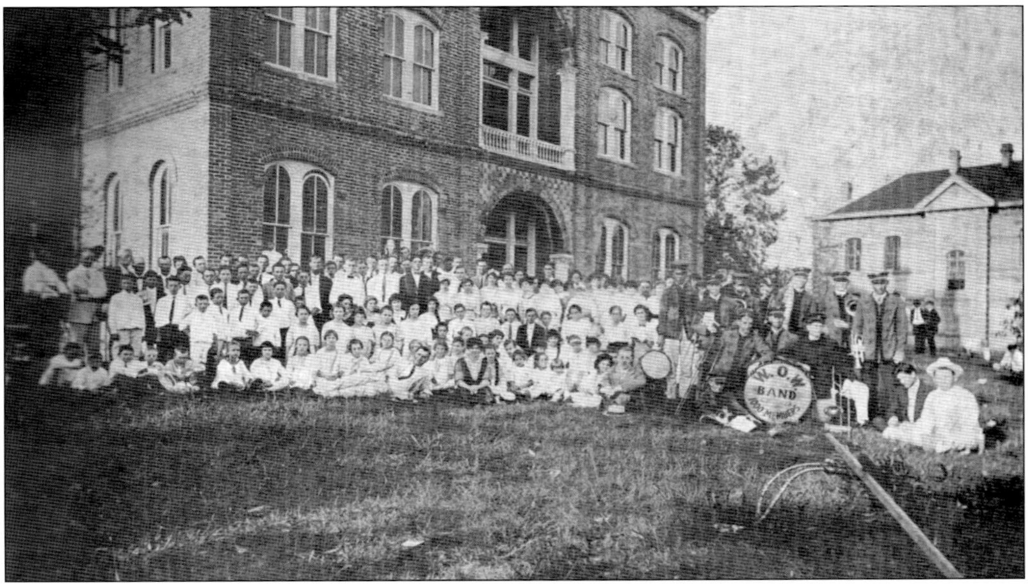

Woodmen of the World sponsored Woodville's first band in 1913. The fraternal organization provided uniforms and instruments for any rural community that could muster the bandsmen and a director. The band played on the courthouse square to entertain during parades, county fairs, and other events. Deke O'Brien described those pictured here as "converts" at a town-wide revival. (Courtesy of TCHS.)

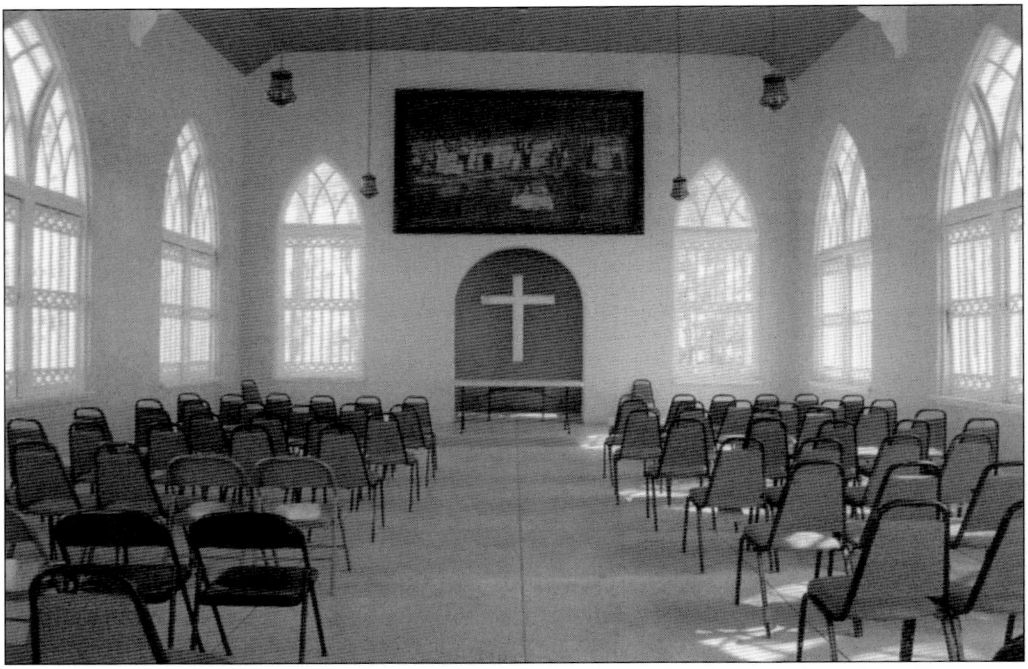

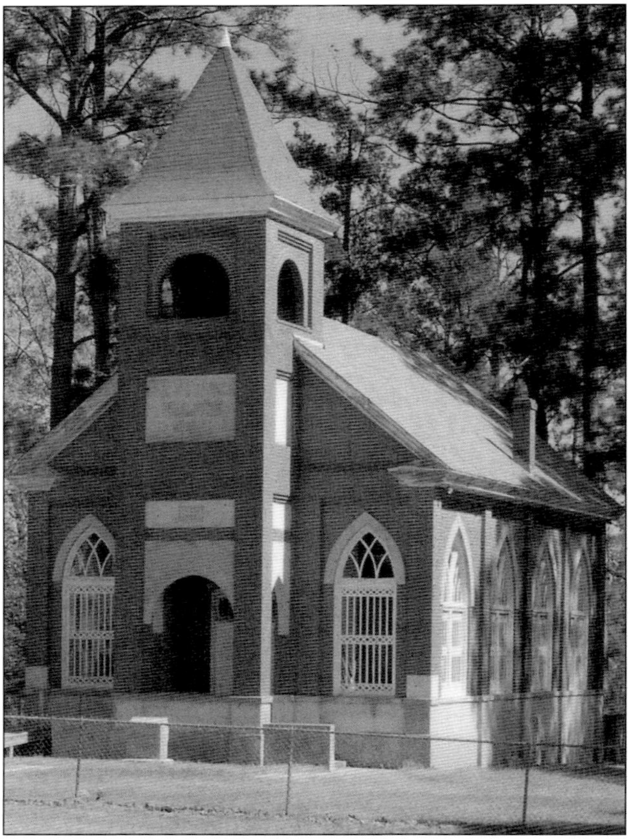

A Baptist minister by calling, Rev. Sam Mann cheerfully baptized any new convert, even the elderly John T. Kirby, who wished to join the Methodist Episcopal South congregation. Kirby's son John Henry commissioned Russian artist Boris Bernhard Gordon to record the event with a painting to be hung in Peach Tree Village Hall when it was built in 1912. Ninety-nine years later, the chapel and the painting still remind visitors of the Kirby family's commitment to family and worship. Former governor Allan Shivers purchased the chapel and the Kirby home property and presented it as a gift to Tyler County. Today, a Christian encampment, Camp Ta-Ku-La, surrounds the chapel and the Kirby home, and the camp staff provides maintenance for those structures. The camp name is taken for the Indian phrase *ta-ku-la*, meaning "peach tree." (Both, courtesy of TCHC.)

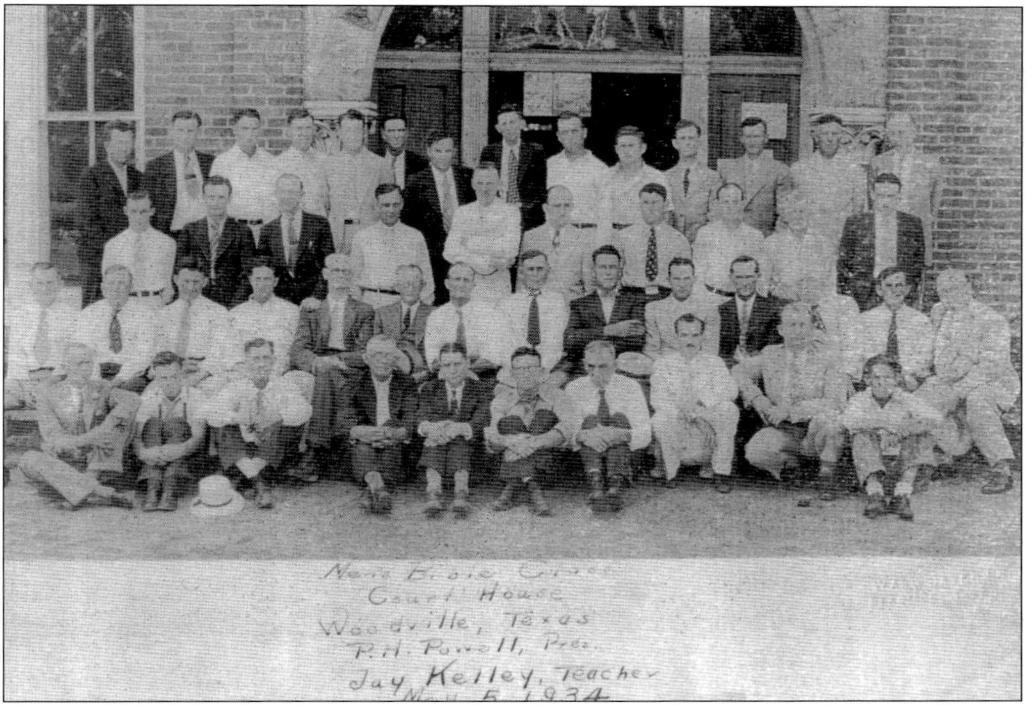

As early as 1934, men from all denominations met on Sunday mornings with their courthouse Bible class teacher Jay Kelley. The lesson concluded in time for members to attend their various churches' morning services. The president of the class, Paul Powell, assigned Bible memory verses to the men each week. Upon meeting members in town later in the week, Powell expected them to repeat the assigned verses or pay $1 into the class benevolence account. Most men went to town prepared to quote the verses, but they still made regular contributions so the class treasury could cover costs of their benevolence projects. (Both, courtesy of TCHC.)

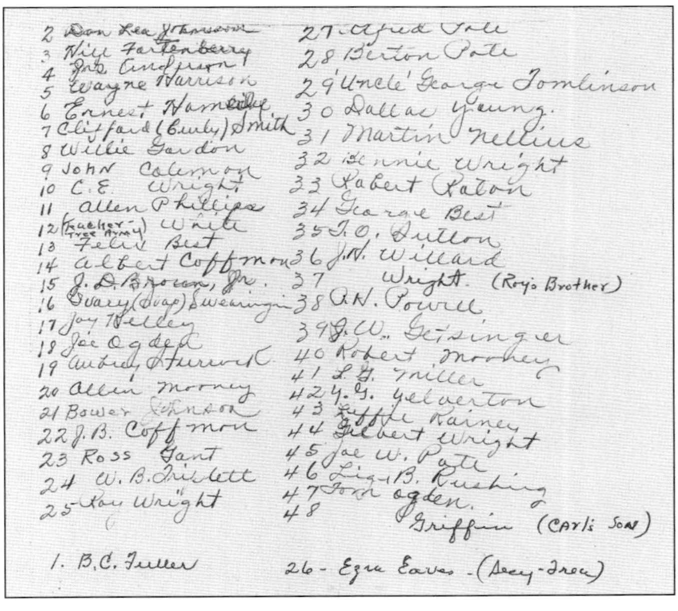

2 Don Lea Johnson
3 Will Fartenberry
4 Jno. Anderson
5 Wayne Harrison
6 Ernest Hamedke
7 Clifford (Curly) Smith
8 Willie Gordon
9 John Coleman
10 C.E. Wright
11 Allen Phillips
12 (Teacher - Tree Army) White
13 Felix Best
14 Albert Coffman
15 J.D. Brown, Jr.
16 Ovary (Soap) Swearingin
17 Jay Kelley
18 Joe Ogden
19 Aubrey Hurwick
20 Allen Mooney
21 Bower Johnson
22 J.B. Coffman
23 Ross Gant
24 W.B. Triplett
25 Roy Wright

1. B.C. Fuller

27 Alfred Toll
28 Burton Pate
29 'Uncle' George Tomlinson
30 Dallas Young.
31 Martin Nellius
32 Bennie Wright
33 Robert Paton
34 George Best
35 T.O. Dutton
36 J.N. Willard
37 Wright. (Roy's Brother)
38 A.N. Powell
39 J.W. Getsinger
40 Robert Mooney
41 L.G. Miller
42 Y.G. Yelverton
43 Luffie Rainey
44 Gilbert Wright
45 Joe W. Pate
46 Lige B. Rushing
47 Tom Ogden.
48 Griffin (Carl's Son)

26 - Ezra Eaves - (Secy-Treas)

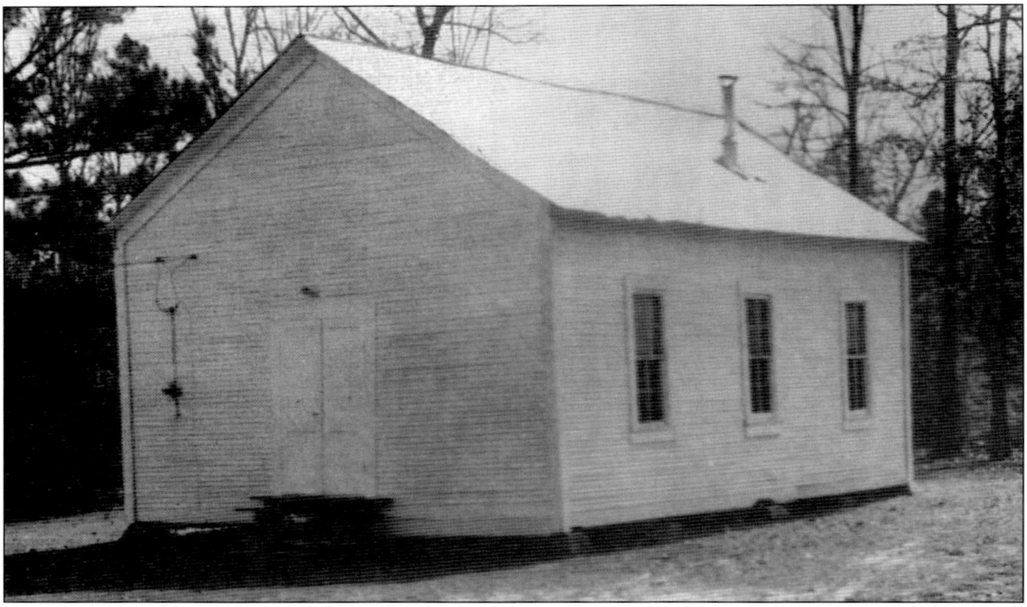

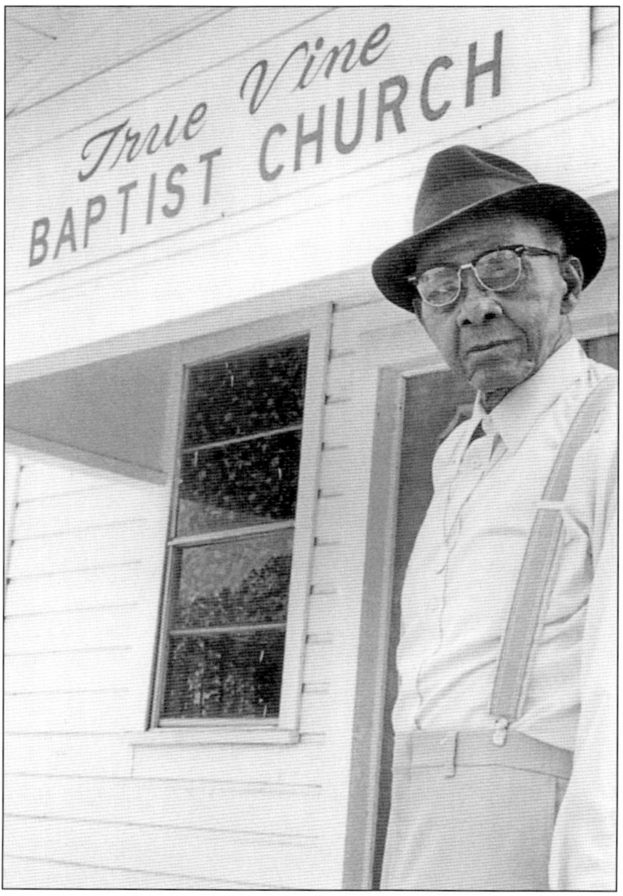

The *Tyler County Booster* reported in October 1940 that the "Hopewell school community has built a two-room log house near the schoolhouse to serve hot lunches in through the winter. WPPA aid can be given as there is a building." Originally located on the Old Emilie Road (now CR 4210), the Hopewell community later moved their church-school building to the newly paved US Highway 190. (Courtesy of Debbie Walker.)

The Reverend Harvey McCartney Sr. began his ministry at True Vine Missionary Baptist Church in Doucette at the age of 12. Assisted by his wife, Gertrude, McCartney continued his ministry throughout his life and contributed to the building of a new worship center dedicated in 2008. Their son Harvey Jr. also served the church as a deacon. (Courtesy of TCHS.)

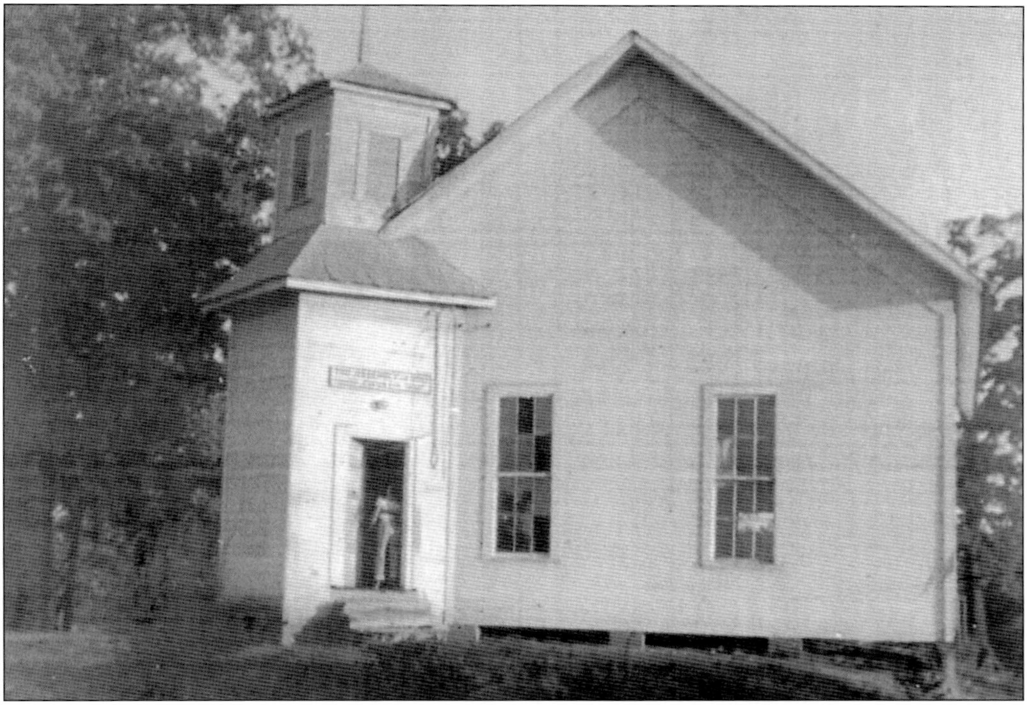

Colmesneil's First Baptist Church grew from a brush arbor meeting held by Rev. Arnold Rhodes in 1883. Built in 1885 and east of current US Highway 69, the first frame structure fell to a turn-of-the-century hurricane. Members soon rebuilt it. In 1947, the congregation moved to its new brick building on FM 256. Congregants donated their former building to the Assembly of God Church, which sold it to Katy Baptist Church. (Courtesy of Debbie Walker.)

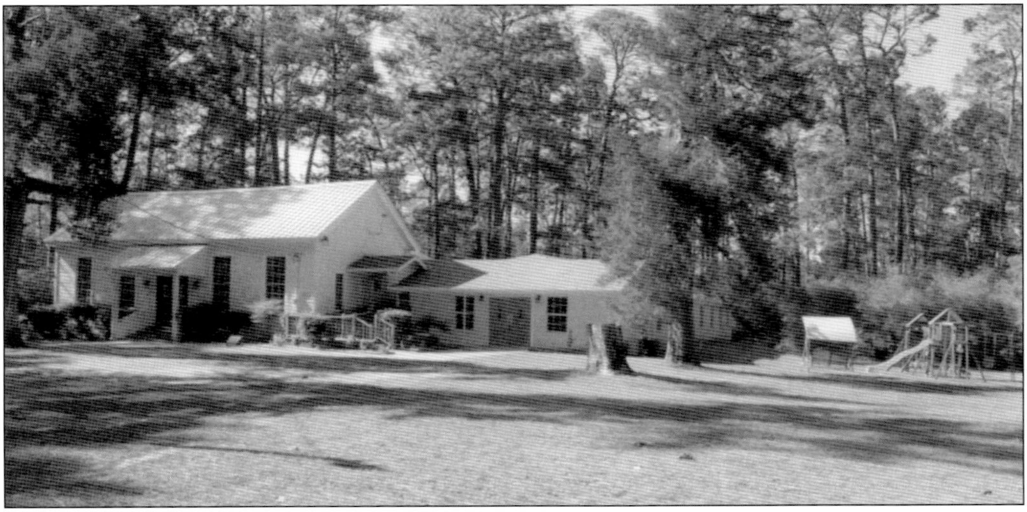

When the Civil War ended, soldiers faced the difficult challenge of returning to their homes. One such soldier was Tom Seamans. Given the shortage of horses, Seamans walked slightly more than 100 miles from Sabine Pass back to his home in the Enon Church community. Perhaps he was fortunate enough to be wearing leather shoes made for soldiers by the Ratcliff family of Spurger. (Courtesy of TCHC.)

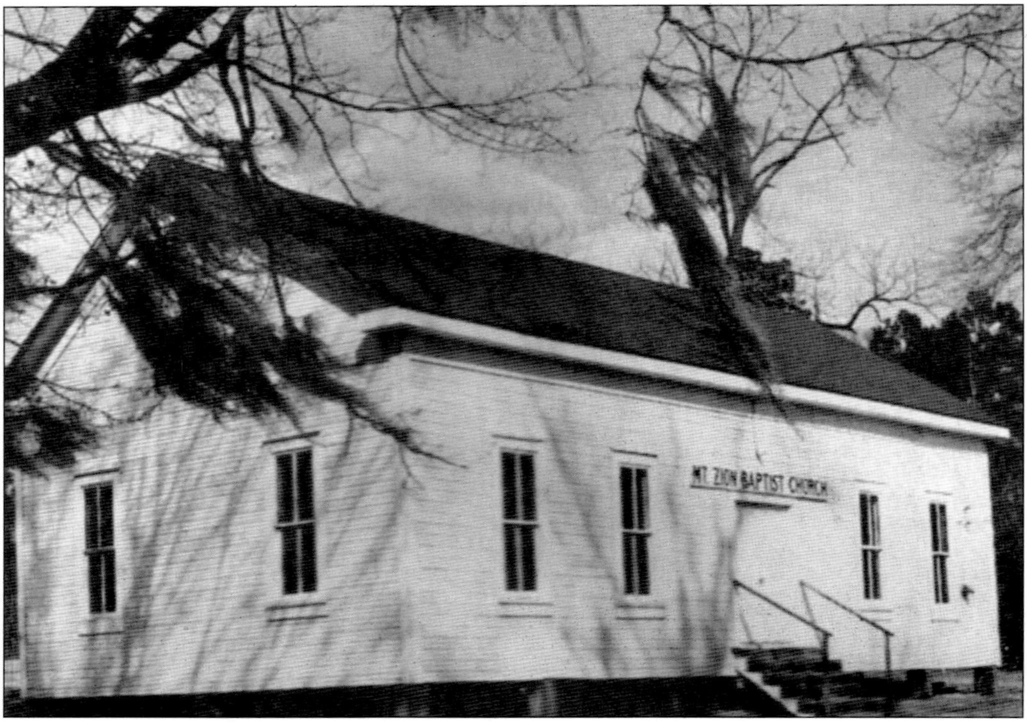

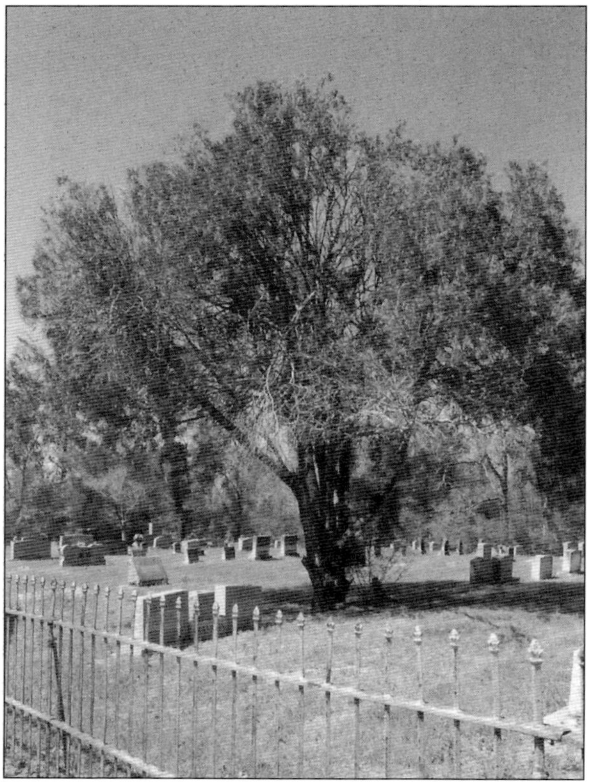

Pioneers organized Mount Zion Baptist Church in the 1830s at a location behind "the old Jim Powell house," which was between Mount Hope and Chester. Later, the church moved to its current location on US Highway 287. The move followed the coming of the railroad and road improvements connecting the new town of Chester to Woodville, the county seat of government. In the late 1930s when Tyler County Courthouse remodeling took place, Mount Zion acquired the ornate iron fence and used it to enclose their cemetery. Although the church disbanded, the cemetery association continues to uphold family legacies and maintain their ties to the peaceful, sandy hilltop. (Both, courtesy of TCHC.)

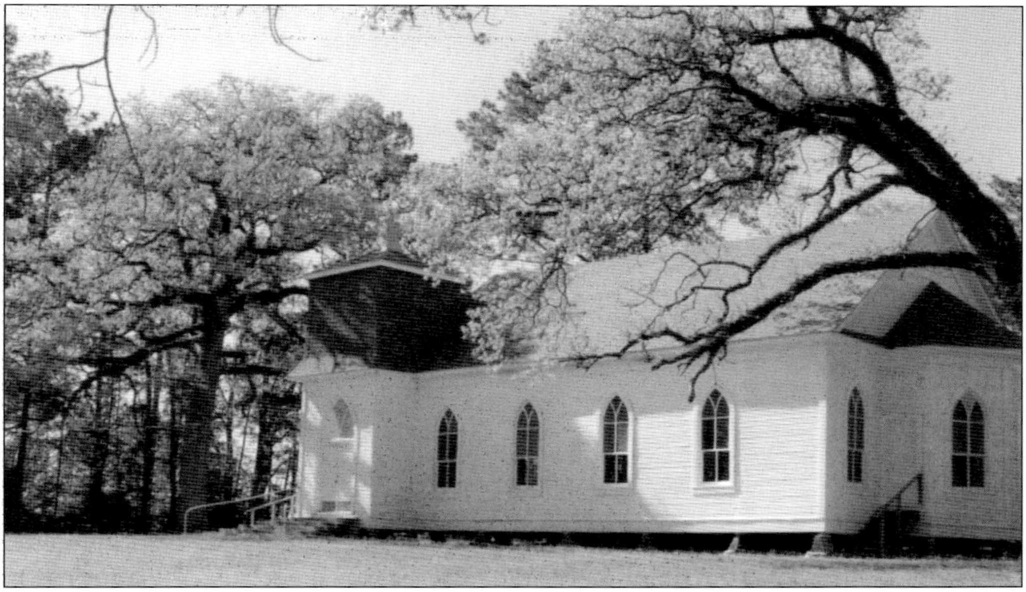

In 1836, James and Tabitha Huff Barnes came to Tyler County with four sons, two married daughters, and four daughters who would marry in Texas. Free land enticed the Barnes family to leave Philadelphia, Mississippi, and begin a new life in the community of Mount Hope. In 1837, an English minister held a brush arbor meeting that led to the formation of the first United Methodist Church in Tyler County. Originally, the church met in a log building, and in 1853, they replaced it with one made of sawn lumber. That building served as the school, church, and lodge. Lodge members later constructed a new building in Chester, but the church stayed at the original location. Mount Hope Cemetery, created at the death of Lucinda Barnes Rotan, occupies part of the front yard of James Barnes's original homesite. (Both, courtesy of TCHC.)

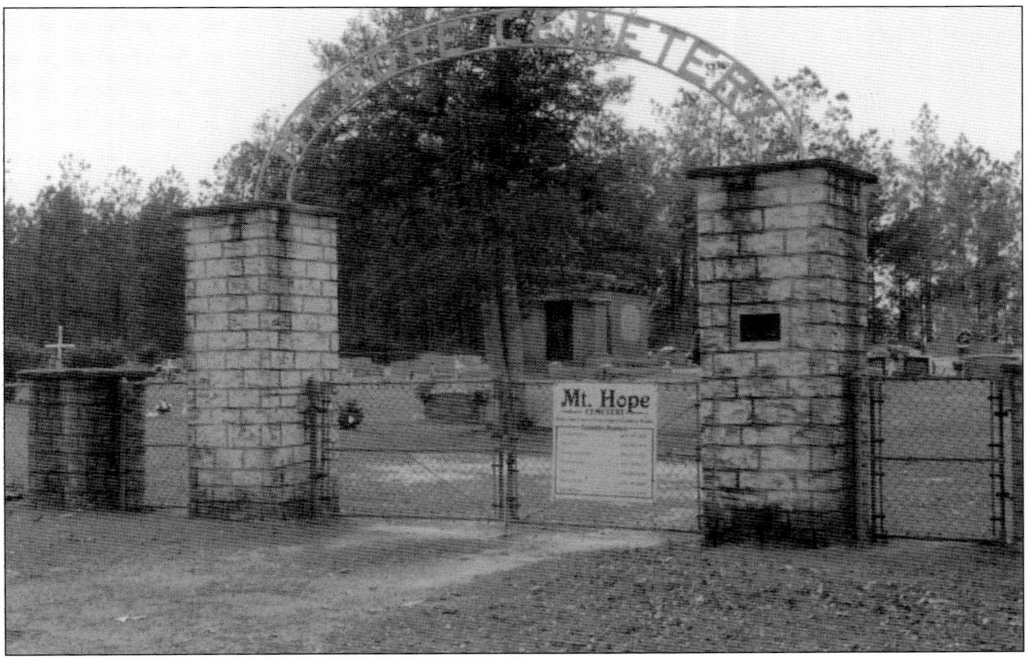

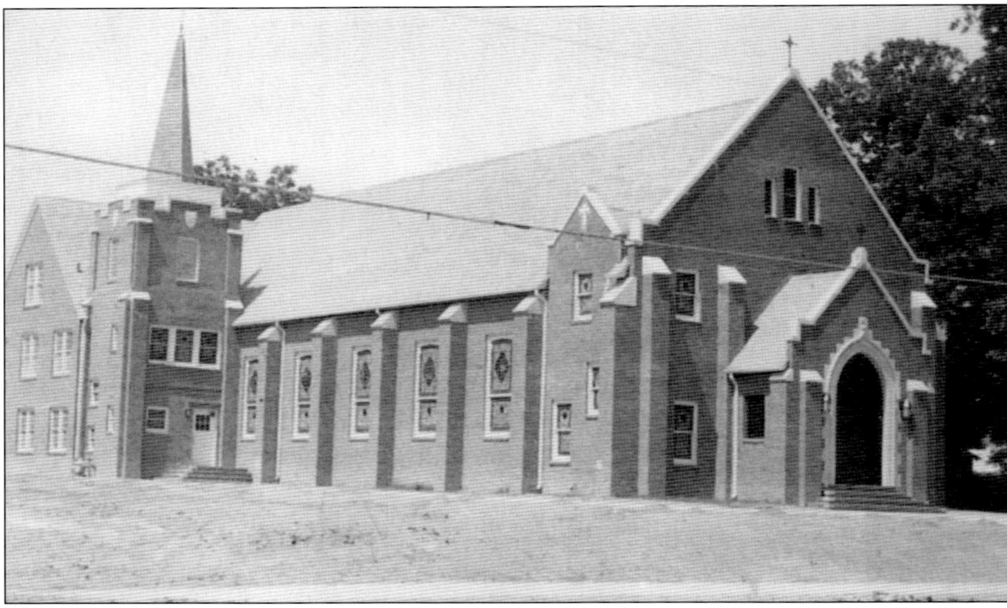

The earliest Methodist congregations began in Woodville before 1849, with the first building being constructed in 1878. Woodville United Methodist Church celebrated its new Gothic-design sanctuary in 1949. It united the north and south congregations, replacing two simple frame structures located nearby. The new building became the hub that had additions of a chapel, classrooms, youth center, and, recently, the Wesley Center for Christian Outreach. (Courtesy of Gladys Best.)

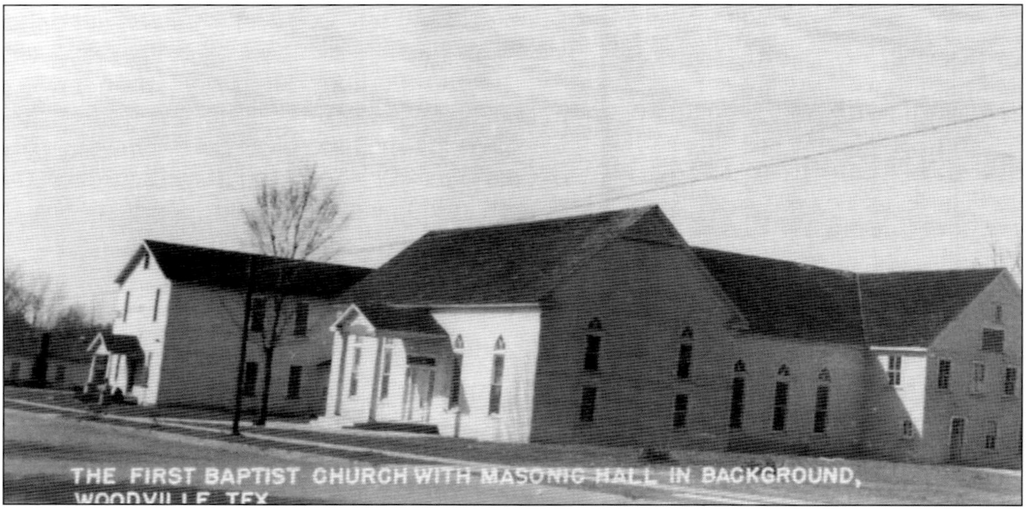

First Baptist Church of Woodville, chartered in 1851, began with a membership of 21 white persons and 26 black slaves. They met in the Masonic hall until 1891, when the church built a one-room frame structure on lots purchased from John Henry and Lelia Kirby. In the 1930s, Pastor Billy Nash led members to expand that building, and in 1950, Dr. L.T. Daniel guided the church to erect the current brick sanctuary. (Courtesy of FBC Woodville.)

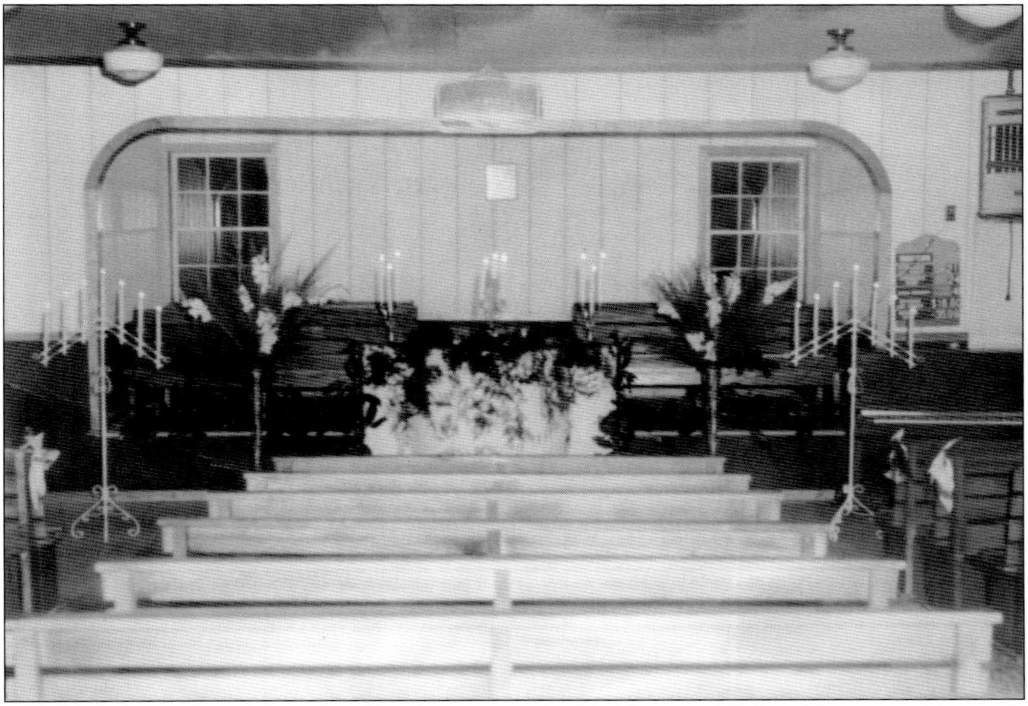

Campground Baptist Church (sometimes called New Shiloh Baptist Church) began in the early 1880s with camp meetings held under spreading trees and often with evening meetings around campfires. The church continues providing religious training and hosting celebrations for families living along FM 256 between US Highway 190 and US Highway 287. A photograph of the 1950s wedding site for Billie Fortenberry and Alford Lee Polk includes a hint about membership activities decades later. (Courtesy of Billie Polk.)

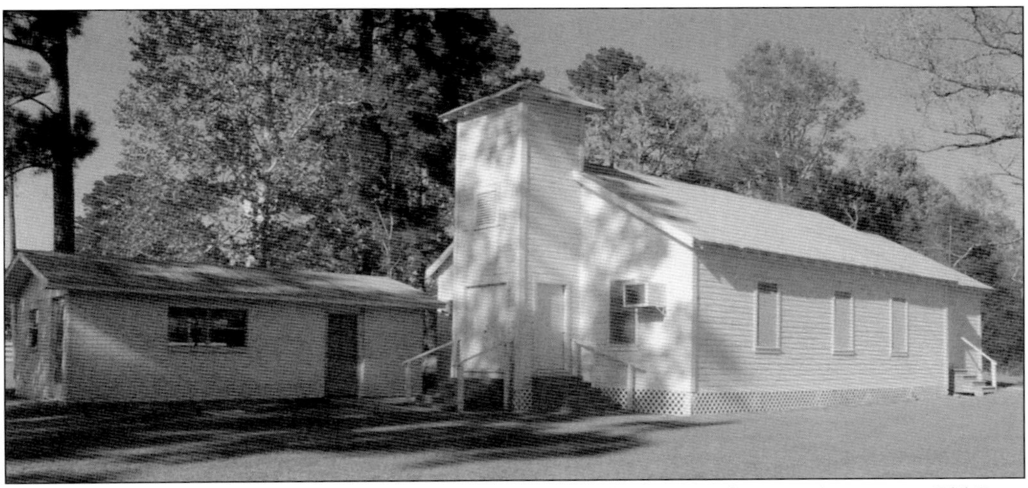

Pine Grove Missionary Baptist Church, founded in the late 1880s, began adjacent to Old Pine Grove Cemetery in Dies. Following a move and a destructive storm, the church found its permanent home on property donated in 1928 by Reverend Henry and Vicey Frazier. The church served as an elementary school from 1948 to 1949. Until his passing in 2011, Pastor Lester Mitchell preached passionate sermons to the faithful Pine Grove flock. (Courtesy of TCHC.)

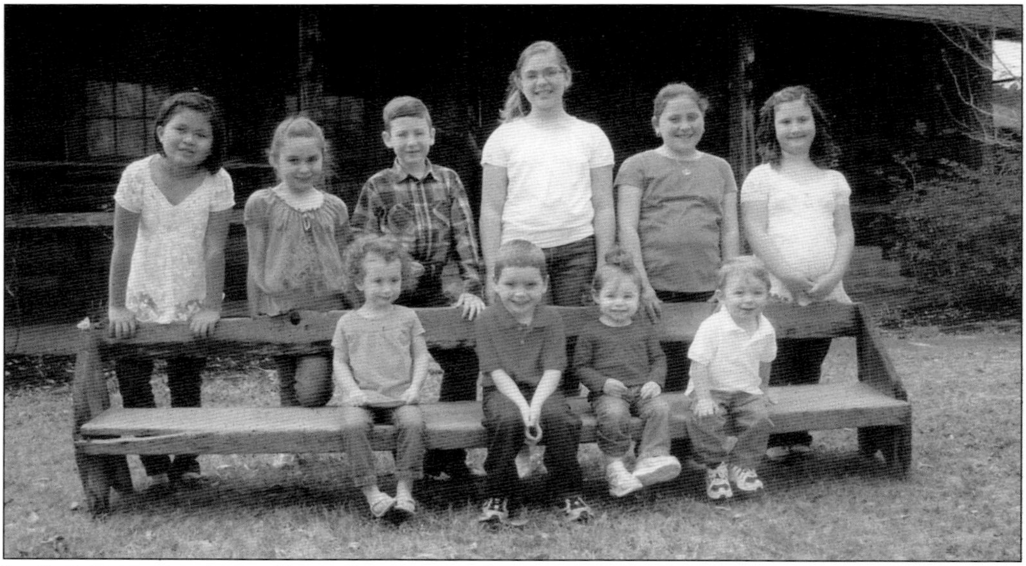

In 1842, James Barclay and his wife, Virginia, chose a scenic hilltop overlooking Big Cypress Creek as the site for their new log cabin. Appointed by Texas president Sam Houston, Barclay served as the first Indian agent to the Alabama and Coushatta Indians living in the area. When visiting Indians waited for their turn with the representative, they used kernels of corn to play "fox and geese" on a game board they had scratched into their host's bench. Barclay built a relationship of trust and mutual respect with these friends. Today, seventh-generation Barclay descendants visit and play on the same bench. The log cabin, with minor modifications (plumbing, electric wiring, and air conditioning) continues as the center for family gatherings. James and Virginia Barclay were buried about two miles away (as the crow flies) in the Hart-Mill Cemetery. (Above, courtesy of Blanche Risinger Shaw; below, courtesy of TCHC.)

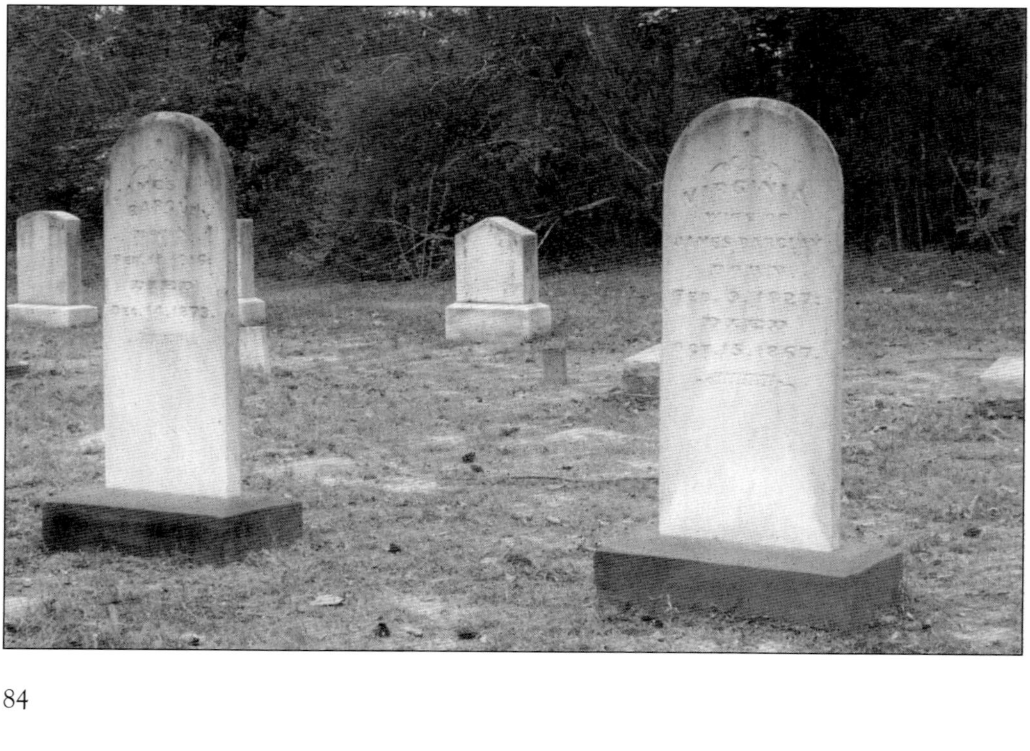

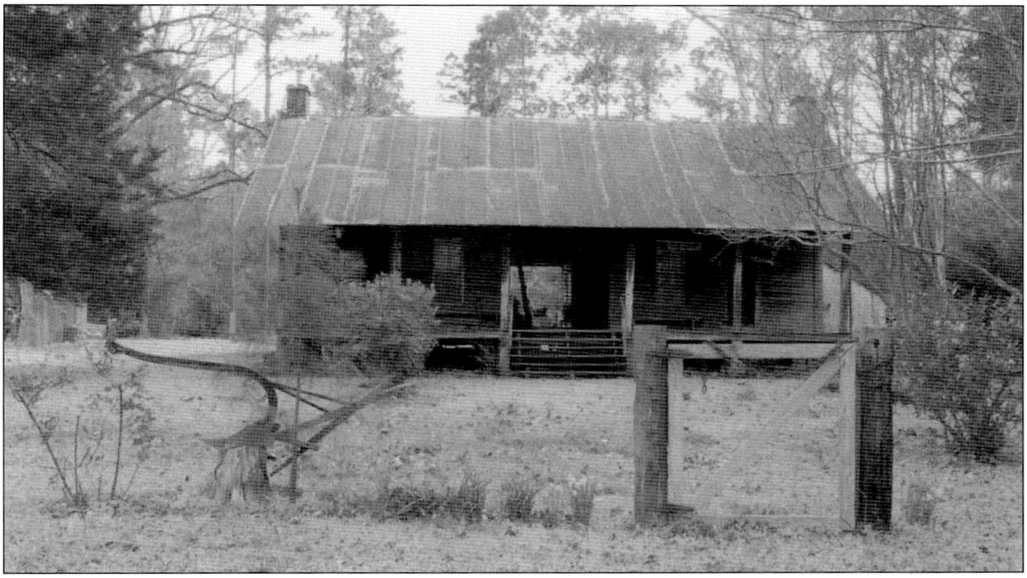

Civil War widow Sara Hicks brought her six children from Georgia to Town Bluff in 1870. John Thomas, William Lewis, and Richard Joel all built homes on what would become Pedigo Loop. It begins at Town Bluff Cemetery on FM 92, passes one Hicks homesite, continues past a dogtrot home built by William Lewis Hicks (above), crosses Camp Branch Bridge, and leads to the Pedigo Cemetery. The loop continues past Abram and Julia Pedigo's home place, passes another Pedigo home and a former Hicks's home that was once used as a store and post office. The road winds between two more Hicks' homes and drops off sharply to return to FM 92. In 1938, the Pedigos' 11 children honored their parents' memory with a stone chapel in the family cemetery. Pedigo descendants and spouses inherit the privilege of being buried there. (Both, courtesy of TCHC.)

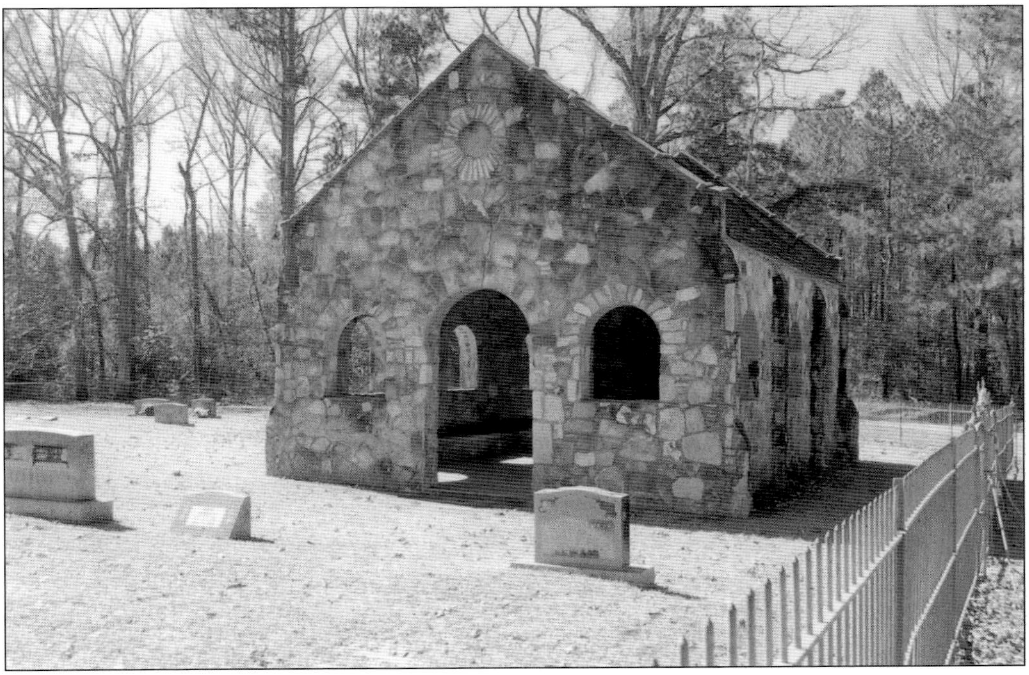

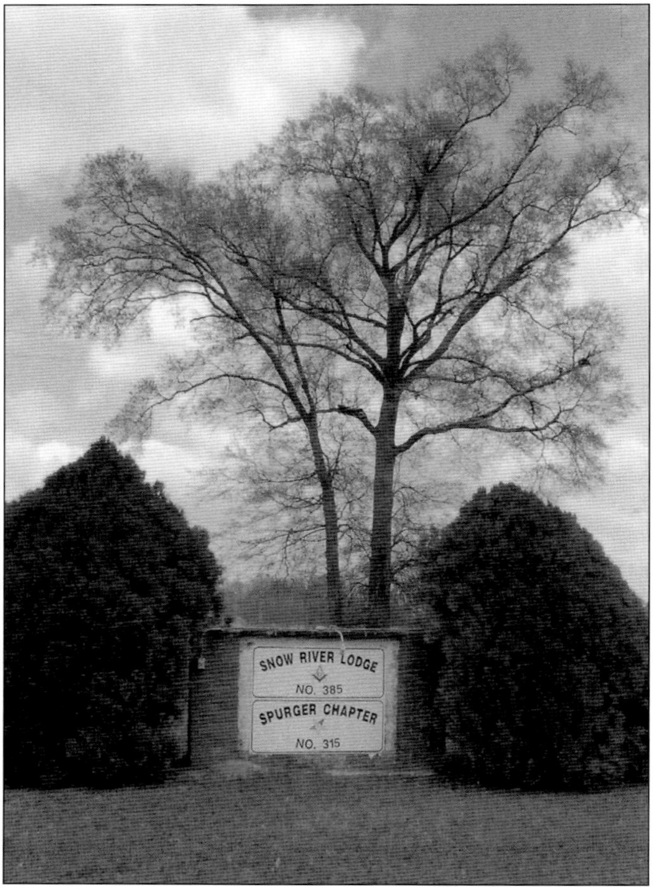

Snow River Lodge takes its name from the Native American name for the nearby river now called the Neches. Legend has it that the earliest settlers along the river banks chose the name Snow River because of the snowy white sand bars that welcomed them to camp in bends of the river. (Courtesy of TCHC.)

Faith and fellowship commonly shared among gatherers at churches and cemeteries also played a part in the daily lives of early pioneers. Men celebrated their providential good fortune when they delivered a full crop of cotton to Pate's Gin, which was located east of the railroad tracks in Woodville. With wagons unloaded and leaving for home, farmers often remarked, "See you next Sabbath, if the Lord's willing and the creek don't rise." (Courtesy of Iva Jo Cook.)

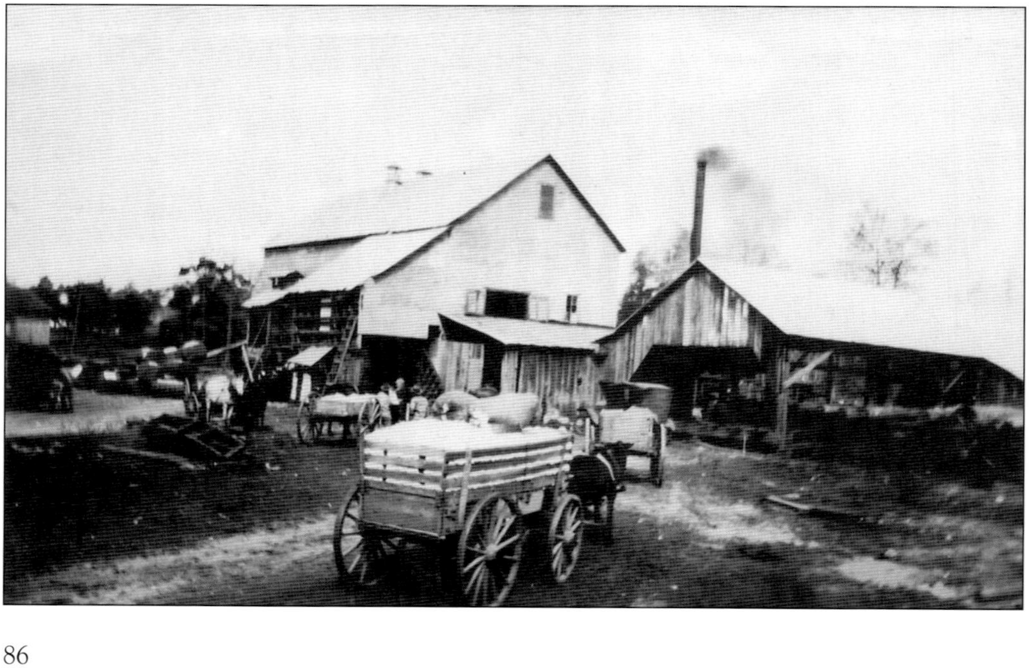

Six

Scholars and Schools

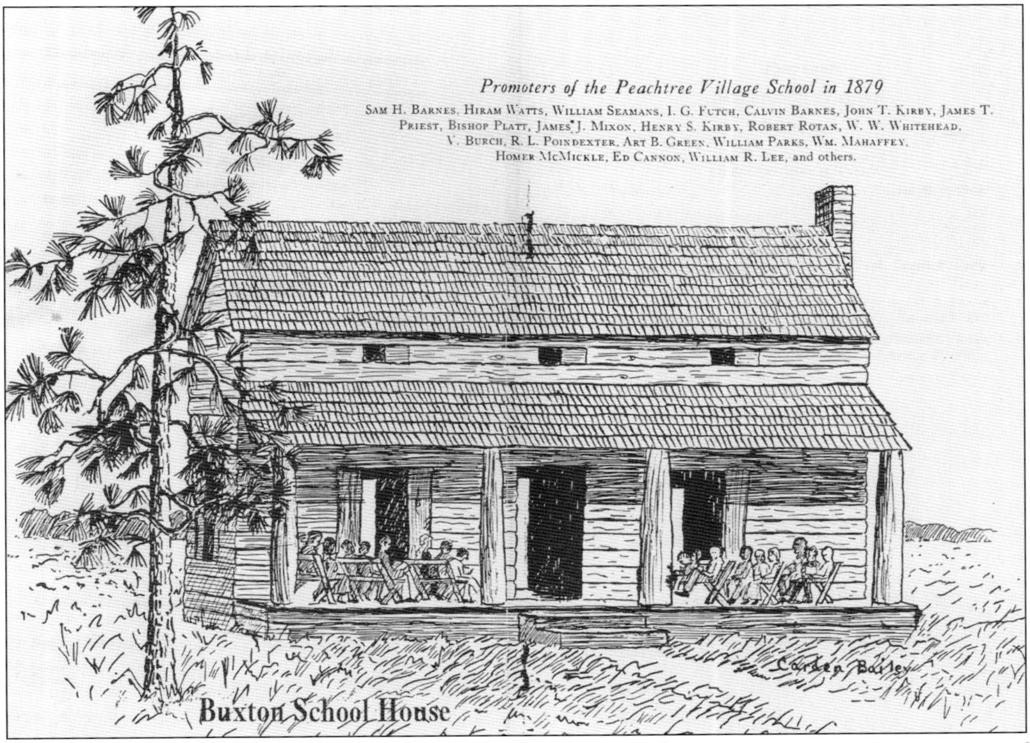

In July 1929, dignitaries from near and far celebrated the 50th anniversary of the opening of Peach Tree Village Crow School. Beginning early in the morning and continuing late into the evening, speeches, singing, dinner-on-the-grounds, and dancing filled both Fridays and Saturdays in Prof. Frank P. Crow's school, which began in 1879 with 75 students attending a six-month period. Students met in a reconditioned log house formerly occupied by freed slaves. (Courtesy of Woodville Independent School District.)

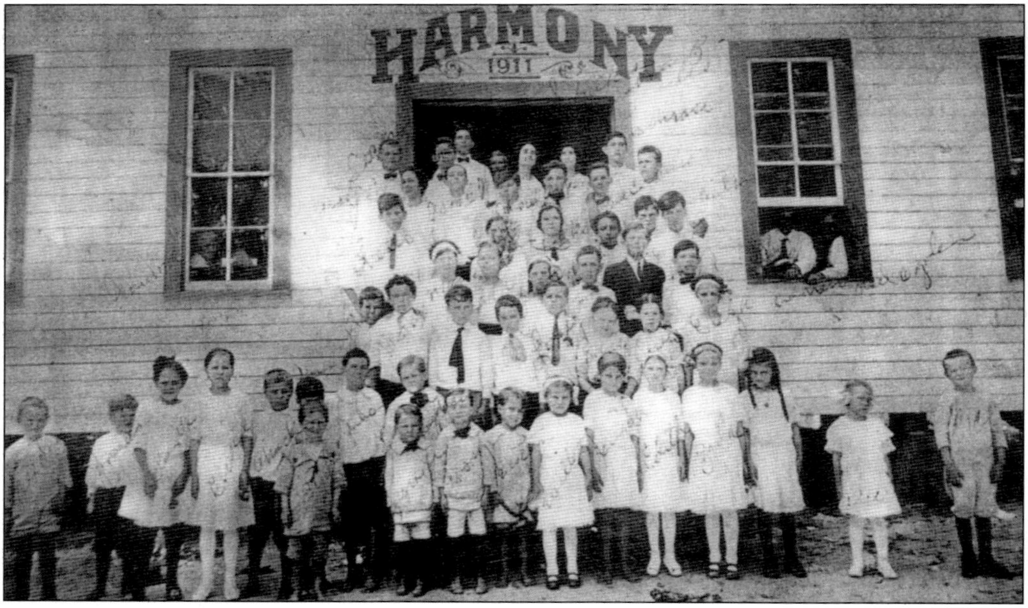

In 1916, county school records show that 54 schools met in 47 districts. As transportation and roads improved, schools began consolidating and continued until the final two schools—Hillister and Doucette—moved their students to Woodville in 1953 and 1955, respectively. Since that time, five districts have continued to educate Tyler County students: Chester, Colmesneil, Spurger, Warren, and Woodville. A photograph of Harmony school children in 1915 reflects the students' true exuberance for life in the country. Young gentlemen scholars of Ira Belt's 1910 school in the Egypt community obviously valued a close connection to the land. Shoes need not be allowed to interfere with their well-grounded feeling. Young ladies, however, knew the importance of looking their best for school pictures and wore their most fluffy hair bows. Boys and girls alike sported their best zippered smiles for the photographer. (Both, courtesy of TCHS.)

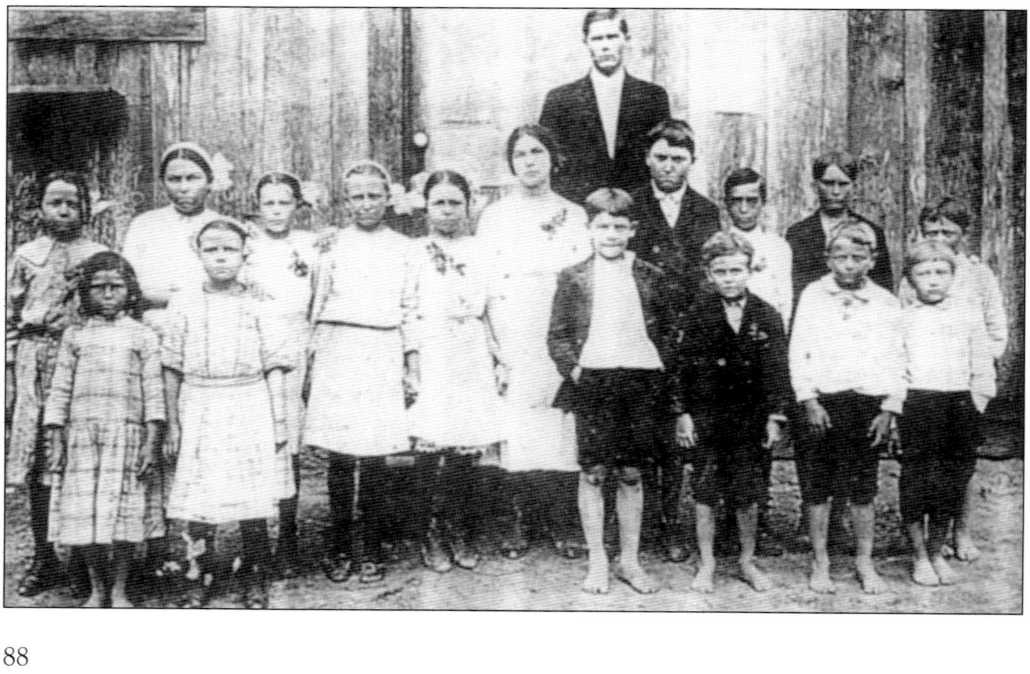

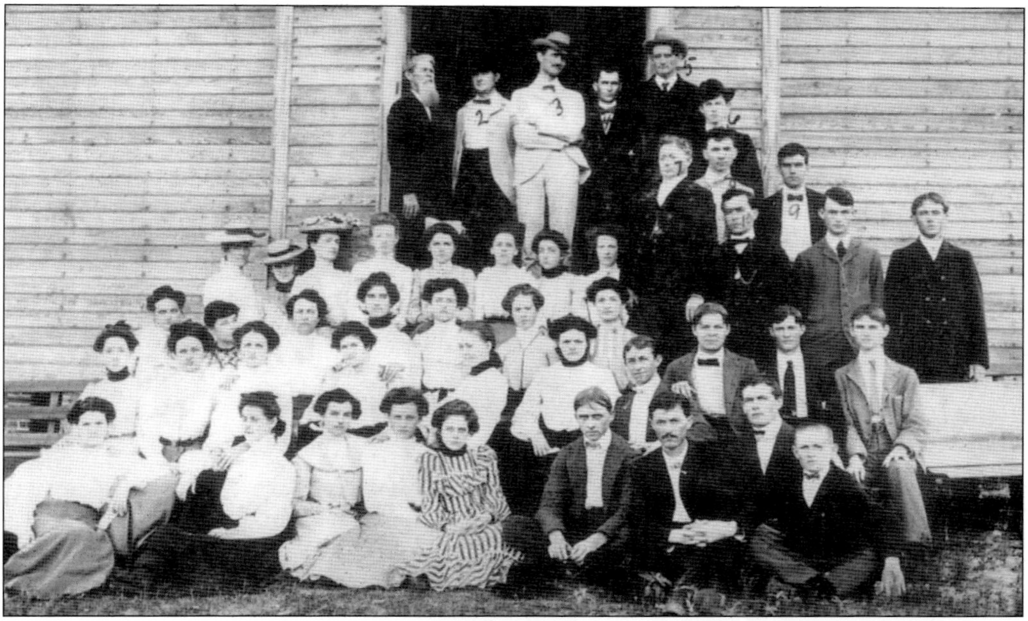

The 1838 legislature used land grants to promote free education in Texas. Continued support came from interest paid on loans made to railroads. Yet, the 1870s found high rates of illiteracy across the state. Beginning in 1879, normal schools responded to the state's need for more trained and certified teachers. The 1905 Colmesneil Normal School offered free tuition for young men and women wishing to become certified teachers. The Sam Houston State Normal Institute, chartered in Huntsville, most likely sponsored the training. Tyler County officials set a goal of offering a school within walking distance (two miles) of each child's home. The number of schools in Tyler County expanded from eight in 1854 to 47 by 1917. Schools prospered. Years later, Shirley Jordan (with Shirley Temple curls) waved goodbye and walked from Joe's Lake to her first day of school. (Above, courtesy of TCHS; right, courtesy of a friend.)

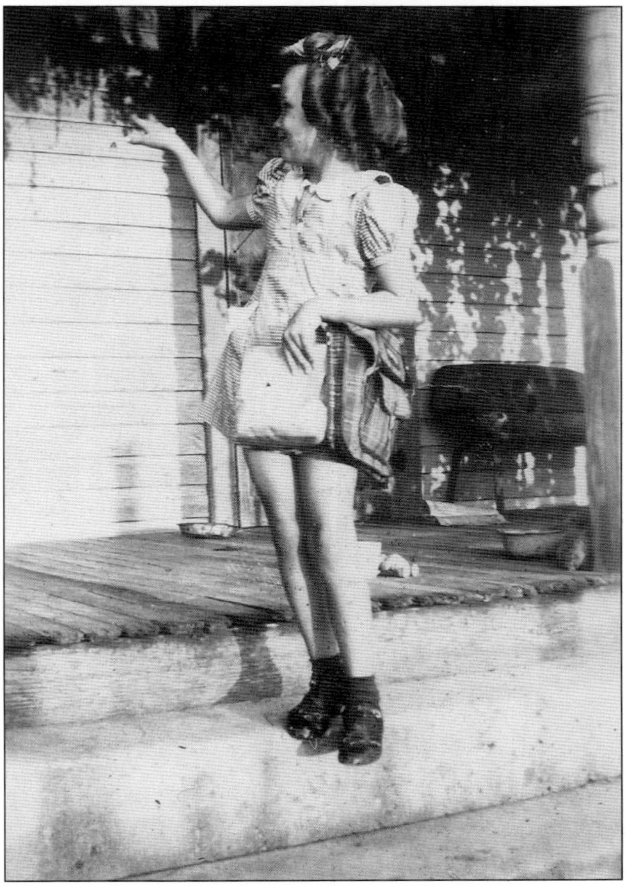

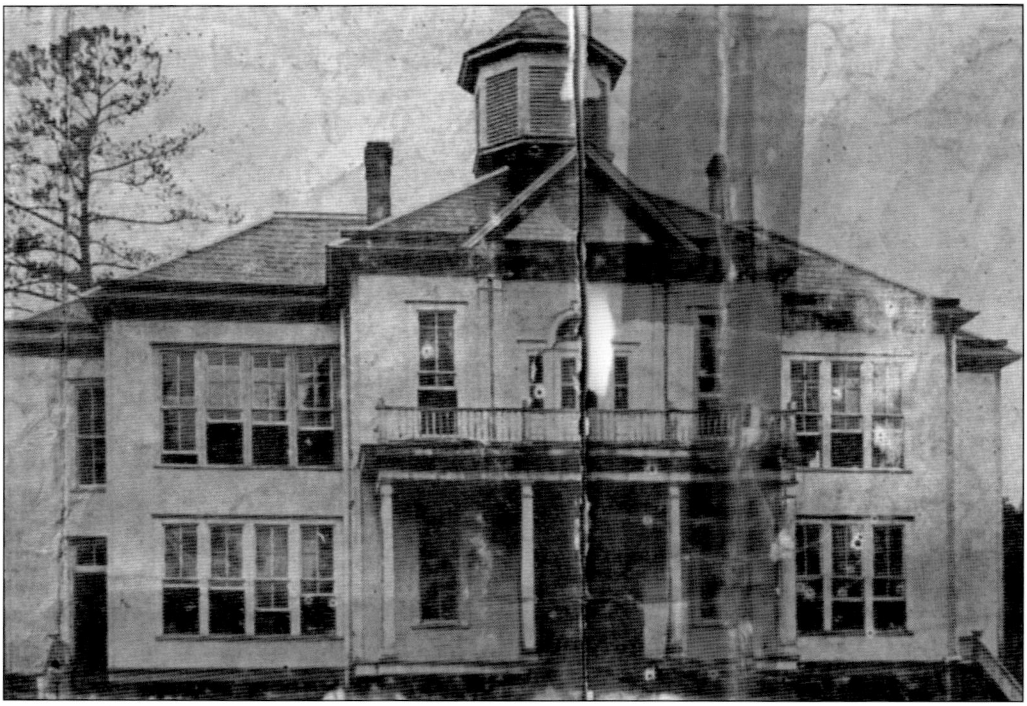

Built for $5,000 in 1903 to specifications of a first-class public building, Tyler County High School belonged to the corporation formed by its subscribers. With main entrances on north and south sides, male and female students used separate entrances on east and west sides. Likewise, they used separate staircases to reach the second-floor auditorium where assemblies and weekly chapel services took place. The building burned in 1924, causing students to once again resort to meeting for classes in churches and the courthouse. Following a successful bond election for $36,000, taxpayers provided the second public school building in Tyler County. Doucette had done the same thing 10 years earlier. The new brick building opened in 1925 and housed all 12 grades. It included indoor restrooms, which were a novelty that required explanation for most of the students. (Above, courtesy of ASLM; below, courtesy of Dan Utley.)

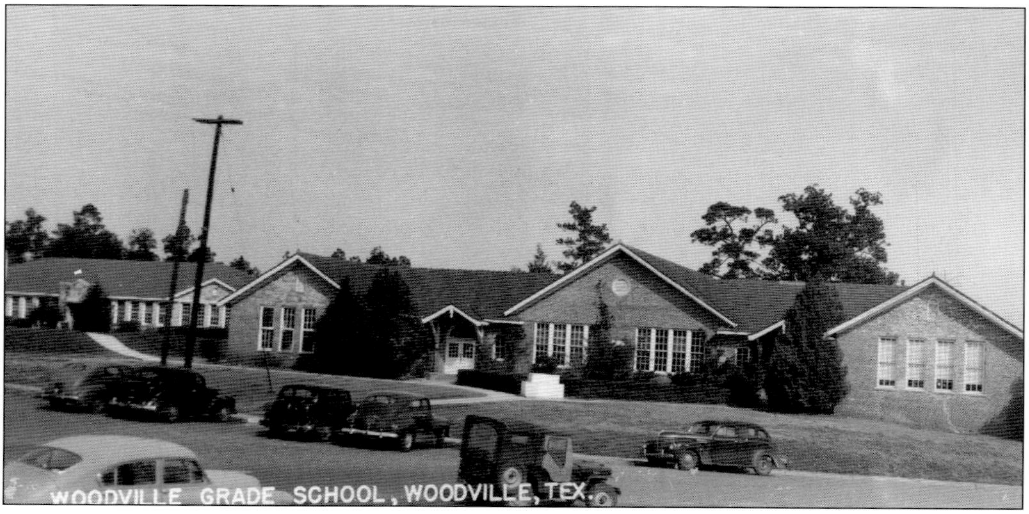

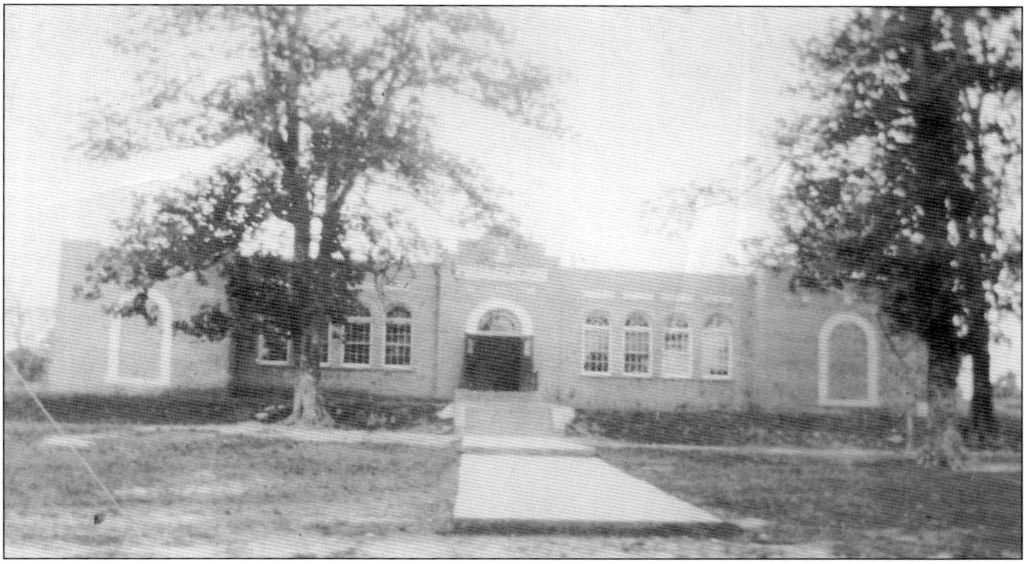

P.I. Hunter came to Tyler County in 1892 with a degree from the University of North Carolina and started his teaching career at Spurger. In 1920, he began as superintendent and teacher in Woodville. There, he guided the consolidation process that grew Woodville's graduating class from nine in 1926 to 25 in 1927. John Henry Kirby and his wife, Lelia Stewart Kirby, saw the need for expansion and donated the land and construction costs for a new building called Kirby High School. Dedicated in 1949, Woodville's gymnasium served sports needs and hosted dances, banquets, and graduations until it was lost in the fire of 2001. School officials cleared the site and demolished the nearby, out-of-date auditorium, then replaced the two buildings with the Kirby Gymnasium, which serves elementary and intermediate assemblies and physical education needs. (Both, courtesy of TCHS.)

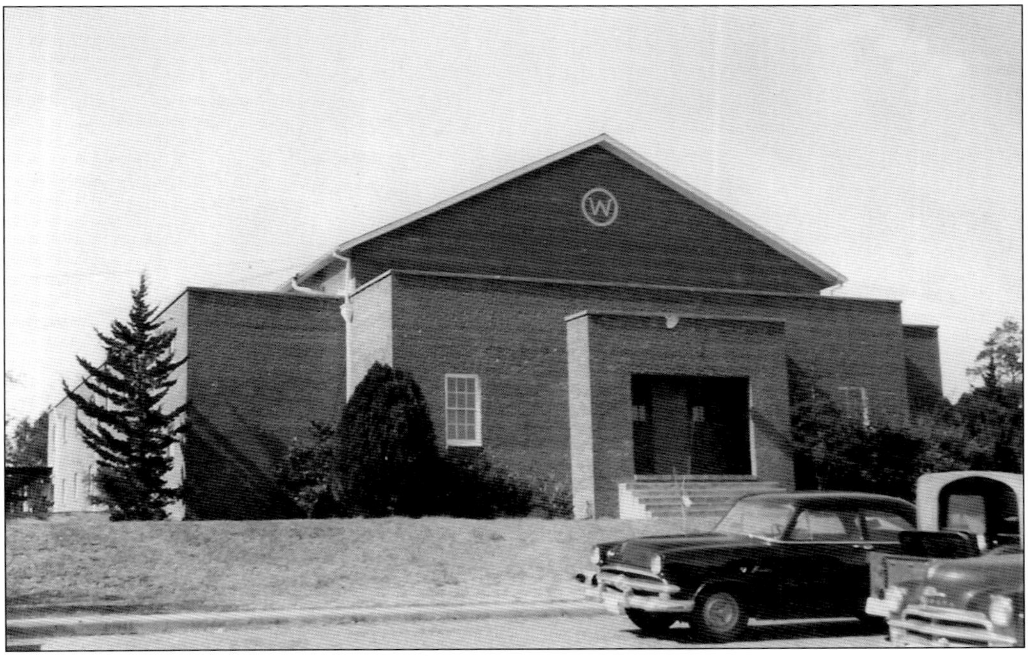

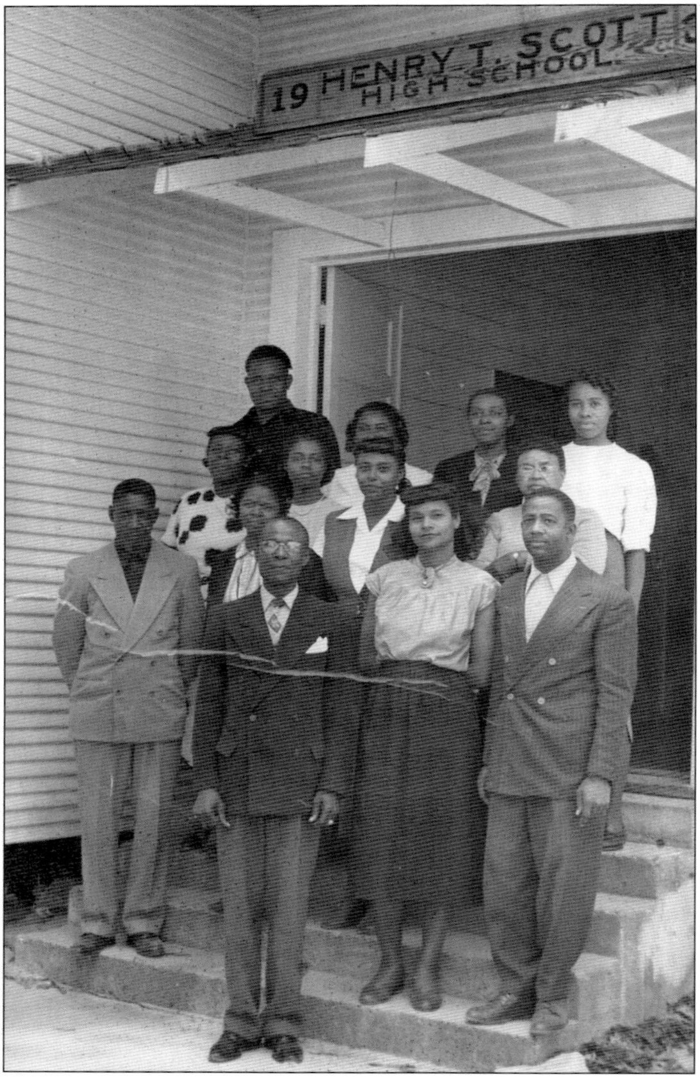

Henry T. Scott and John K. Canada made lasting improvements to education in Tyler County. Scott, a barber, organized a system for teaching African American students in churches and lodges before he earned a degree from Prairie View A&M University. Beginning in 1920, Scott worked with P.I. Hunter to plan for a real school building. He solicited financial support from community members and his own earnings, which resulted in the Henry T. Scott School being built in the early 1930s. Canada came to Scott School as principal in 1947. Canada's vision and steady leadership brought immediate and continuing improvements to the school buildings, faculty, and student activities. Canada managed Scott School's growth during the era of school consolidation. The faculty increased from eight to 25. Student enrollment grew from less than 100 to an average of 500. (Both, courtesy of Mayme Canada Brown.)

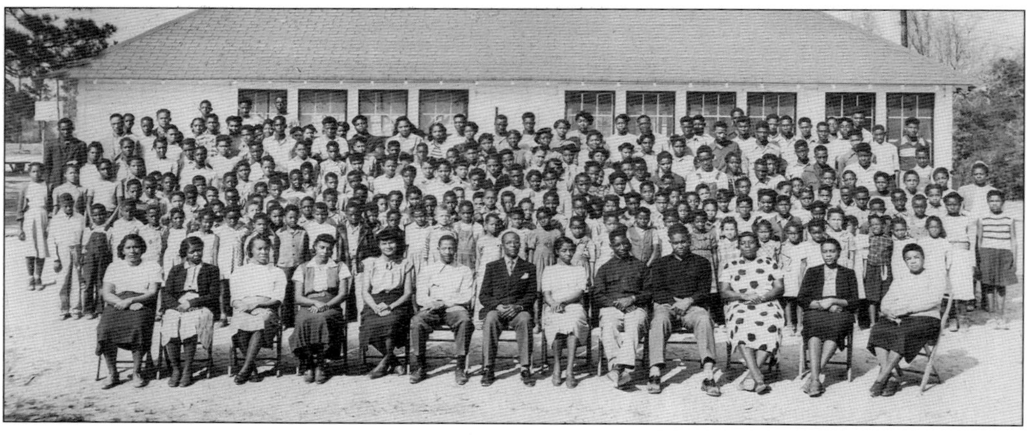

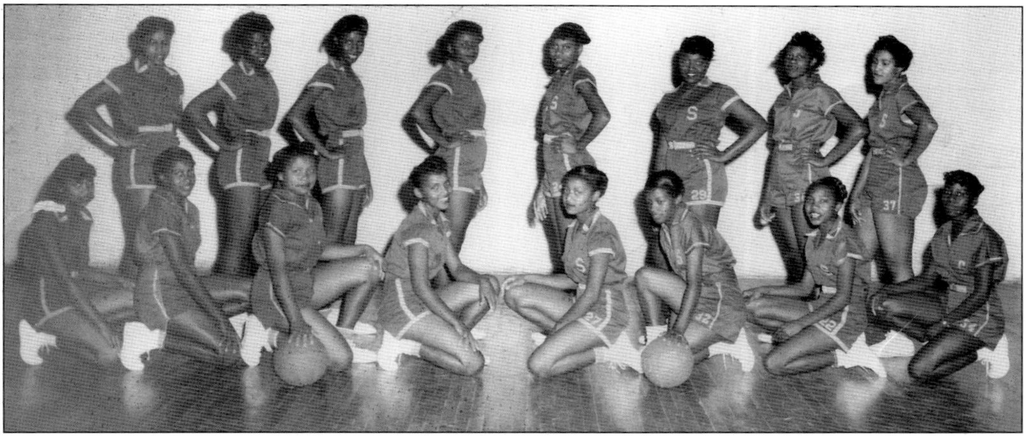

Principal John K. Canada's vision of improving learning opportunities for African American students led to expansion of curricular and extracurricular activities. Vocational programs in homemaking and agriculture gave students skills that they used at events, like the annual mother-daughter and father-son banquets. Business courses and a music program added practical and artistic training for students. With the cooperation of the Scott School's Businessmen League, the PTA, and the Woodville Independent School District School Board, a much-needed gymnasium became a reality. Acting on the proposal of Maggie Barlow, the school board named the gym after Principal Canada. Student athletes made good use of the new gym. Under the leadership of coach Alonzo Richardson, girls' basketball teams won many tournaments. (Both, courtesy of Mayme Canada Brown.)

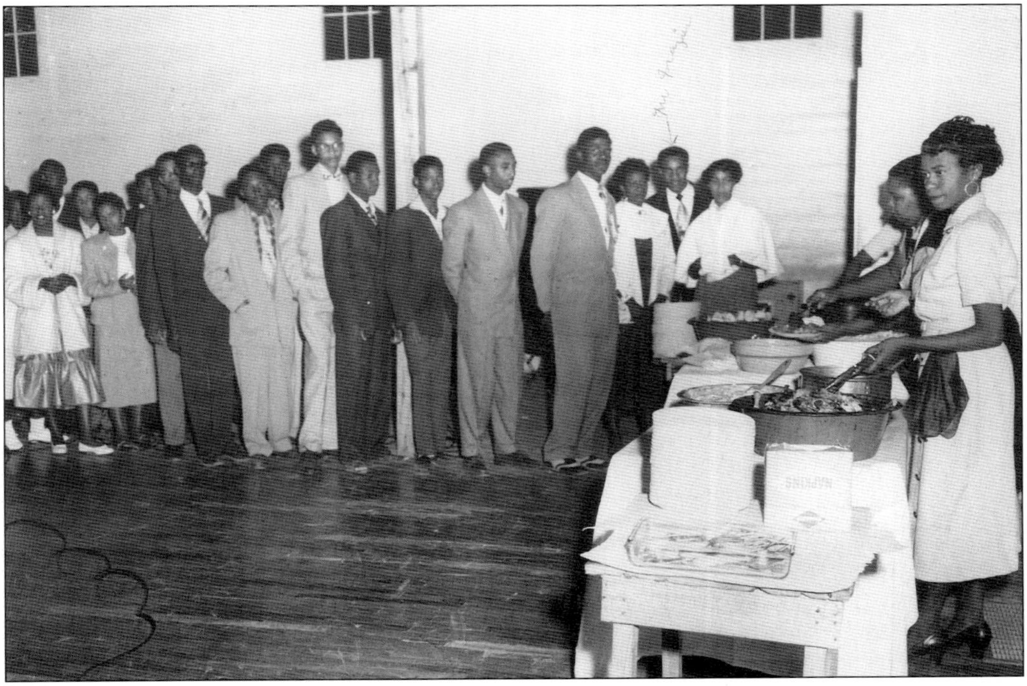

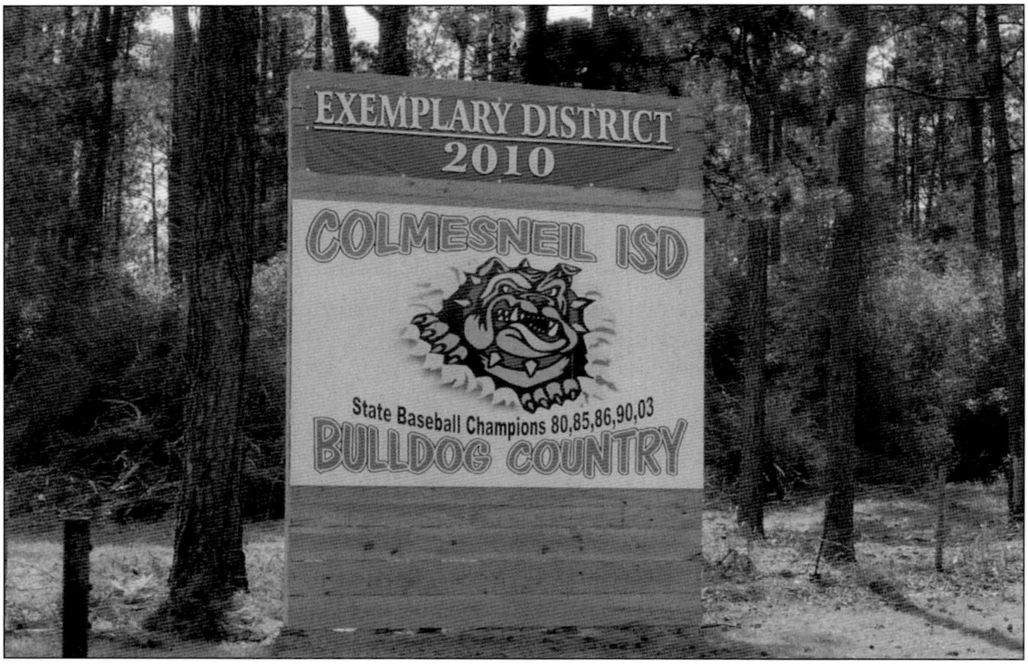

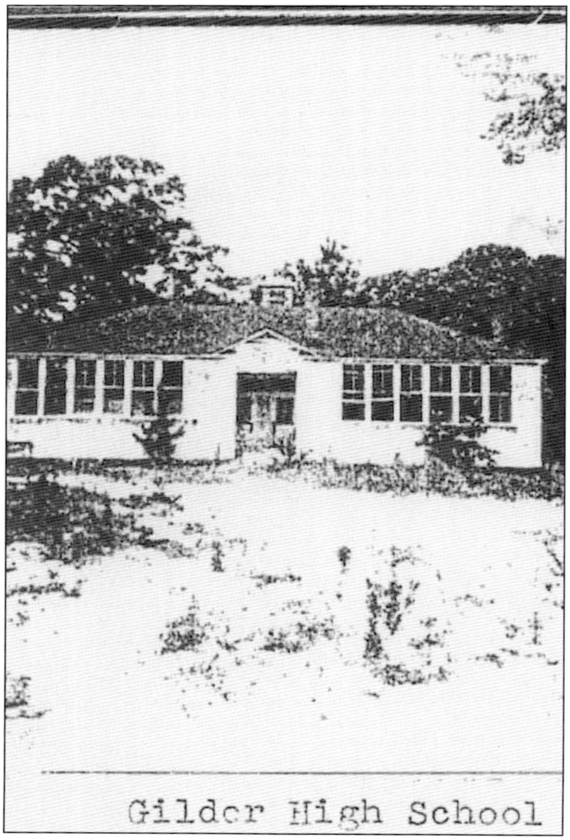

Exemplary schools do not exist by accident. Colmesneil's record of academic and athletic successes reflects the vision and commitment of leaders to meet high expectations with hard work and determination. Like today's school leaders, Issac James Gilder focused on student achievement from the time he began as principal of Colmesneil's African American school in 1909. He saw students move from a simple log structure shared with a church to a furnished, three-room schoolhouse. Later, he led in the expansion of that building to include two more classrooms and indoor restrooms. His efforts did not go unnoticed, and the school board chose to name the new building in his honor. Gilder retired in 1949. (Above, courtesy of TCHC; left, courtesy of TCHS.)

Lee A. Taylor became superintendent of Colmesneil Independent School District (CISD) in 1929, just weeks before Black Tuesday and the beginning of the Great Depression. In those difficult years when unemployment was the norm, he led the school to focus on activities and projects in which students could learn and do things to help their community at the same time. Successful sports teams had always been important in Colmesneil, and as a Bulldogs coach, Taylor continued that tradition. He helped supervise the construction of Lake Tejas, which provided jobs for young men, entertainment for the community, and extra funds for the school. He worked with Judge Wheat to establish the first annual Tyler County Dogwood Festival. After 41 years as superintendent of the same school, Taylor retired in 1970. He left a legacy of community service and kept a lifetime collection of friends. (Both, courtesy of CISD.)

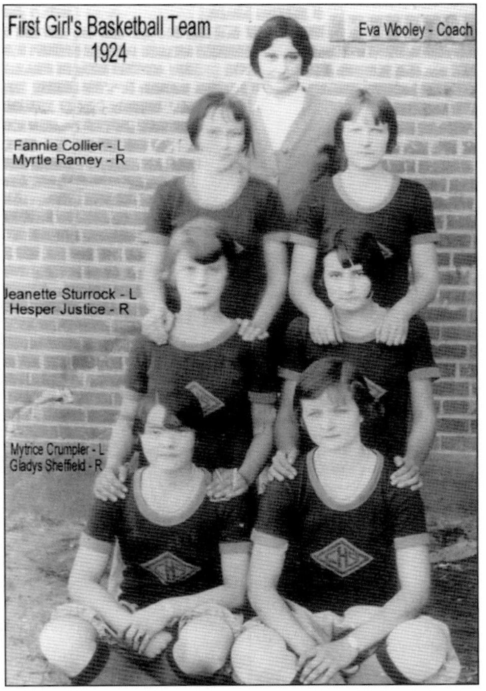

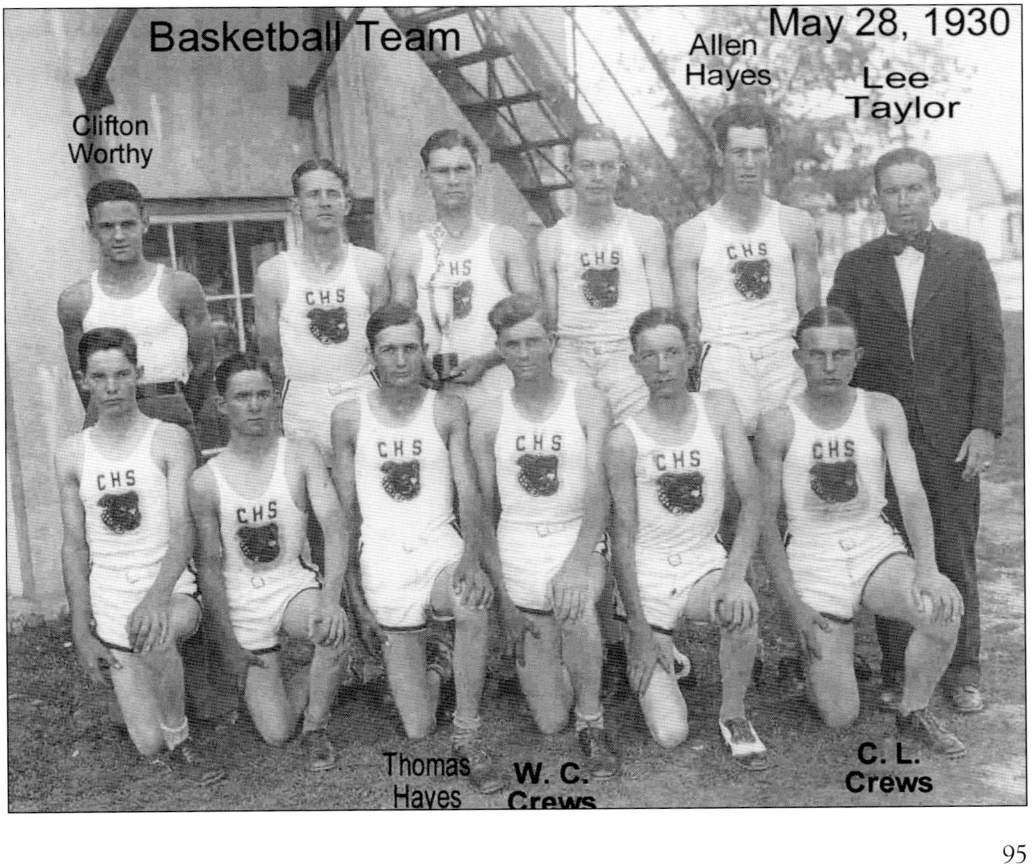

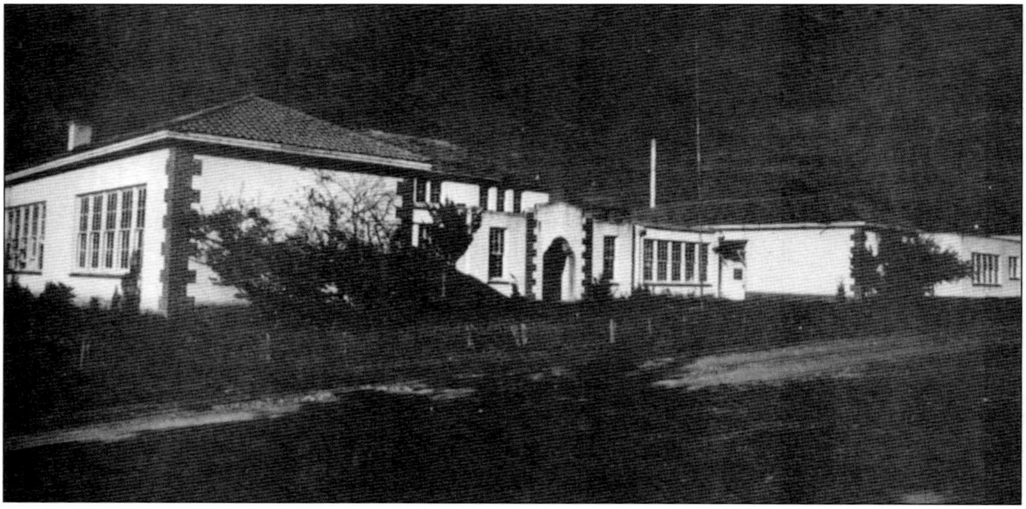

Fresh air filled the halls of Chester Independent School District when the doors opened in the fall of 1945. The school, constructed a few years earlier by the Civilian Conservation Corps, welcomed students whose families and friends were returning from military duty in World War II. Those students produced their first school yearbook in the spring of 1946 and dedicated it to veterans, saying, "To those gallant boys and girls of our school who served in our armed forces. We salute you and wish you well in the victorious future." The era that followed in the 1950s saw the addition of many extracurricular activities at the school. One such activity, baseball, began in 1951 and produced five district championships and two bi-district titles by 1957. (Both, courtesy of Chester Independent School District.)

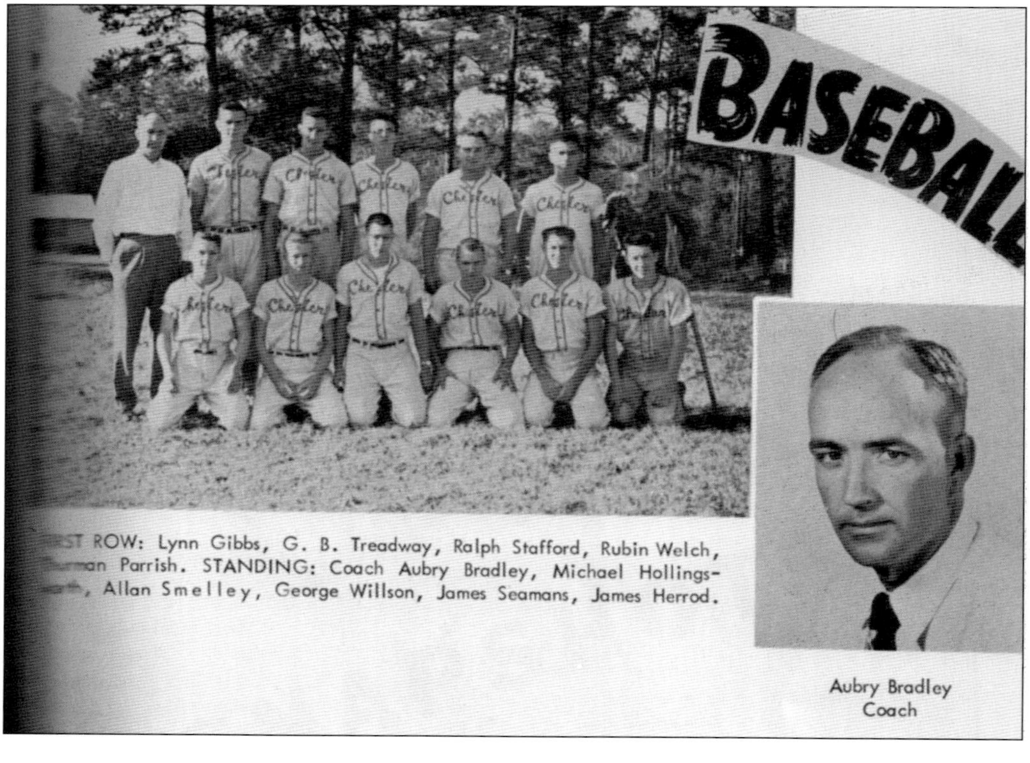

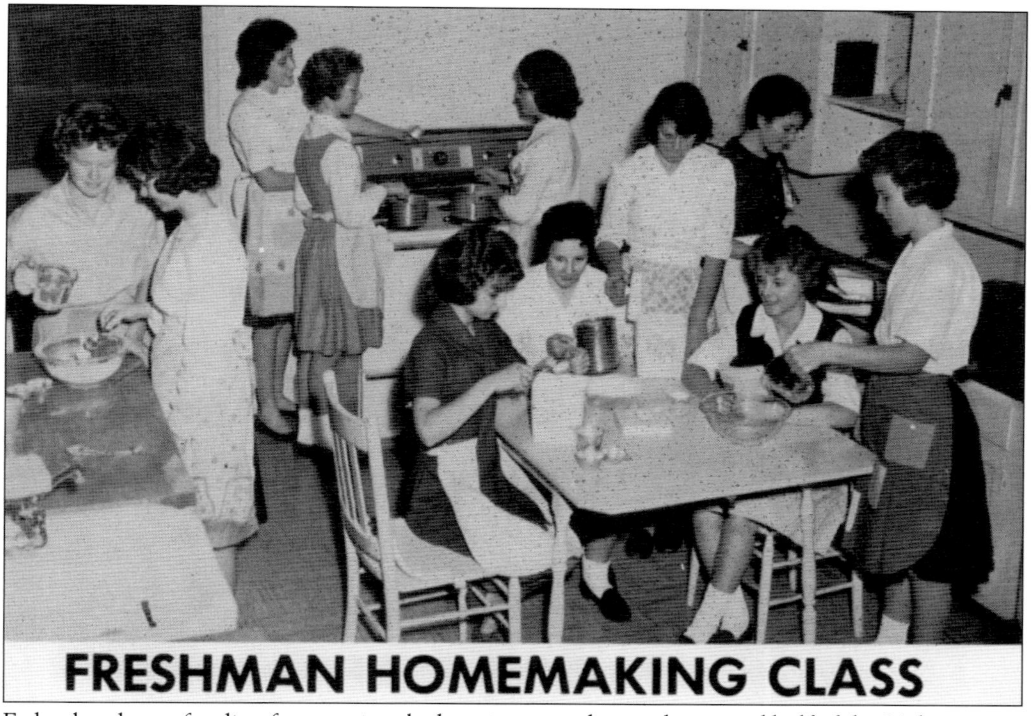

Federal and state funding for vocational education grew during the second half of the 20th century. Homemaking (later called home economics) and vocational agriculture classes expanded their focus to include career-related training and skills needed to manage a home, farm, or ranch. Who knew then that Rusty Hughes—named "Mr. Personality" by his classmates and football captain by his teammates—would apply skills learned at Chester High School in his future work as precinct commissioner? (Both, courtesy of Chester Independent School District.)

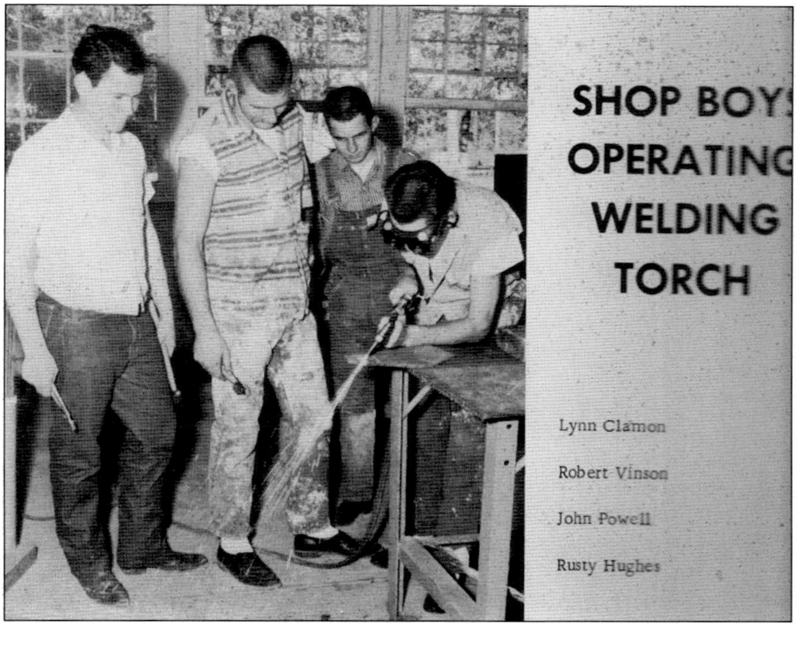

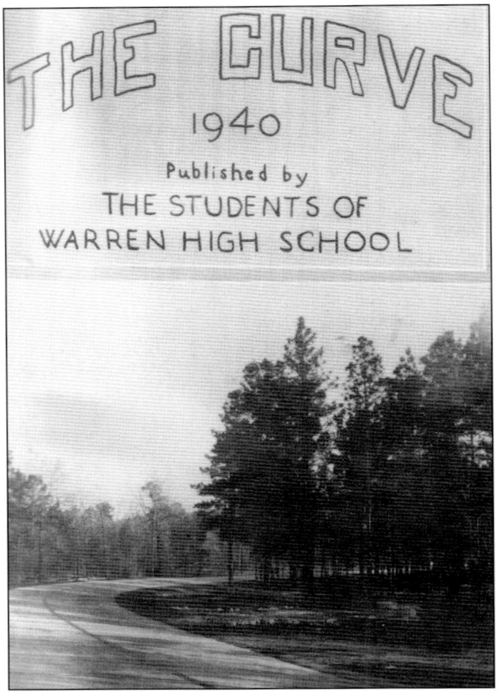

Early records of Warren Independent School District show that students there have taken great pride in representing their school, whether in academics or extracurricular activities. The exuberant 1935–1936 girls' basketball team was only one of a long string of award-winning teams. In 1940, Warren High School published its first school yearbook. The senior class chose the cover image and wrote these words of explanation: "In naming this, our first Warren High School Annual, we considered the fact that our small town has been built on a double curve; together with the fact that, after all, our life cycle is in reality a curve. If, in future years, when the tide of life is beginning to turn backward, someone may recall pleasant memories while glancing at this book, we shall feel that our efforts have not been in vain." (Both, courtesy of Warren Independent School District.)

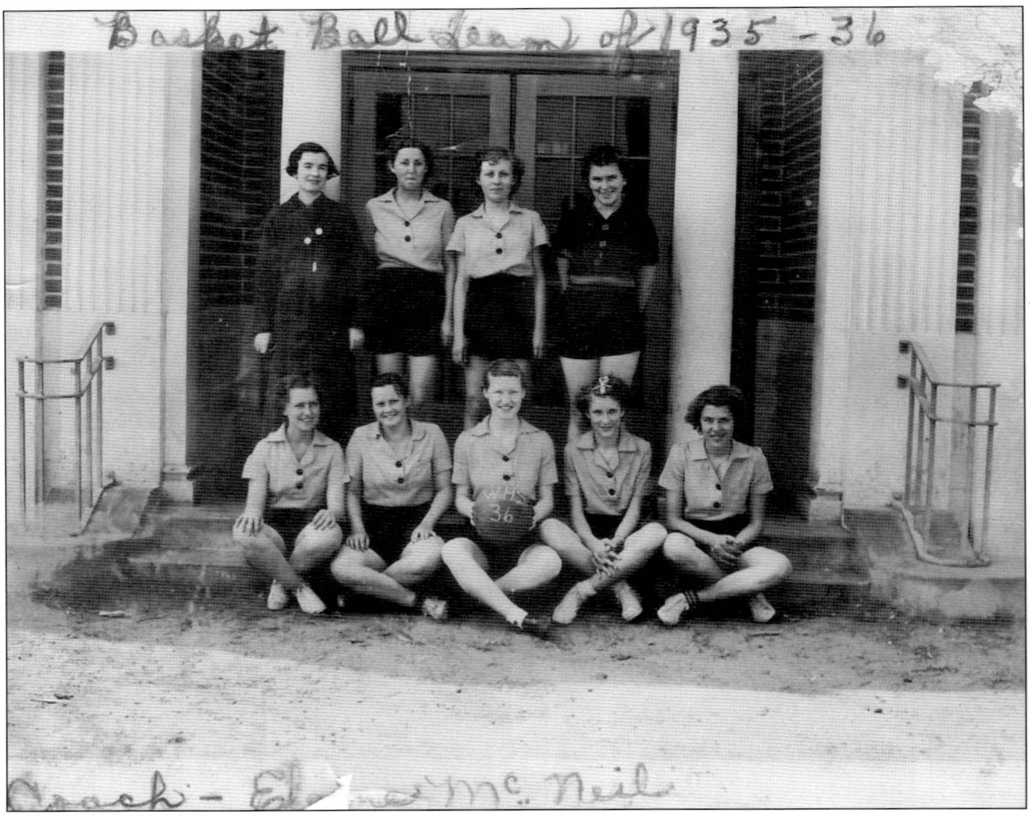

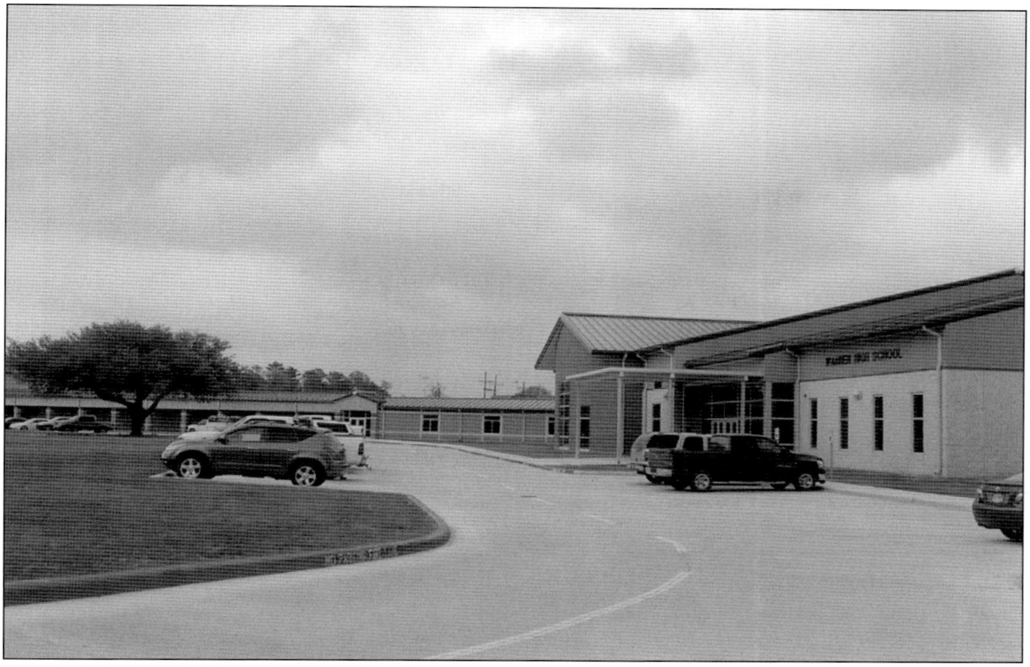

In the 21st century, pleasant memories continue to be developed at Warren High School (above) and Fred Elementary School (below). New buildings with state-of-the-art technology and attractive classrooms offer a learning environment that encourages students to strive for excellence. Visitors to these campuses find faculty and administrators who believe in a school and community partnership as stated in this Charles Wells quote: "The school will teach children how to read, but the environment of the home must teach them what to read. The school can teach them how to think, but the home must teach them what to believe." Warren Independent School District's vision statement expresses a belief that every student should be prepared to achieve success in life through innovation, motivation, and discipline. (Both, courtesy TCHC.)

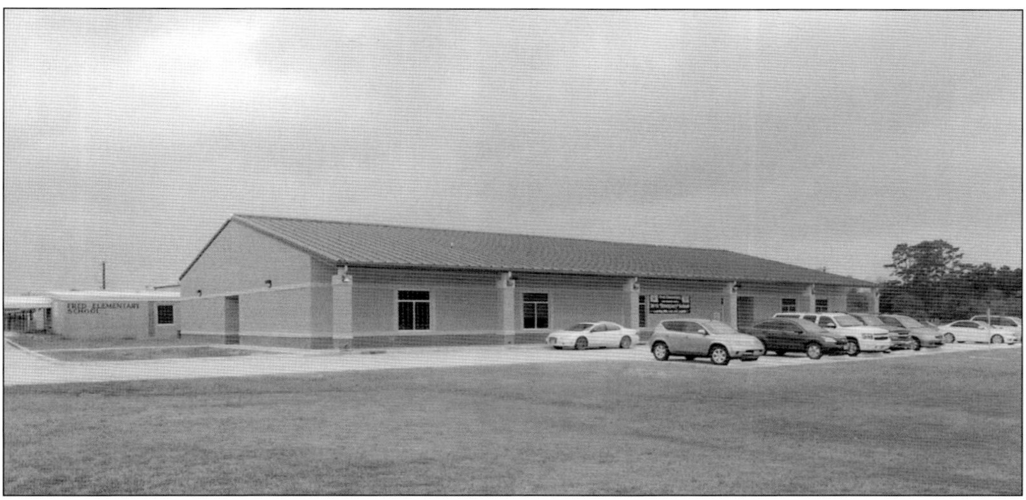

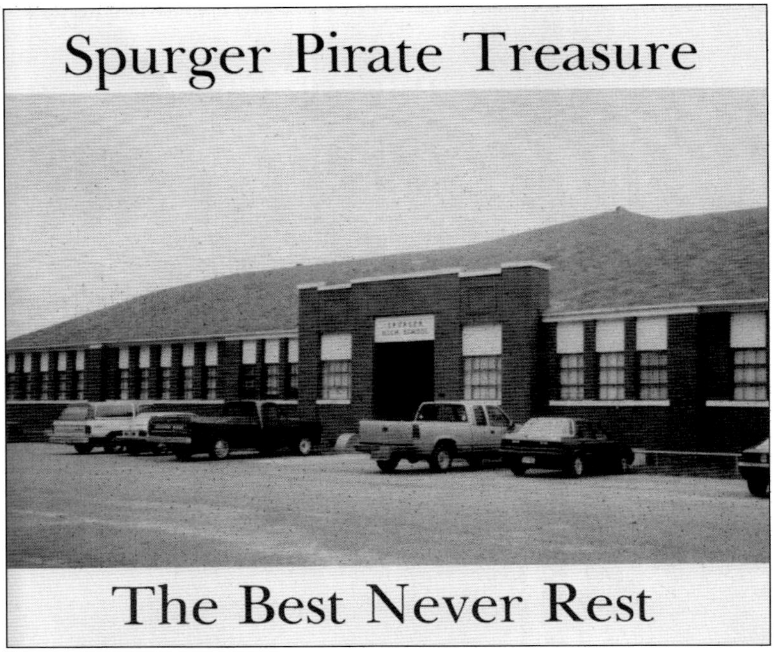

The original Spurger School yearbook, first published in 1945, took the name *Pirate Parade*. That name continued until the staff dropped "parade" and used the simple name *Pirate* in 1968. The annual publication took a new name and a new slogan in 1993 as *Pirate's Treasure* and *The Best Never Rest*. (Courtesy of Spurger Independent School District.)

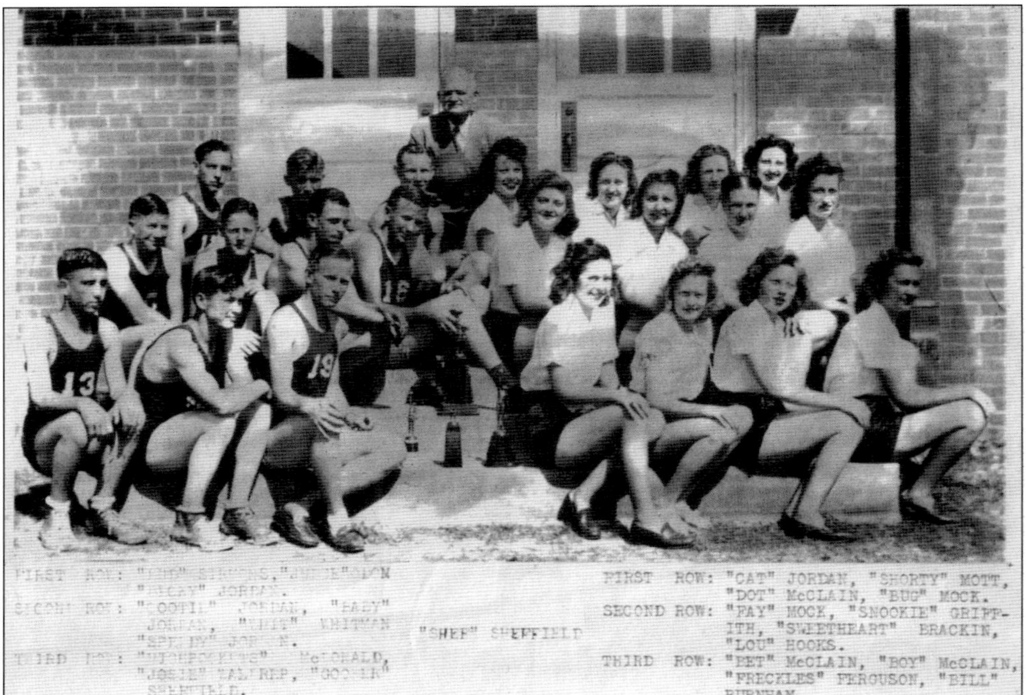

Coach E.E. Sheffield and the boys' and girls' basketball teams of 1945 set up the Tyler County sports tradition that continues six decades later. Spurger is still the team to beat. After a brief experience trying six-man football, the school and community decided to stick with basketball, baseball, and track. Winning records indicate they made a good choice. (Courtesy of Spurger Independent School District.)

IN HONOR OF THOSE WHO SERVED

The following heroes of America were from
Spurger Rural High School:

Bill Brown
Travis Cain
Robert Mott
Bernice Mott
Aden Jordan
L. G. Jordan
Audie Sloan
John Luman
Leon Dean
Billy Peavy
W. B. Harper
Wayman Baker
Spek Shaw
Avon Crosby
Kyle Hooks
Earl Yawn
Pete Hollis
Bob Brisbin
J. C. Hicks
Felix Hooks
Lee Sirmans
James Hooks
David Hooks
Billie Mott
Jack Shaeffer
Joe Warren
Monroe Warren
Elic Bowers
Marice Severs
Thomas Mock
Curtis Hooks
Mickens Hooks
Gurvis Sheffield
Marlin Jordan

Garnett Burnham
Harman Jordan
Jimmie Jordan
Tommie Jordan
Dick Jordan
Prentice Jordan
Jack Sheffield
David Sheffield
Earl Glenn Sheffield
Richard Sheffield
Fred Jenkins
Howard Jenkins
Mooney Hicks
Harvey Waldrep
Ray Waldrep
Wallace Odom
Adnell Odom
Julian Hutto
Herman Grission
Carlos McClain
Earl McClain
Robie Levins
Clyde Dulaney
Dan McKinnis, Jr.
Nolan Morgan
Douglas Bingham
Lockey Lee Hicks
Elden Brisbin
Forrest Collier
Marvin Ramer
Johnnie Ramer
Frank Collier, Jr.
Robert C. Wilson
William Ramer

Hewey Loveladv
Presly Lewis
Earl Ferguson
Billy Stewert
Charles Ray Stewert
James Sheffield
Wilbur Sawyer
Tarance Bingham
Douglas Crosby
Clenton Richards
Eddie Severs
Artie Lee Willis
John M. Holstead
M. L. Bingham
Carroll Sheffield
Thomas Anderson
John Wesley Knight
Escar Swearington
Fred Swearington
Walter Winkle
Robert Lee Peavy
James Sirmans
Myles Harcel
Evert Phillips
Joe Bailey Phillips
James Hebert Bell
J. D. McDonald
John McDaneld
Ella Jea Mott
Nathen Jordan
Millard Burcks
Raymond Calaway
Aster Whitman
Dorothy Brisbin

Following World War II, students at Spurger High School expressed their patriotism by dedicating their yearbook to local veterans. The book opened with these words: "To the Veterans of World War II, who gave their time and their lives for their country, we dedicate this PIRATE PARADE of 1947. To those who marched over the many miles of rough ground, to the heroes who flew in the air in fair or stormy weather, and those that went down in the sea, we hereby pay tribute." More than 100 young men and women from Spurger answered the call to serve their country and protected their fellow citizens. (Courtesy of Spurger Independent School District.)

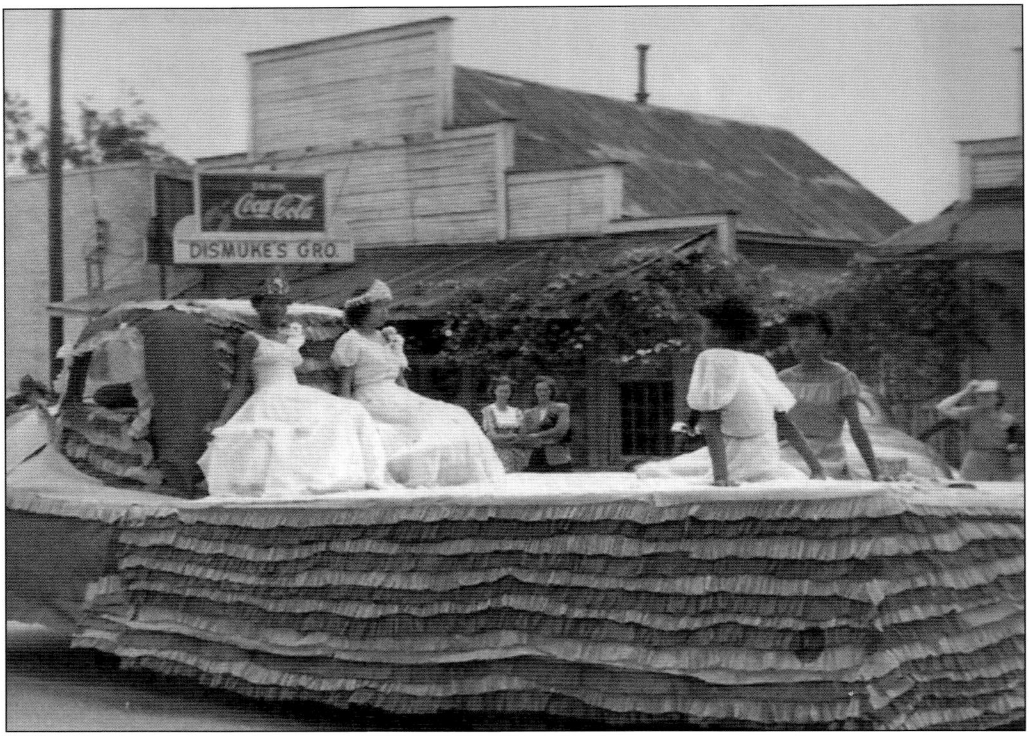

Crowns, fluffy dresses, and frilly floats made homecoming festivities memorable for young ladies. Football teams and homecoming parades made their debut with African American students in the 1950s. Merchants like Charlie Dismuke looked forward to having extra people downtown to enjoy the parade and possibly to buy a pint of ice cream. (Courtesy of Mayme Canada Brown.)

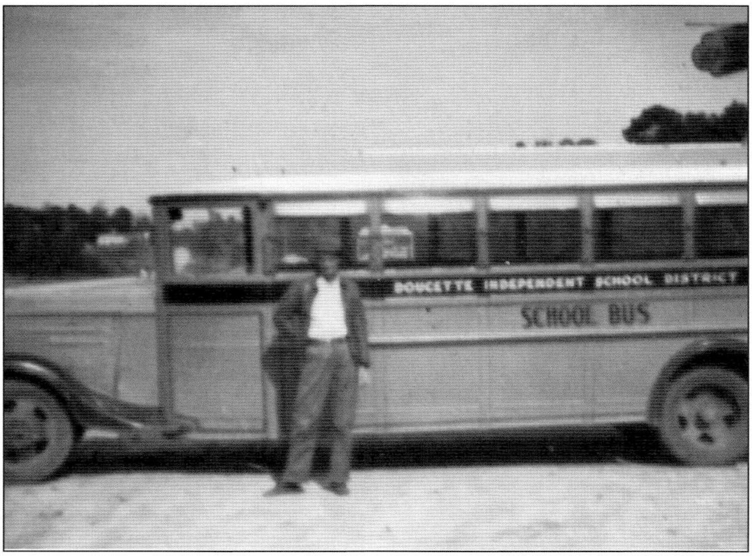

J.C. Clark recalls watching the kids from Doucette load into Cleve Miles's school bus at the end of a busy day. Dallas Young rode along to keep order, and he stood by the door at the back of the bus, inviting students to join him. "All aboard for Doucette," he called out in his booming voice. The bus filled quickly and puttered away on the dusty street. (Courtesy of Bertis Best.)

Seven

House Calls to Hospitals

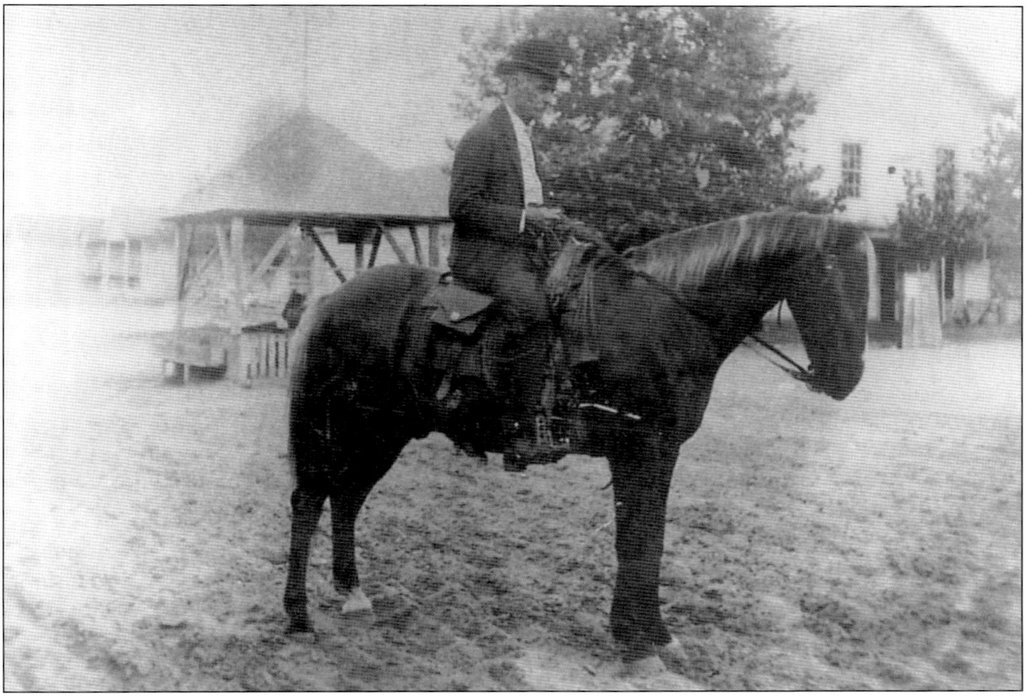

In 1852, twelve-year-old William Martin Van Buren Stewart came from Alabama and settled in the Cherokee community with his family. In 1867, after serving in the Civil War, he married Sarah Jane Crow, and they operated a hotel in Colmesneil. He received his medical certification in 1881 and practiced as one of 25 doctors in Tyler County until 1906. He died in 1917. (Courtesy of CISD.)

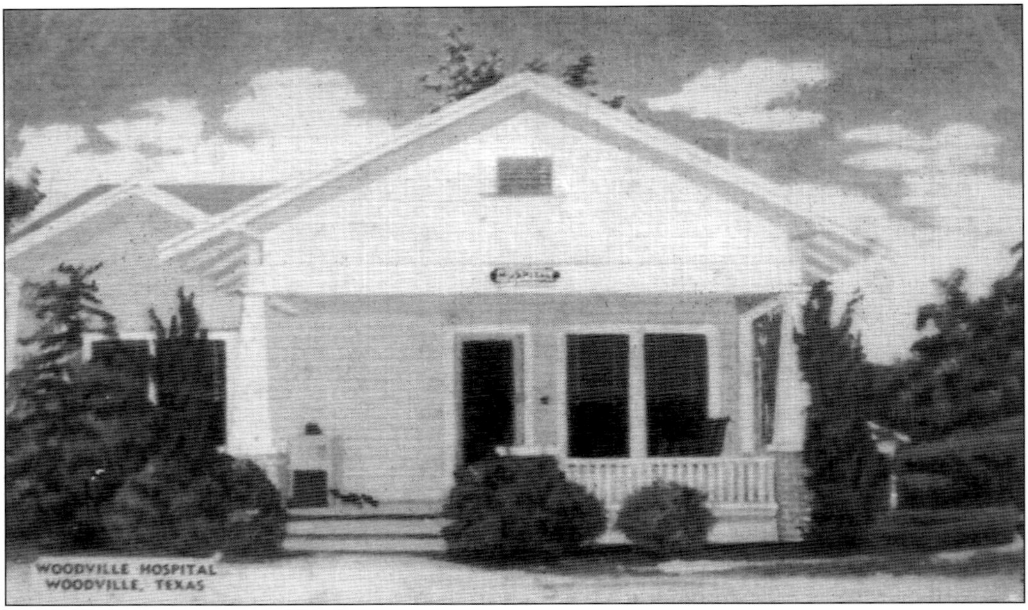

Dr. Watt Barclay opened his hospital on Pine Street in the late 1930s. The hospital contained two wards that each had two beds—one for females and one for males. In addition to making house calls all over the county, he saw patients, delivered babies, and performed surgeries in the hospital. A 1940 edition of the *Tyler County Booster* reported that John Reid was "recovering nicely" following an emergency appendectomy at the local hospital. (Courtesy of Shirley Rawls.)

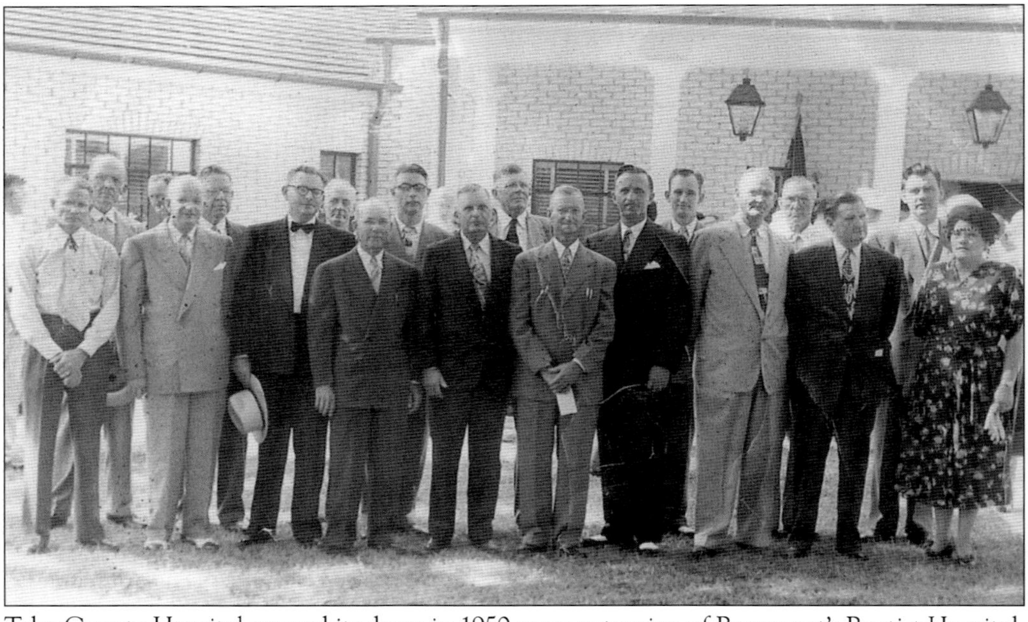

Tyler County Hospital opened its doors in 1950 as an extension of Beaumont's Baptist Hospital. After a few years of operation, the county took responsibility for the hospital and created a taxing district to provide necessary financial support. In its six decades of existence, the hospital has undergone numerous expansions, including the most recent expansion for emergency room and laboratory services in 2004. (Courtesy of TCHC.)

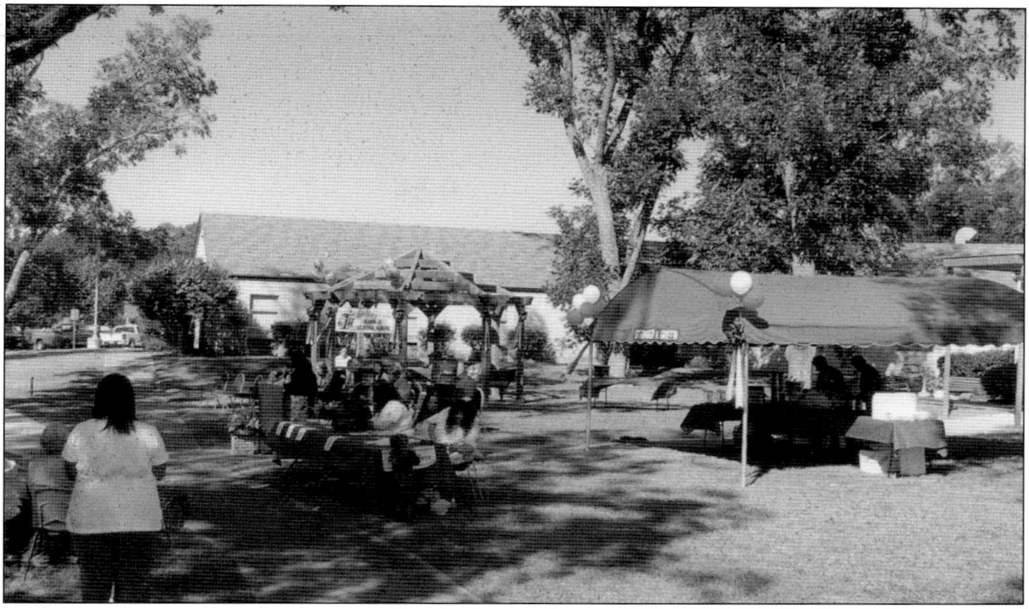

Tyler County Hospital School of Licensed Vocational Nursing began in an attic storage space that was converted to a classroom in 1960. Beginning with a class of less than a dozen, the school now offers training for 72 students in each class. Graduates excel on state licensing exams and find employment all over Southeast Texas. Pictured, the school celebrated its 50th anniversary on October 8, 2010. (Courtesy of Tyler County Hospital.)

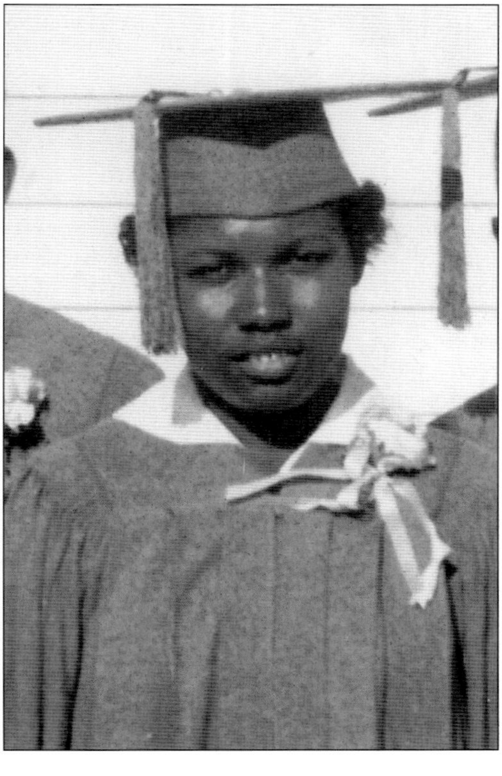

In 1957, Marie Moye made history as the first African American student to graduate from Lamar University's School of Nursing as a licensed vocational nurse. She returned to her hometown, Woodville, and worked with Dr. Watt Barclay and nurse Edith Hatton at Tyler County Hospital as a scrub nurse in surgery. She also delivered babies as a midwife in the community. Moye retired in 1991, having delivered more than 500 babies. (Courtesy of Mayme Canada Brown.)

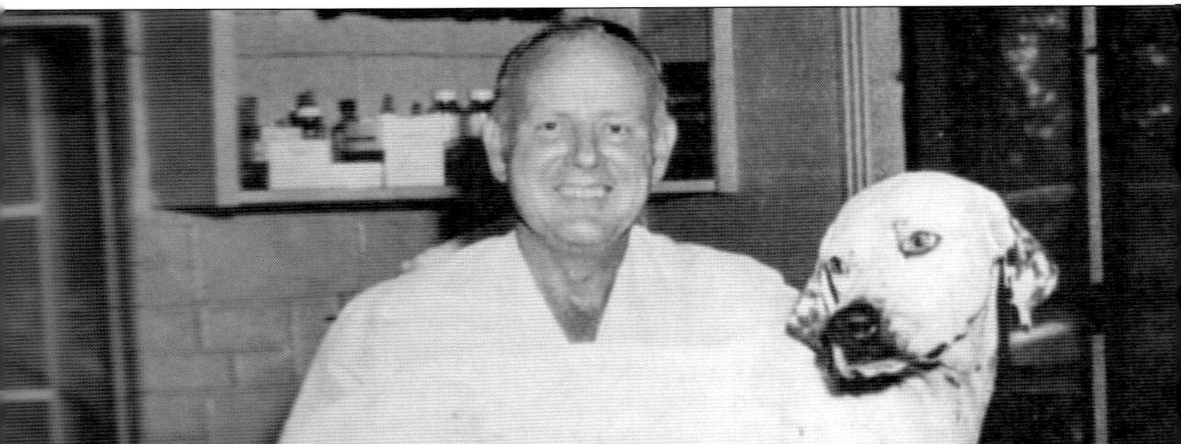

If there were a book naming outstanding teams that made a good difference in this world, Tyler County's medical team would top the list. Beginning in the early 1950s, Doctors Garner, Burton, Gilchrist, Swearingen, Radford, Jinnette, and Babin attended to the medical and dental needs of the people. Dr. W.S. Nichols (pictured) opened the county's first veterinary clinic and cared for every kind of animal—from puppies and hound dogs to colts and quarter horses. In addition to managing successful practices, all of these gentlemen contributed their energies to community improvements. Having chosen Tyler County as home for their families, they all served on school and bank boards, in civic organizations, and in their churches. (Courtesy of Woodville ISD.)

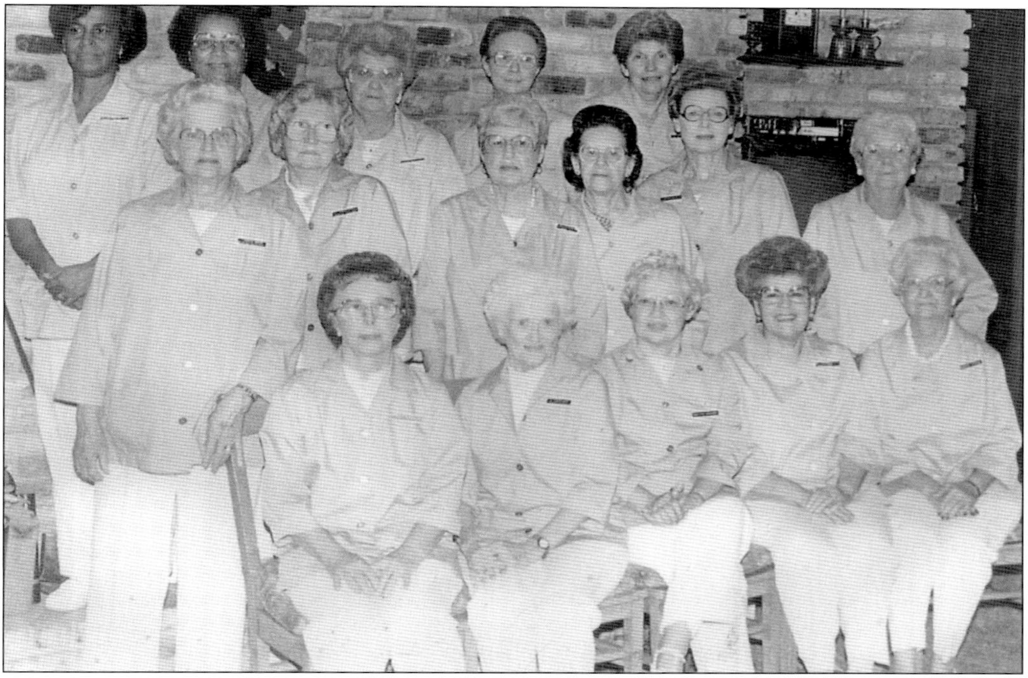

Beginning in the 1960s, the Tyler County Hospital Auxiliary became a strong force for good. Under the early leadership of Dr. Ivison Grimes's wife, Eva, the auxiliary did such work as shelling and freezing peas from local gardens to provide meals for patients. Now, in addition to volunteering at the information desk and conducting service activities on the patient wing, the group also manages a well-stocked gift shop. With their income from sales, the auxiliary provides for improvement and expansion of services at the hospital. In 2004, one such project included the purchase of items needed to furnish the newly built emergency room wing of the hospital. (Above, courtesy of TCHS; below, courtesy of TCHC.)

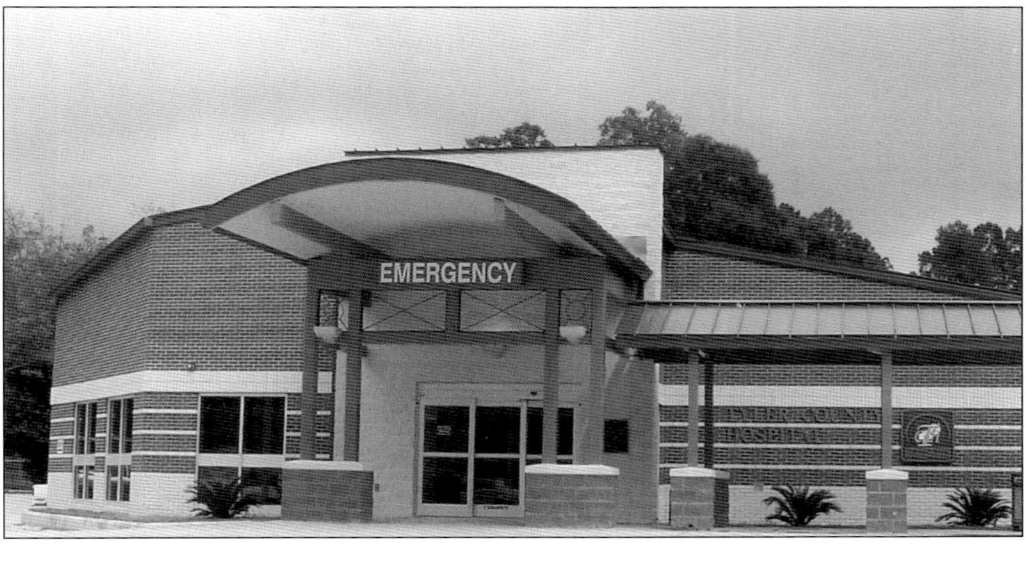

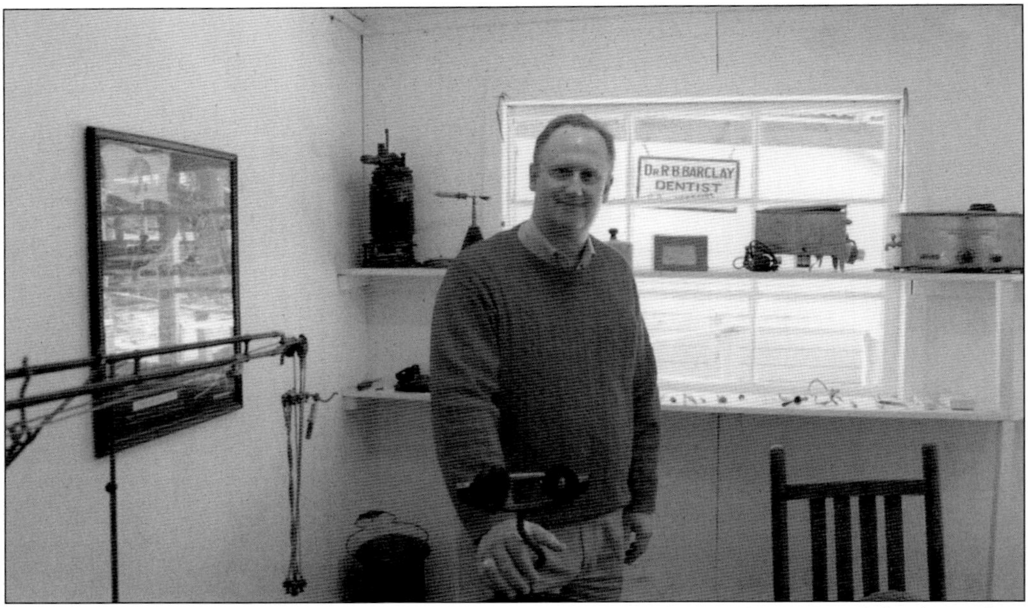

Lee Mann, great-nephew of Dr. R.B. Barclay, reminds Tyler County old-timers of the days when patients climbed the stairs to reach the dentist office above the original Citizens State Bank (now offices and shops). Through arrangements made by Dr. Brian Babin, the furnishings from Doctor Barclay's old office are now on exhibit at Heritage Village. (Courtesy of TCHC.)

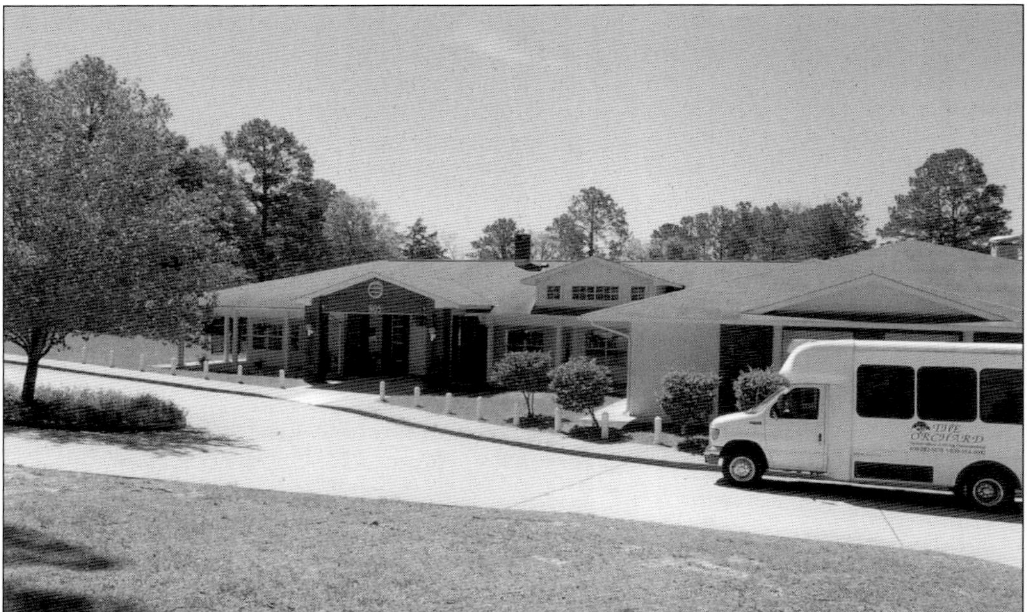

With the arrival of the 21st century came the county's first assisted living complex called the Orchard. The facility takes its name from its location on property that had been part of the Reid family's pecan orchard. Efficiency apartments include kitchenettes and patios, while common meeting areas offer dining and socializing rooms. An in-house beauty salon and "people mover" van service add benefits for Orchard residents. (Courtesy of TCHC.)

Eight

SERVICE ABOVE SELF

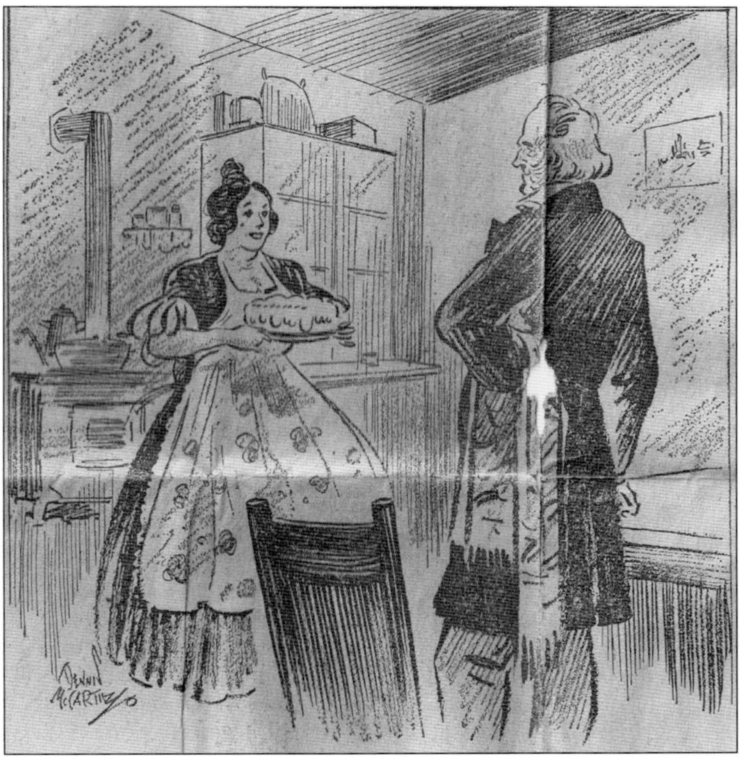

Gen. Sam Houston, who was later president of the Republic of Texas, sometimes visited Tyler County. Once, the ladies of Emilee prepared a "bolted cake" for him. Having no flour, they used a bolt of cloth to sift corn meal until it became fine enough for a cake. In 1933, "Uncle" John Rotan told a Beaumont newsman about watching Houston pack the cake in his saddle bag and state he would eat it all before his next stop. (Courtesy of ASLM.)

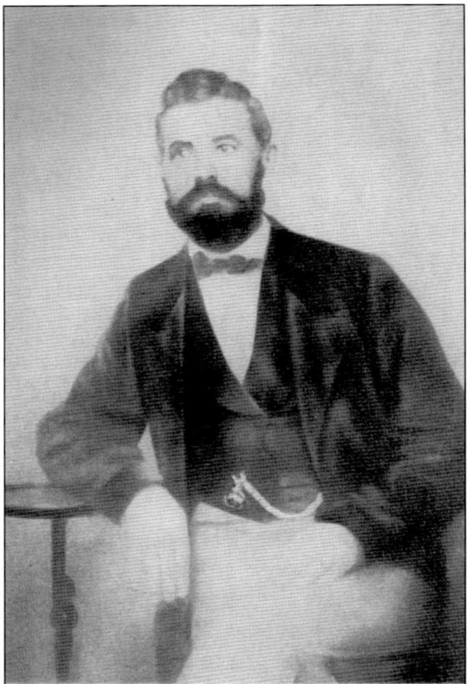

P. A. Work, Colonel, C.S.A.
Commanding 1st Texas Infantry Regiment
Hood's Texas Brigade

In April 1861, after voting at the Texas Secession Convention to leave the Union, Capt. Philip Alexander Work, who was later a lieutenant colonel, returned to Woodville and formed a 220-man company. The Woodville Rifles fought in Lee's Army of Northern Virginia. Following the war, Work rejoined Terry's Texas Rangers. Upon retirement, he received pensions from the Union for his work as an Indian fighter and from the Confederacy for his war service. (Courtesy of ASLM.)

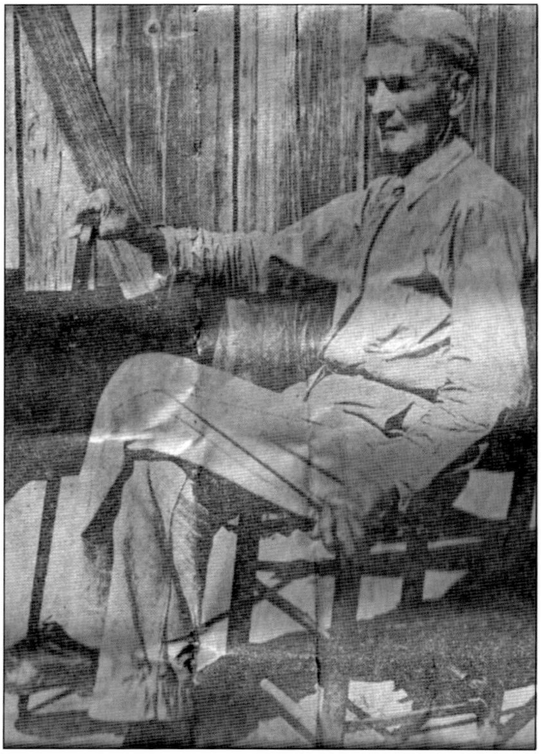

A few days before his 90th birthday in 1932, uncle Tom Seamans told a Beaumont reporter about his Confederate soldier experiences at Sabine Pass, including his eye-witness report of a firing squad execution of a captured deserting officer. Following the war, he continued farming cotton. With workers, he hauled 50 bales of cotton from Peach Tree Village to the "little old town" of Houston, which had one cotton warehouse. (Courtesy of Bertis Best.)

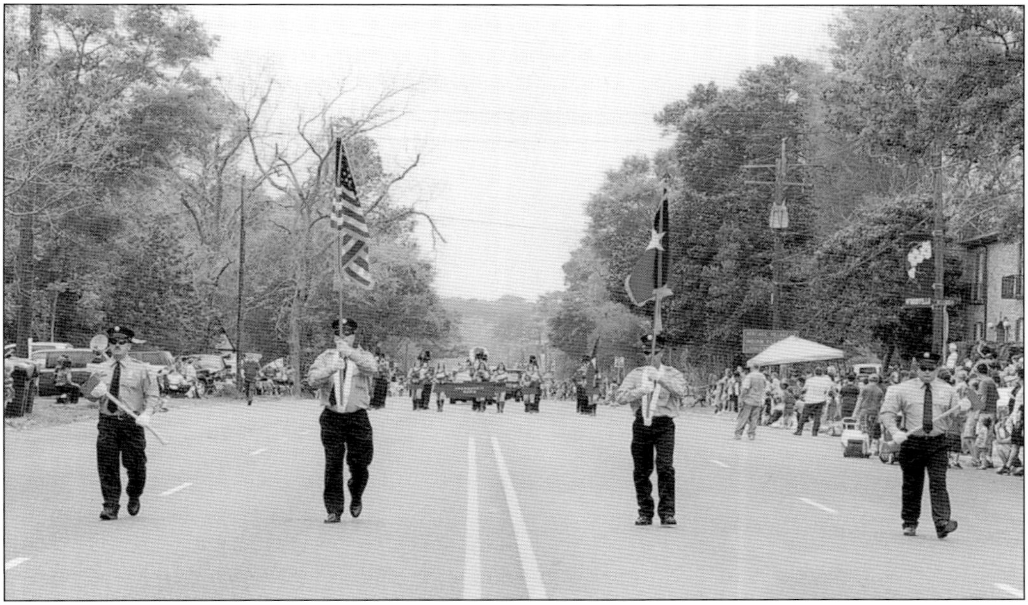

A total of nine volunteer fire departments protect lives and property in Tyler County. Many of these units formed as early as the 1940s and encouraged citizens to contribute to the cost of trucks and other firefighting equipment. Though trained primarily for emergency situations, firemen proudly formed a color guard when invited to lead a traditional Tyler County Dogwood Festival Parade. (Courtesy of Jim Powers.)

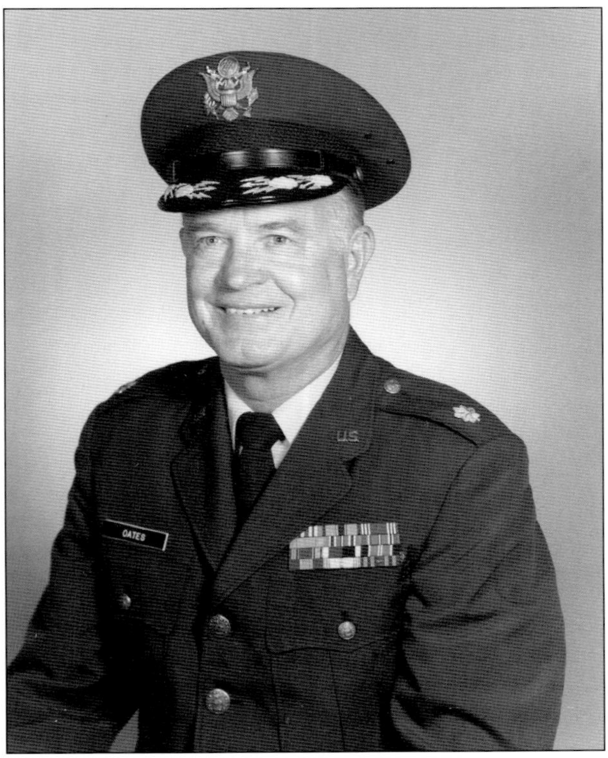

An Air Force veteran of 31 years, including 13 years in Europe and World War II service, Lt. Col. Elmer Ray Oates retired in 1971. He continued to demonstrate proper flag etiquette wherever the opportunity arose. Even at age 90, he set the tone for all parade watchers when he stood to salute as the flags passed him and others on the lawn of Woodville United Methodist Church. (Courtesy of Dorothy Oates.)

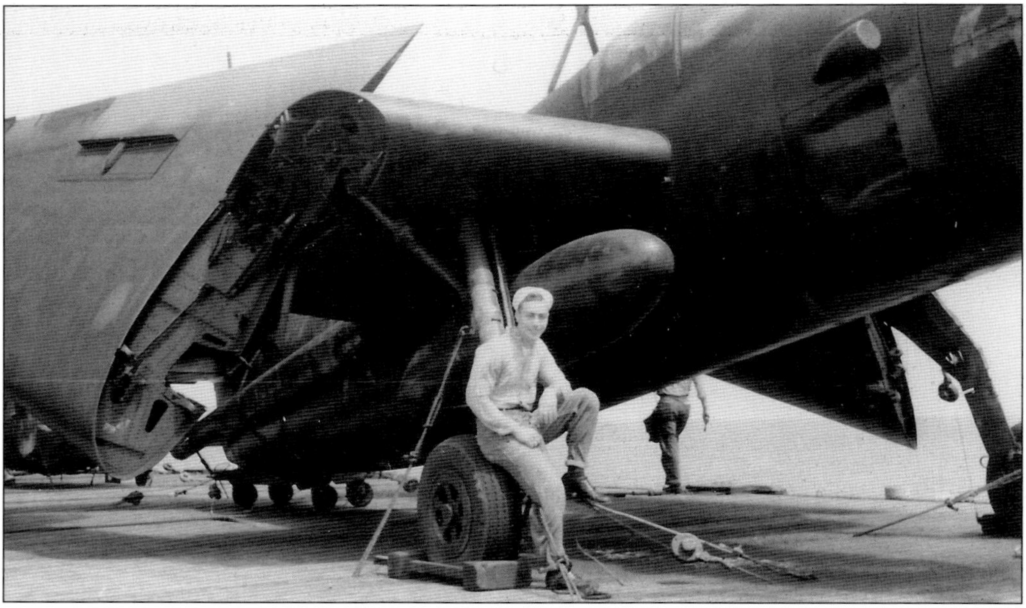

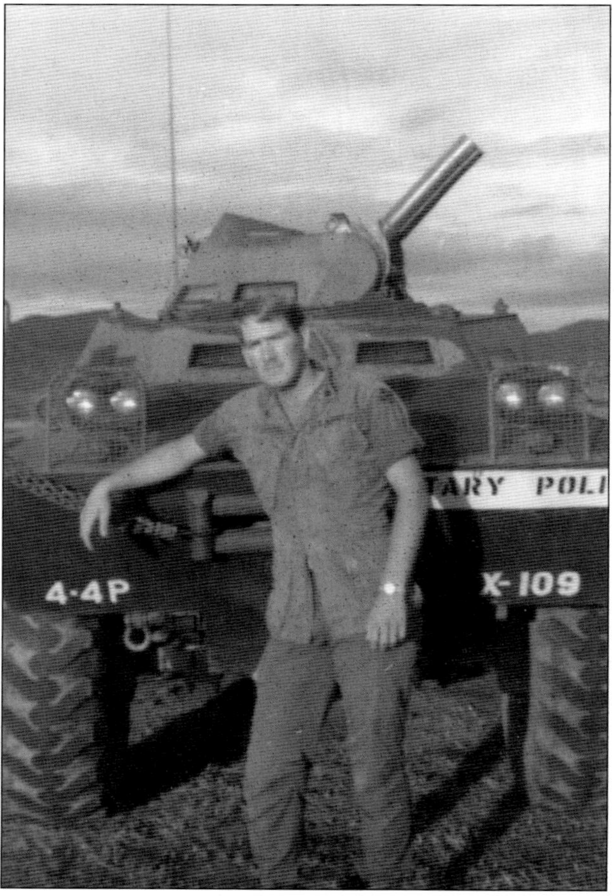

In 1952 to 1954, Maxie Young served two tours of duty on the USS *Essex*, the Navy's largest aircraft carrier with more than 100 planes and helicopters onboard. His work as an aviation hydraulic metalsmith prepared him for a 30-year career with Mobil Oil and Mobil Chemical. Young's experiences in the Philippines and Korean waters brought him to a new awareness of the blessing of living in the United States. (Courtesy of Joyce Young.)

Spc. Jerry Tolbert served in the Army from 1969 through 1971 and spent one year in Vietnam with the 4th Military Police Company, 4th Infantry Division. One of many Tyler County patriotic youth serving in an unpopular war, Tolbert expressed his appreciation for the good people of Tyler County who always treated him respectfully and welcomed him home as a hero. (Courtesy of Anne Tolbert.)

Sgt. Derrick Maloy, a popular graduate of Woodville High School, enlisted in the Army and took his young family abroad for a portion of his tour of duty. Stationed first in Italy, and later in Korea and Saudi Arabia, one of Maloy's assignments included conducting cleanup activities following Desert Storm. (Courtesy of Dorian Maloy.)

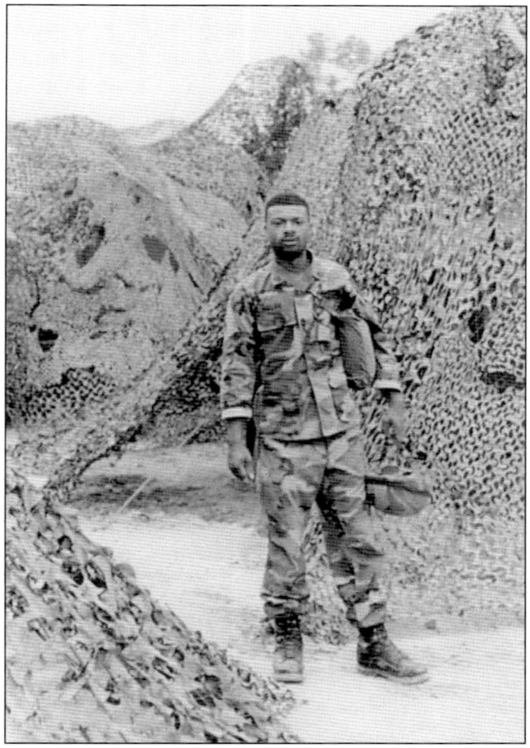

CWO3 Wesley Charles "Chuck" Fortenberry paid the ultimate sacrifice with his unit in the US Army, 1st Cavalry, 1st Battalion, 227th Regiment. On Easter Sunday, April 11, 2004, he flew his attack helicopter to heroically save American ground troops from enemy combatants and gave his life in the process. A monument stands on the courthouse lawn denoting his awards: Bronze Star, Purple Heart, Air Medal, and Distinguished Flying Cross. (Courtesy of TCHC.)

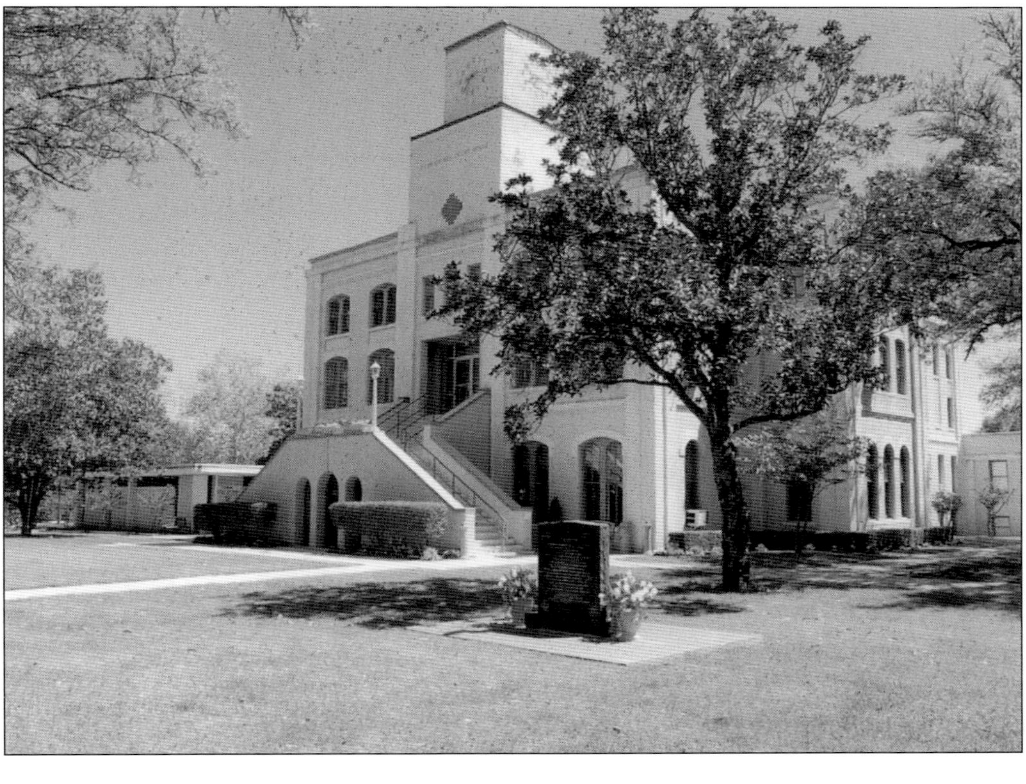

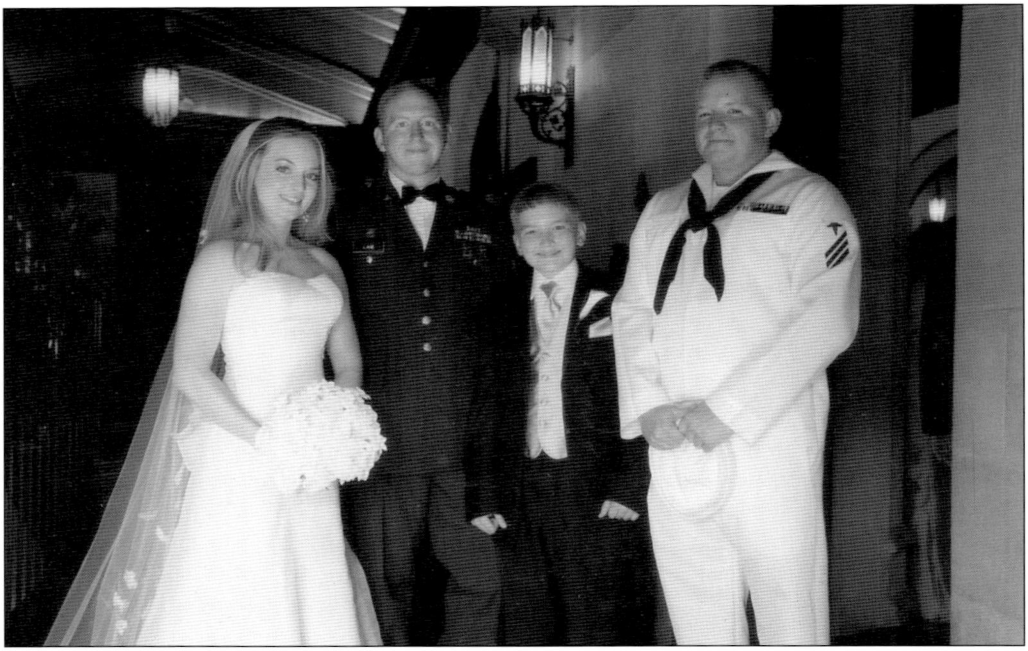

Strong family ties have sustained Tyler County folk through their time of service in the military. Brothers Sgt. Evan Lane (left) and PO3 Barret Lane (right), a hospital corpsman, volunteered for military service in difficult times. Evan served in South Korea, Qatar, and Iraq in an engineering battalion demolishing improvised explosive devices. Barret volunteered for special attachment to a Marine unit and served as a medic in both Iraq and Afghanistan. The men secured leaves to celebrate their cousin Elizabeth's wedding with their younger brother Will and other family members. Another distinguished Tyler County military family is that of US Air Force captain Alex Gazzaway. His family (below) received the prestigious National Military Family Association's title of 2008 Family of the Year. The award recognizes those families who have made the most of the adventure of military life and conquered its challenges. (Above, courtesy of Anne Garner; below, courtesy of US Air Force.)

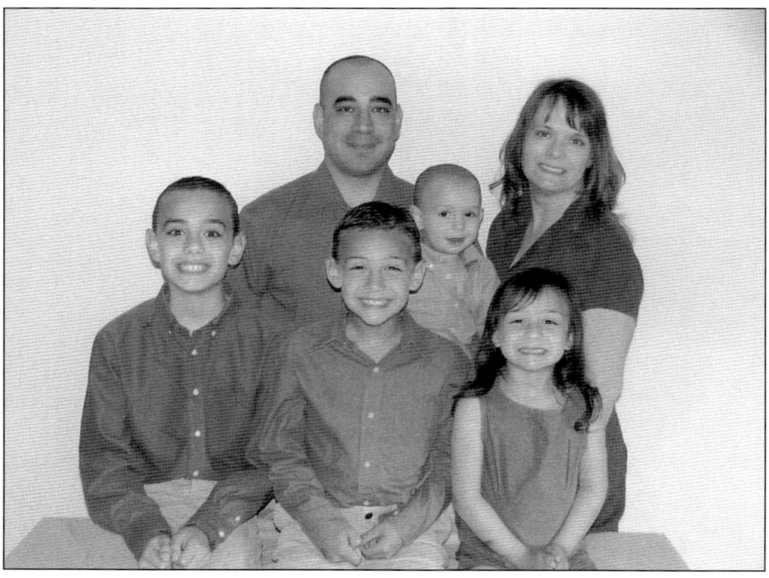

Nine

Ceremonies and Celebrations

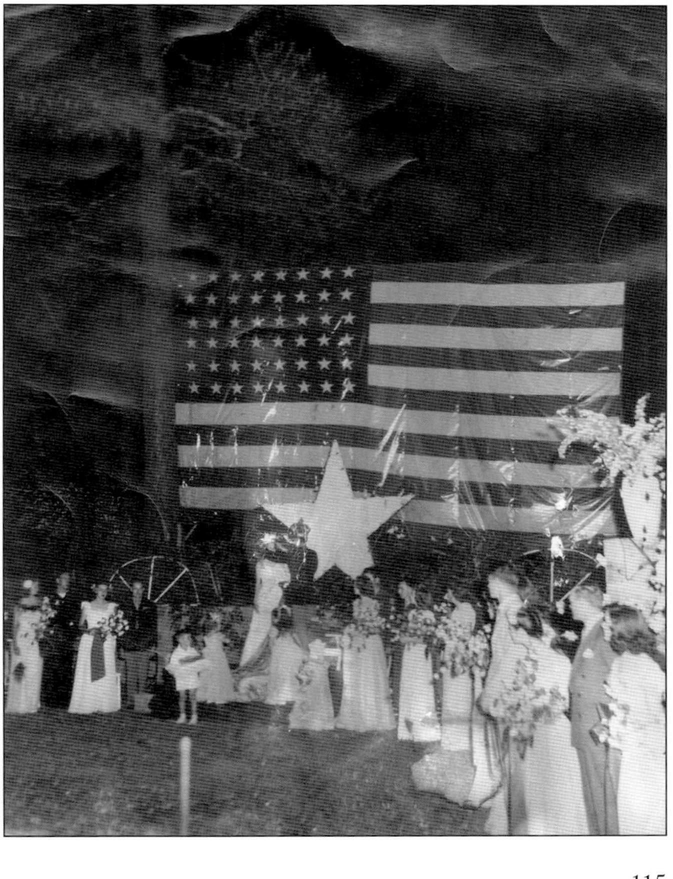

The 1946 Tyler County Dogwood Festival gave Tyler County folk the perfect combination of events to celebrate. As Judge Wheat so eloquently stated, it was "Dogwood Time in Tyler County." Most importantly, the festival honoring the beauty of springtime could also honor the young men home from military service in World War II. King Elmer Ray Oates crowned queen Helen Sheffield at the third festival, which established the continuation of an annual tradition. (Courtesy of TCDF.)

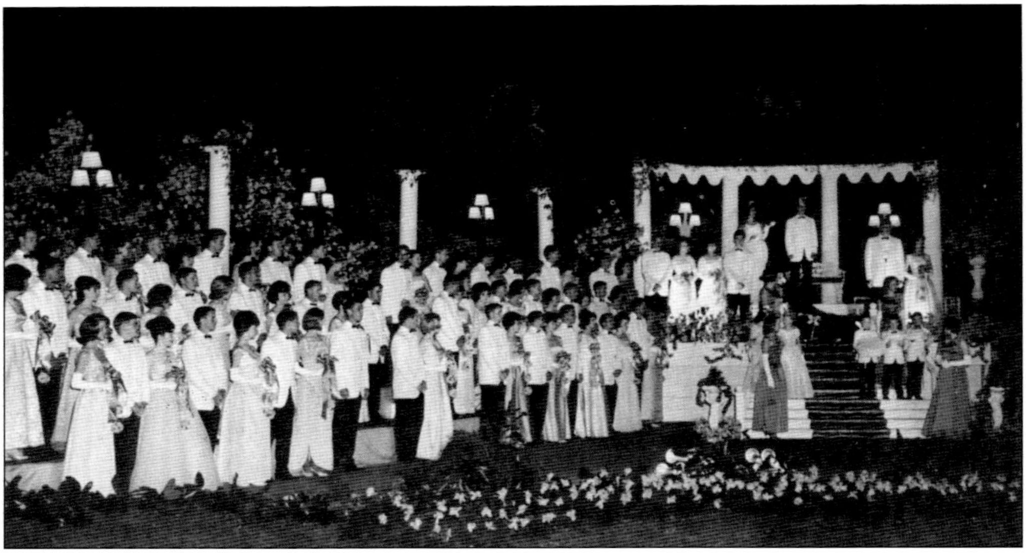

In 1963, queen Terri Daniels's court joined her on a throne fashioned as a colonial garden setting. As always, mounds of paper azaleas decorated the stage with a backdrop of lacy dogwood trees. Yellow jasmine and wisteria vines filled the towering pine and hardwood trees to complete the picture. The royal court awaited its entertainment: a historical pageant and a sky full of pyrotechnics. (Courtesy of TCHC.)

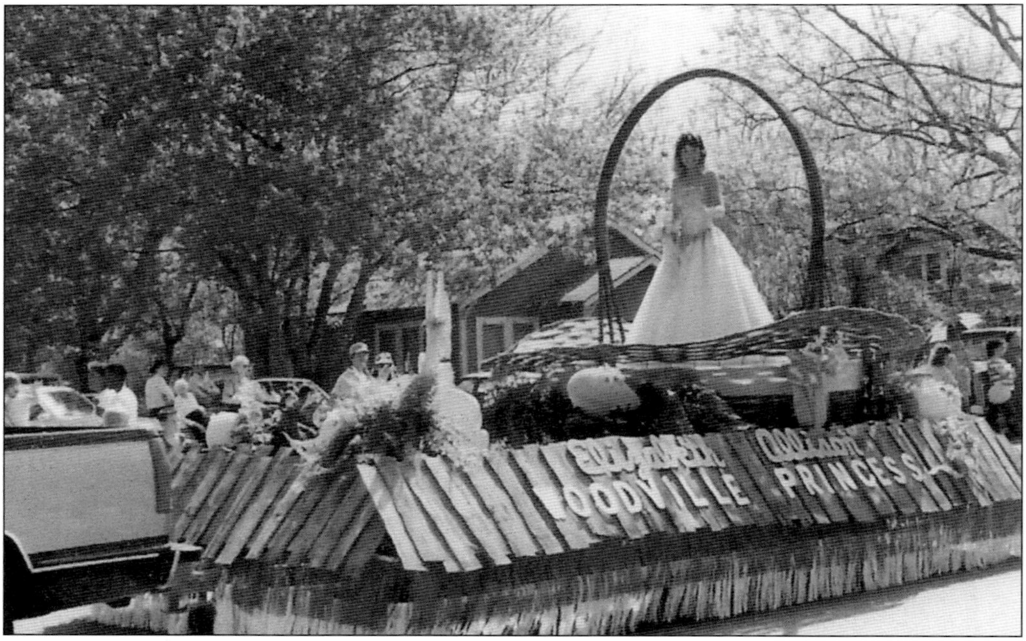

In 1988, Woodville princess Elizabeth Allison's float featured two events that shared one weekend: Easter and the Tyler County Dogwood Festival. Michael Watts applied geometry skills from Jim Hays's mathematics class to calculate the elliptical basket design. He then led vocational agriculture students in building the float. Through the years, when Easter and the Dogwood Festival occurred on the same weekend, local churches have made use of the beautifully decorated amphitheater to host Sunday services outdoors. (Courtesy of Beth Allison.)

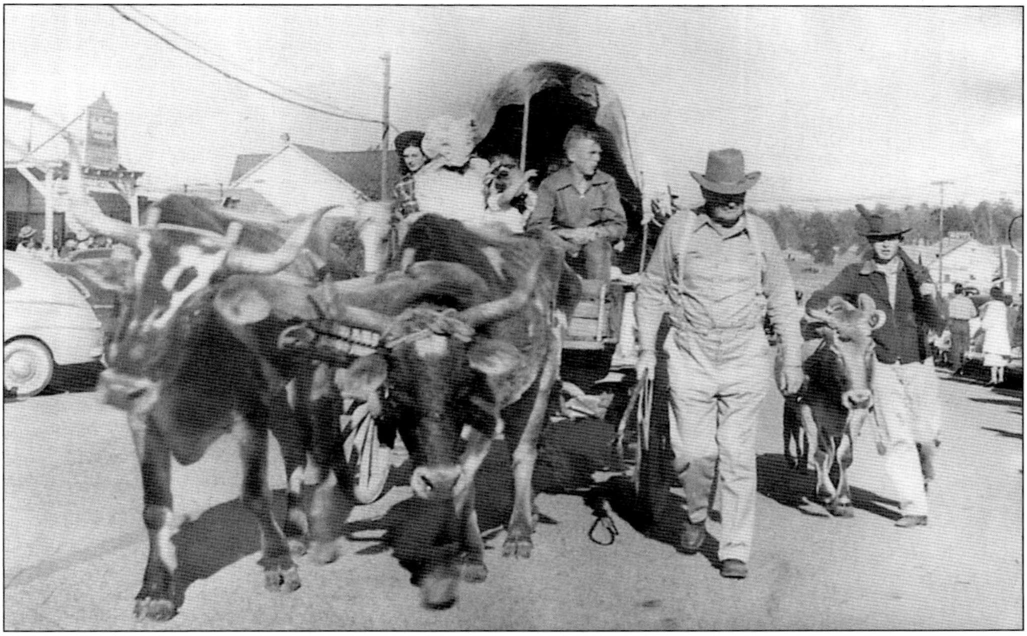

Jethro Holmes (front, walking) took his team of oxen, Tom and Jerry, to entertain audiences across Texas, sometimes going as far as San Antonio to exhibit pioneer travel at the Institute of Texan Cultures. Walking from their home on Town Bluff Road, they made regular appearances in the annual Tyler County Dogwood Festival Parade as well as in the historical pageant. (Courtesy of TCHS.)

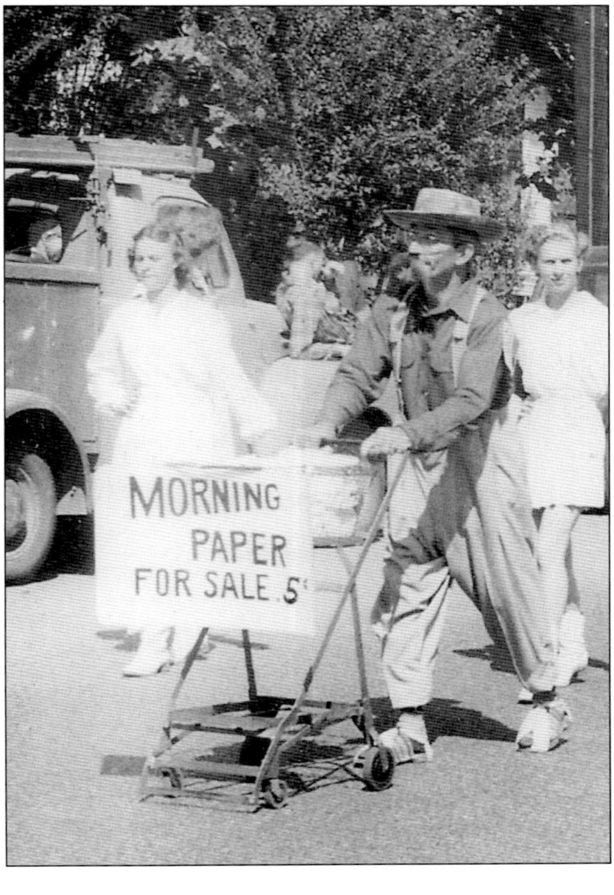

Early festival-goers always looked forward to seeing Roy Pate in the Tyler County Dogwood Festival Parade. Pate's sometimes subtle and always unpredictable entries made everyone laugh. Once, the product he advertised in his shopping buggy turned out to be different than the expected newspaper. His "Morning Paper" looked more like the Sears Roebuck catalogs, and a few rolls of soft white paper. (Courtesy of TCHS.)

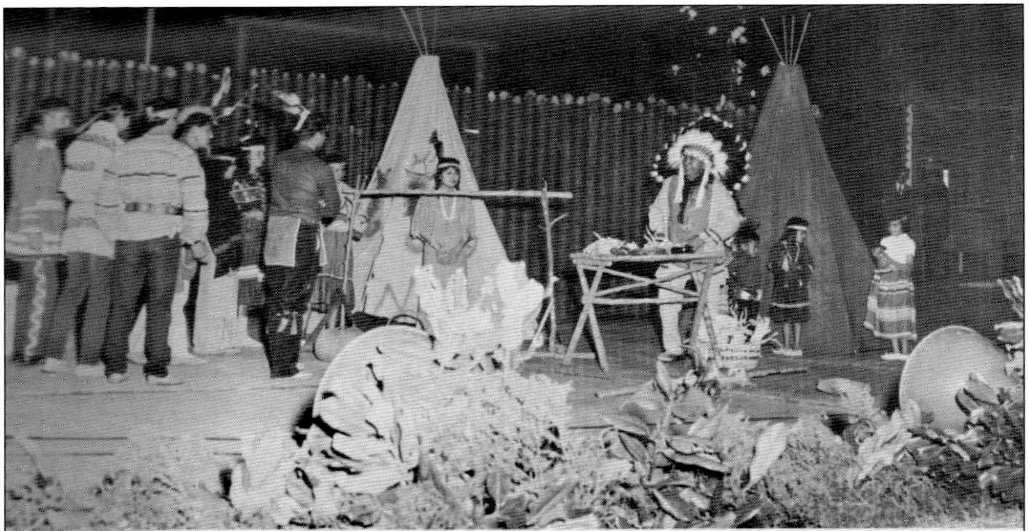

Scene from the 1966 Pageant "Texas Under Mexican Rule" written by Mrs. R. L. Brockman. This scene is from episode titled "The Indian Village."

Judge James E. Wheat encouraged development of pageants to reenact colorful events in county history. Designed as entertainment for the royal court, pageants depicted the grand heritage shared by Tyler County residents. Each year, Wheat conducted research on a different historical topic and wrote a detailed review for the annual Dogwood Book. Those reviews later became pageant themes. (Courtesy of TCDF.)

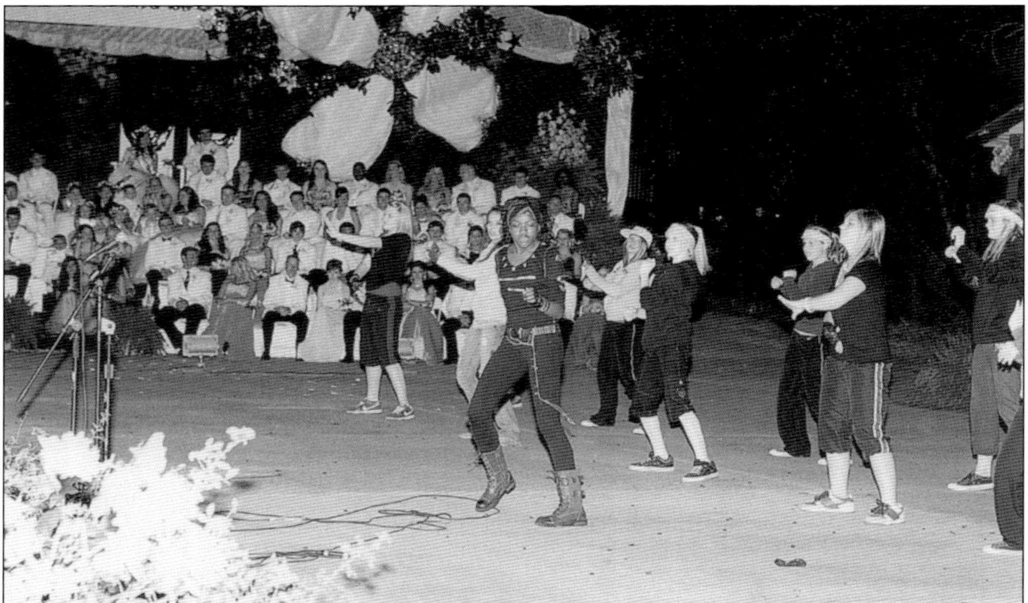

As technology improved and interests broadened, festival entertainment began to focus on musical reviews referring to more contemporary history. Now, local artists write, produce, and enact dramas on stages designed, built, and decorated entirely by volunteers. Dorian Maloy and her backup troop performed Michael Jackson's "Bad" in the 2011 historical play. (Courtesy of Jim Powers.)

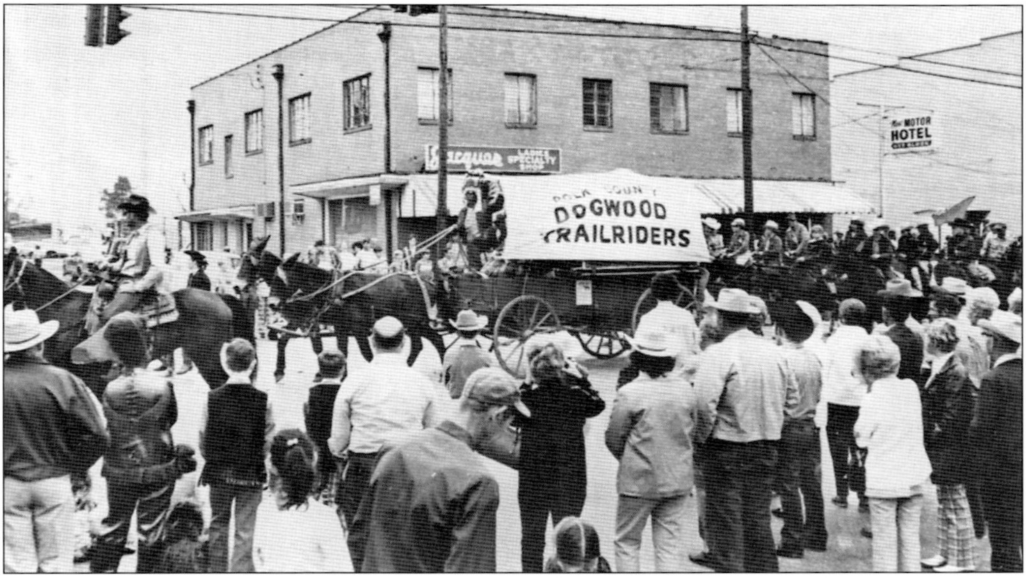

The year 1970 saw an addition to the Tyler County Dogwood Festival, which was the first Western Weekend. Trail rides from all over Southeast Texas converged in the county on Friday. Those riders joined royalty floats, wagons, and surreys to fill a Saturday afternoon parade. A "Western Queen" contest took place at the rodeo arena, along with goat and calf scrambles. Teen and adult dances concluded the event in traditional boot-scootin' style. (Courtesy of TCDF.)

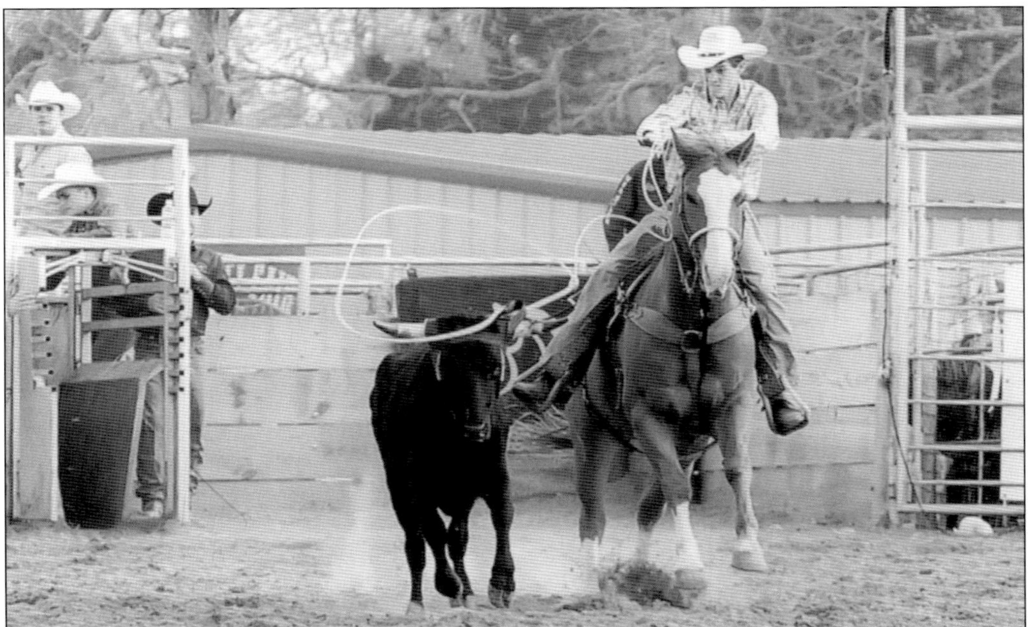

Four decades later, Dogwood Western Weekend still draws an energetic crowd. Dustin Mason practices roping year-round at his grandparents' home in Doucette. Charles and Shirley Rawls enjoy watching him bring his skill to the steer-roping event. Dustin's mom, Tracy, and sister Shelby sponsor trail rides throughout the year as benefits for families with emergency needs or just for the fun of riding. (Courtesy of Jim Powers.)

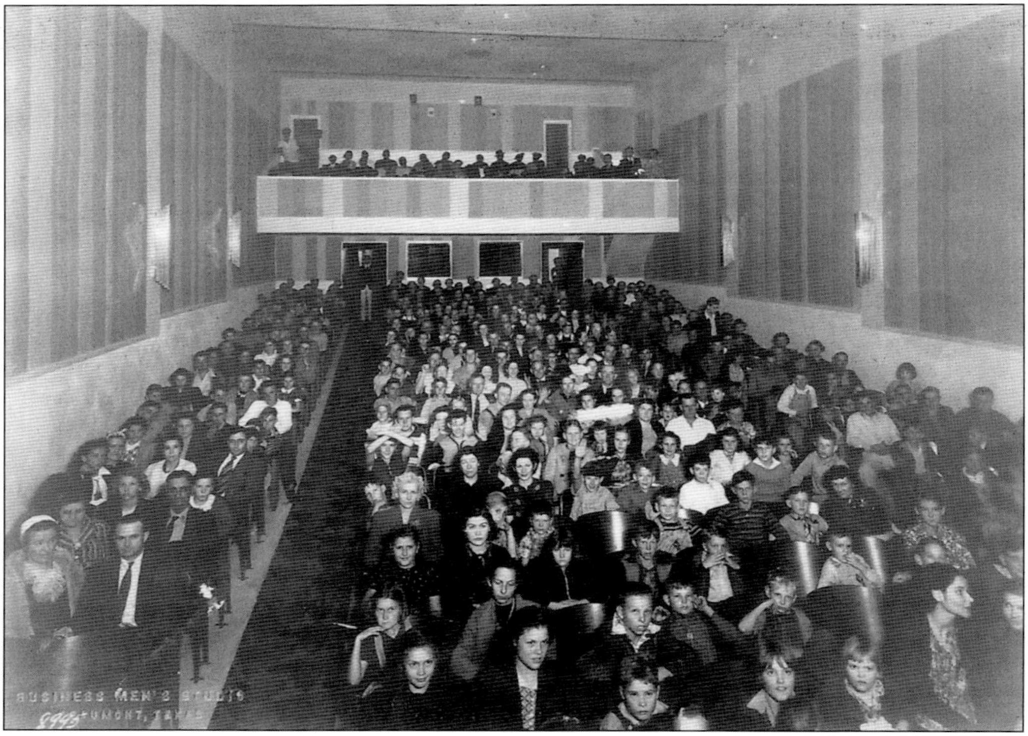

Stars of stage and screen entertained 1950s audiences. A couple could take in a movie with popcorn for less than a $1 at the Fain Theater in Woodville or the Dogwood Drive-in on US Highway 69. At Hillister Elementary, Kathleen White's expression class presented its Easter program featuring hatboxes that were decorated by pupils Gladys Best, Janice Smith, Barbara Allison, Becky Ogden, Sharon Allison, Paula Allison, Jenny Clow, and Dixie Ogden. (Above, courtesy of TCHS; below, courtesy of Gladys Best.)

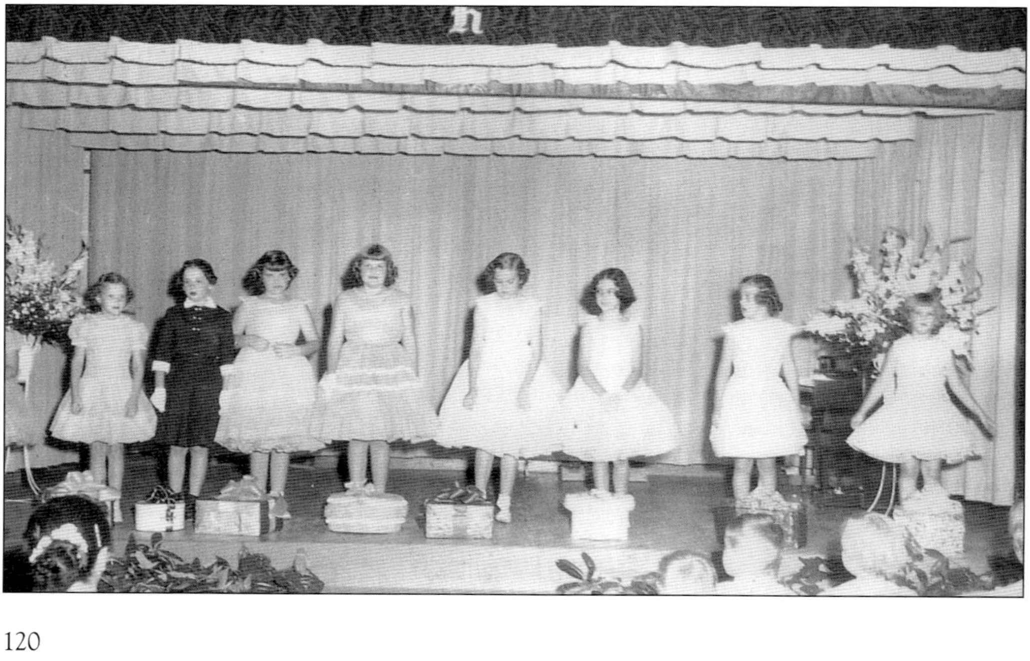

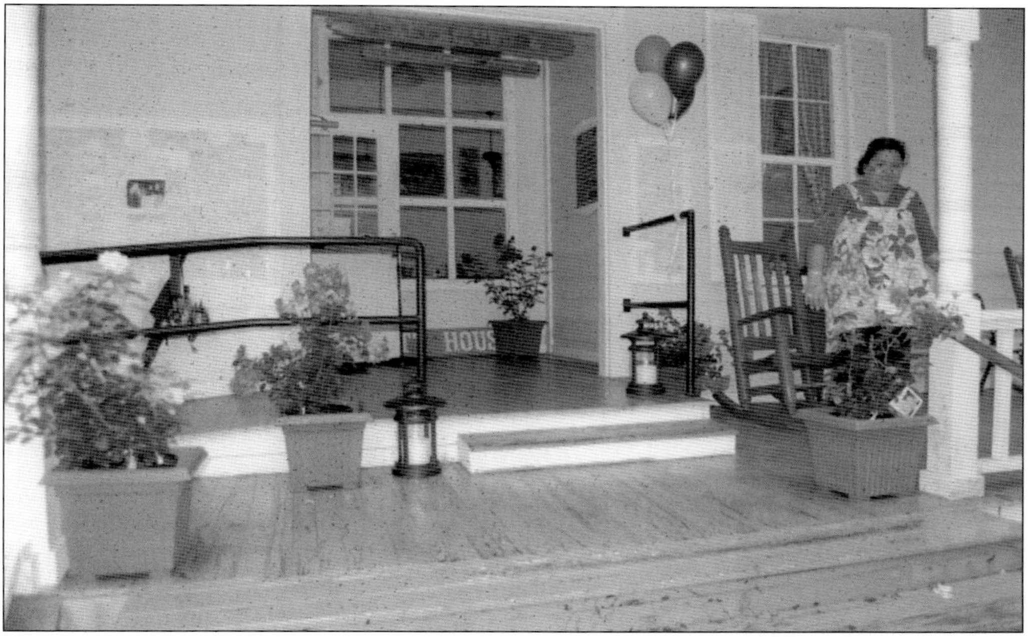

Ofeira Gazzaway welcomes guests to the Pickett House for family-style meals seven days a week and also for special events like birthday parties and receptions. Heritage Village founder Clyde Gray negotiated to bring the building to the Heritage Village from Midway, which was where it had served as a schoolhouse. With ongoing maintenance and improvements made by the Tyler County Heritage Society, the restaurant continues to delight tourists and local families. (Courtesy of TCHC.)

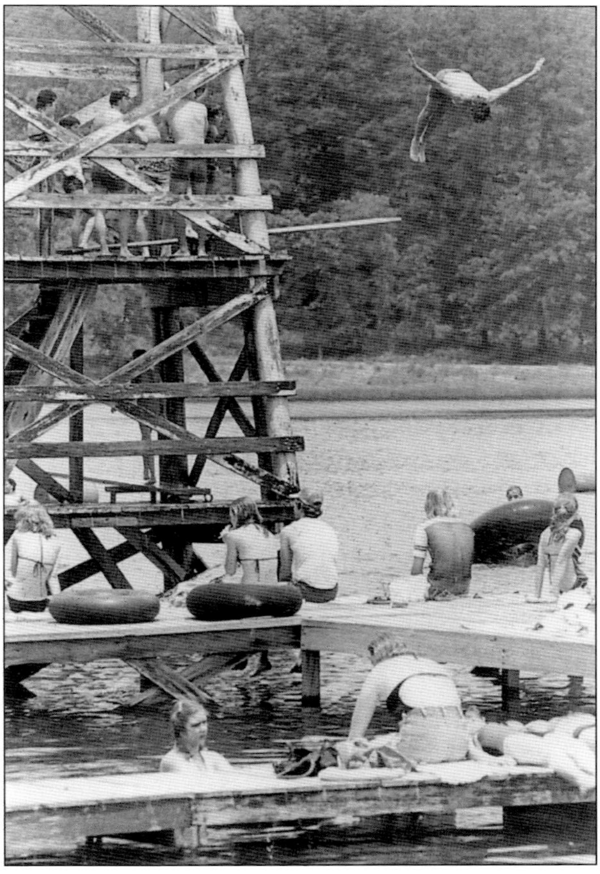

Built during the Great Depression by out-of-work young men who took jobs in the National Youth Administration, Lake Tejas continues to invite swimmers and picnickers of all ages. The Colmesneil Independent School District owns and manages the property, using the proceeds from tickets and the concession stand to support extracurricular activities for students. (Courtesy of CISD.)

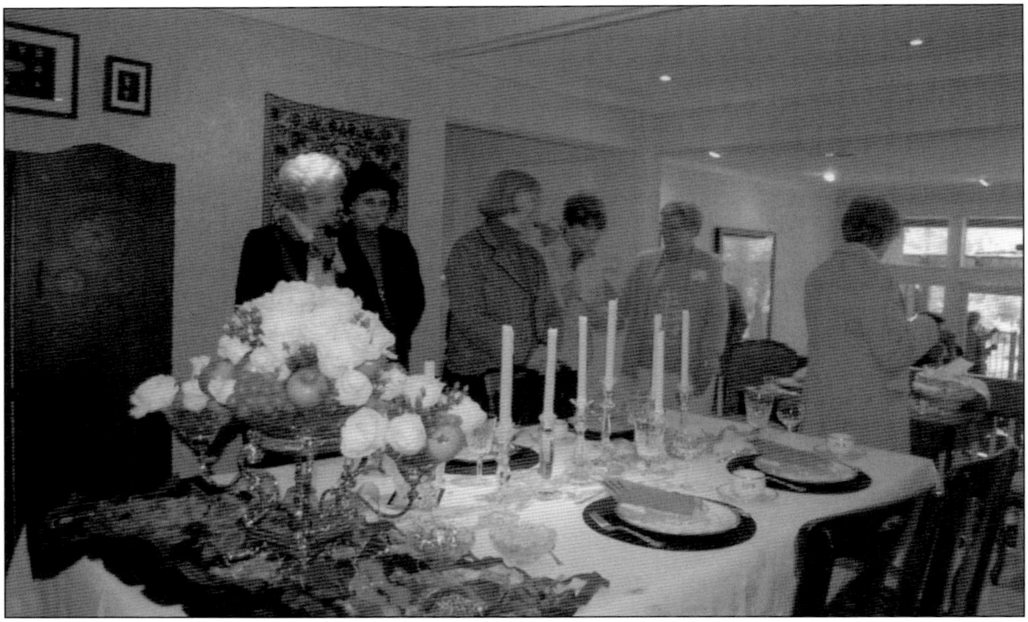

Every community in Tyler County holds benefit functions to raise funds for such things as student scholarships, new fire engines, Relay for Life, or families with special needs. From bake sales to auctions, from bird feeders to handmade quilts, from barbecues to crawfish boils, events bring people together for good causes. One such event is the annual Christmas Tour of Homes, which has been hosted by the Woodville ladies clubs for more than 35 years. (Courtesy of TCHC.)

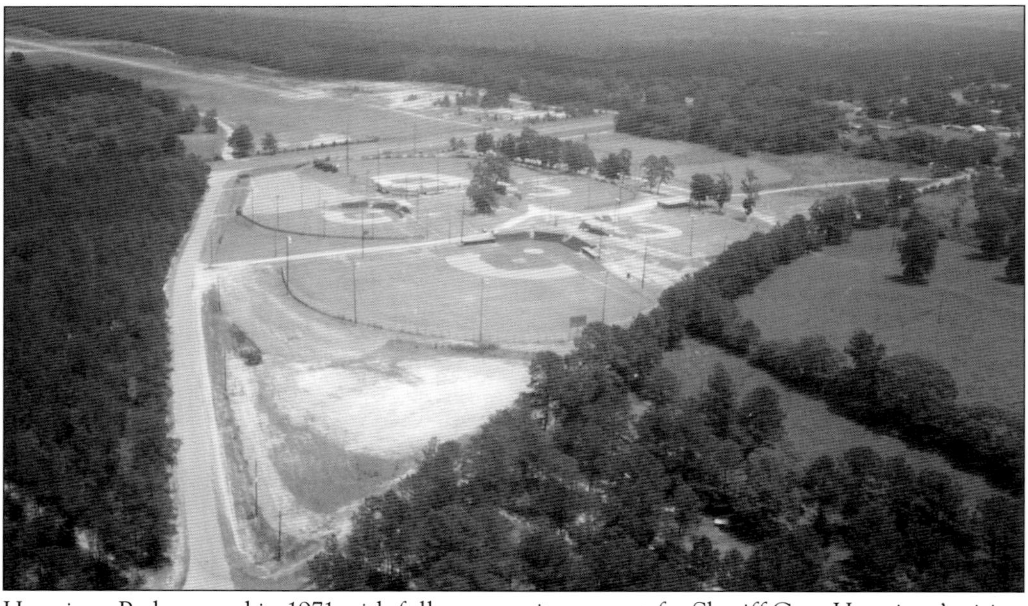

Hennigan Park opened in 1971 with full community support for Sheriff Gary Hennigan's vision to provide top-quality baseball training for all children in Tyler County. Support continued and the park developed from the original three fields to six. Many of the first young players on these fields grew up to coach their own children there. Tyler County All-Stars continue to win championships, sometimes at the state level. (Courtesy of Debbie Hennigan.)

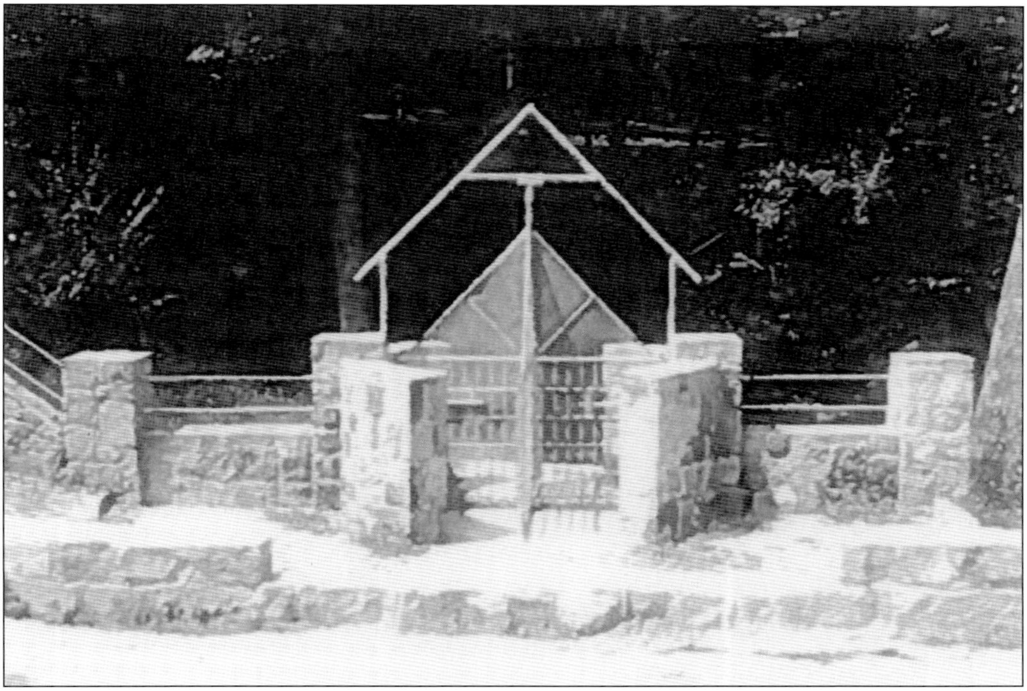

During and following the Great Depression, John Wingate served as road foreman for the old Texas Highways Department (now TxDOT) in a region including Tyler County. He had the vision for creating roadside parks where travelers could stop for a picnic in scenic surroundings. In 1930, he guided the construction of the first such park on land donated along Cow Creek near Newton, Texas. In 1934, with the encouragement of Judge Wheat and the chamber of commerce, Wingate supervised the building of Kirkley Springs Park on land donated by Long Bell Lumber Company. At the time, the 10.5 acres adjoined Highway 106, which has since become US Highway 287. In addition to providing a scenic rest stop for weary travelers, the park continues to be used as it was when it was new: for school, church, family, and friendly gatherings. (Both, courtesy of TxDOT.)

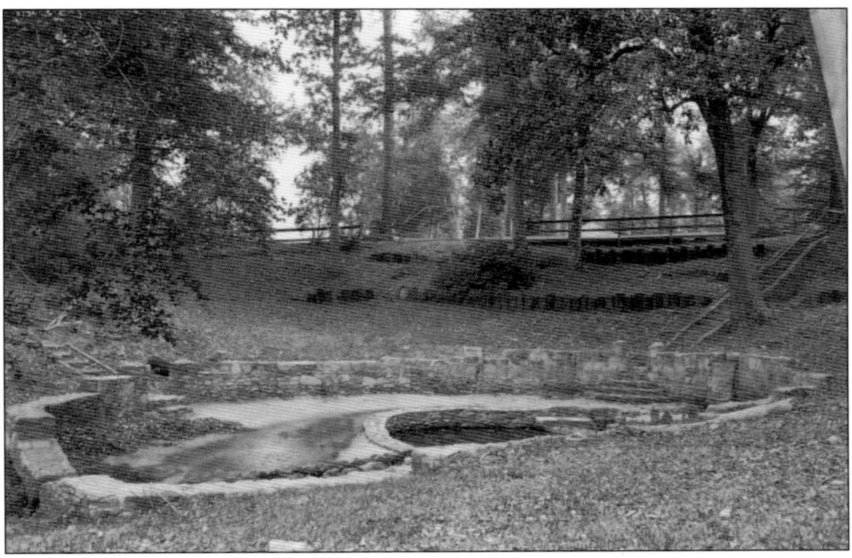

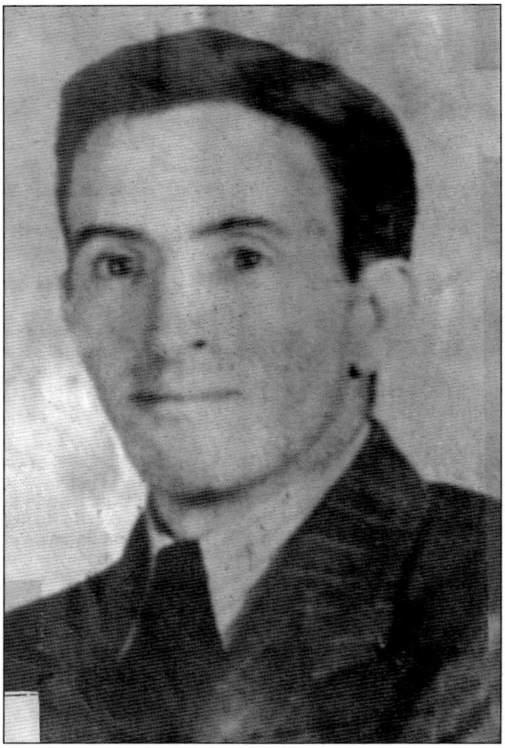

Many student athletes helped put Tyler County's name on the map. In the 1930s, after graduating from Kirby High School, Bob Phillips attended Stephen F. Austin State College in Nacogdoches. There, he continued his outstanding performance in track and field events. He represented the United States in the World Olympics in the 1930s and later became inducted into the Stephen F. Austin State University Athletic Hall of Fame. From 1956 to 1958, Zelmo Beaty led Scott High School Panther basketball teams in state championship play. After high school, he continued his education at Prairie View College, and upon graduating he played professional basketball with teams in St. Louis, Atlanta, and Oregon. (Left, courtesy of ASLM; below, courtesy of Mayme Canada Brown.)

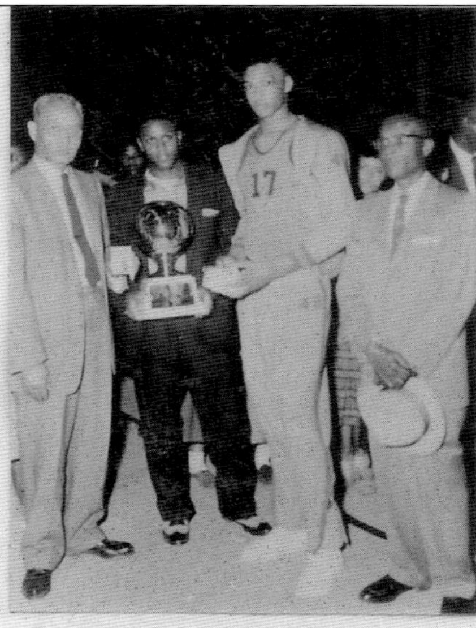

Receiving the Trophy

Left to right:

Mr. O. J. Thomas: State director

Coach: Mr. John E. Payton

Player: Zelmo Beaty

Principal: Mr. John K. Canada

John Elliott (right), a Warren High School graduate, and Hugh Lynn Pitts (below), a Kirby High School graduate, made history playing college and professional football. Elliott answered a draft with the New York Jets after graduating from the University of Texas. With his help, the Jets won Super Bowl III against the Baltimore Colts. Pitts, discovered as a Kirby High School junior by a scout looking at another player, played center for Texas Christian University. After a Southwest Conference Championship in 1956, he went on to play for the Los Angeles Rams. Both men enjoyed successful business careers in oil field service and real estate industries. (Right, courtesy of Warren Independent School District; below, courtesy of TCHS.)

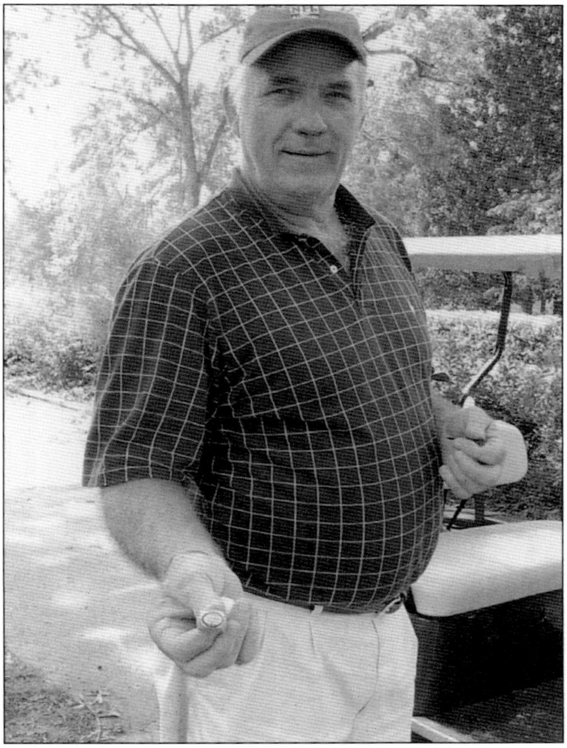

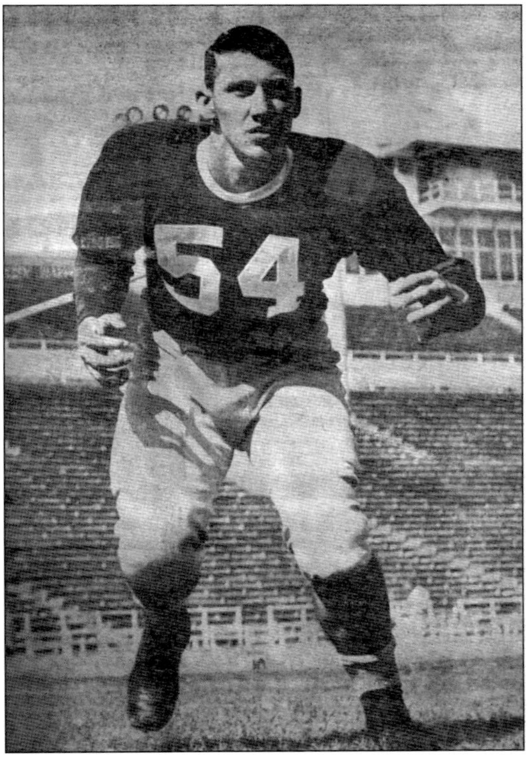

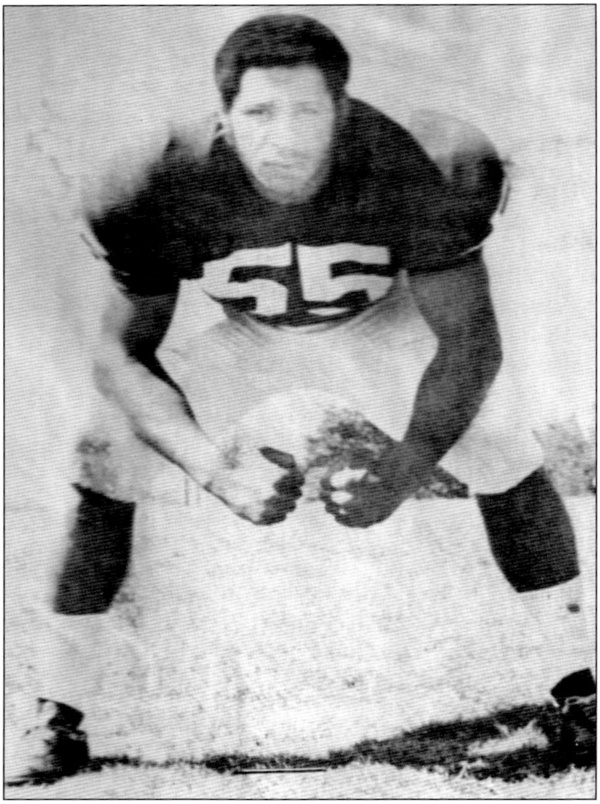

In 1966, Richard Gill and his brother Willie made history as the first black students to attend the previously all-white Kirby High School (KHS). Coach Charlie McGinty recruited the athletes to play football at KHS in the first year when African American students could choose which school to attend. McGinty credited Richard for providing leadership that led to a smooth integration of the two schools in the following year. From Woodville, Gill signed with North Texas State University and played three years there as a linebacker. Gill's untimely death in 1969 followed complications from a knee injury. Tyler County's African American community celebrated another first when they followed Mayme Canada Brown's leadership to establish a day honoring the memory of Martin Luther King Jr. with a parade and other activities, seen below. (Left, courtesy of Woodville Independent School District; below, courtesy of Mayme Canada Brown.)

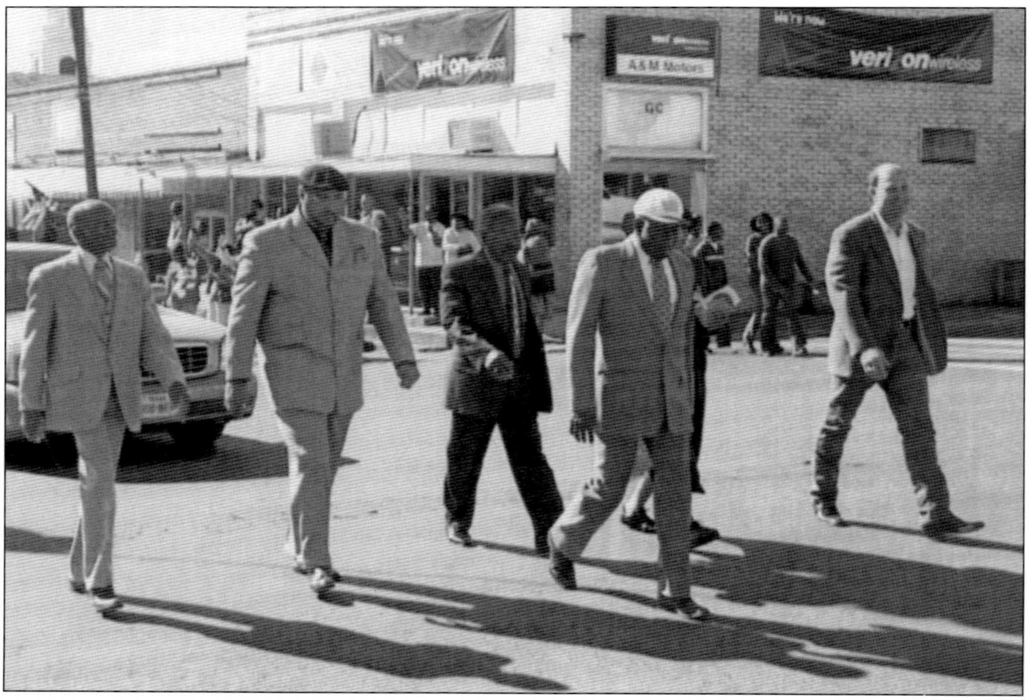

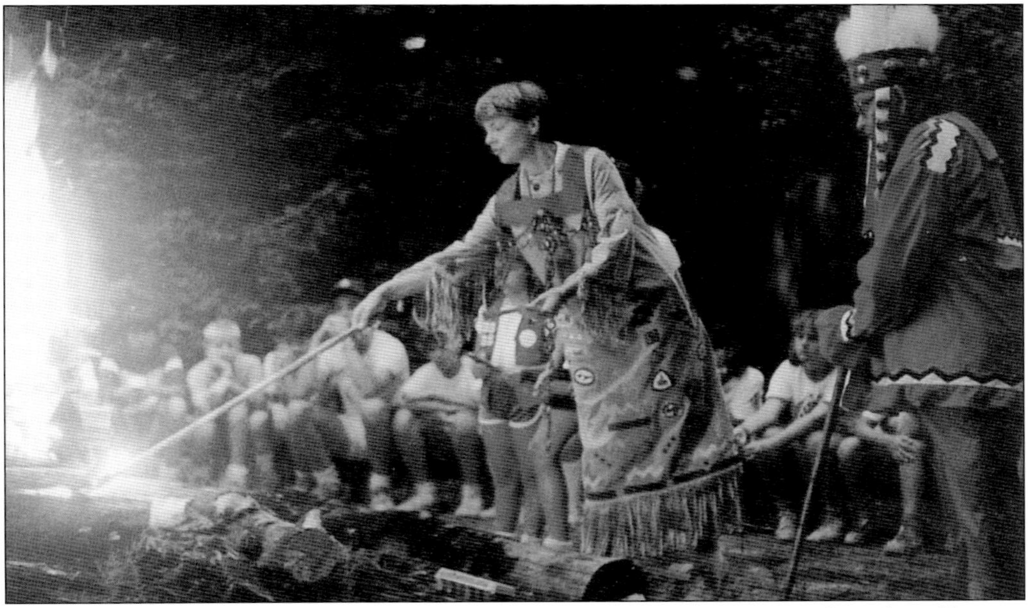

From the early 1950s, Camp Niwana has provided rustic camping experiences for girls and boys in Southeast Texas. Chief Fulton Battise from the nearby Alabama-Coushatta Reservation enjoyed participating in ceremonial campfire events. Today, fourth-generation campers participate in activities that encourage them to develop campfire ideals focused on the motto WOHELO (work, health, and love). (Courtesy of Darby Kethan.)

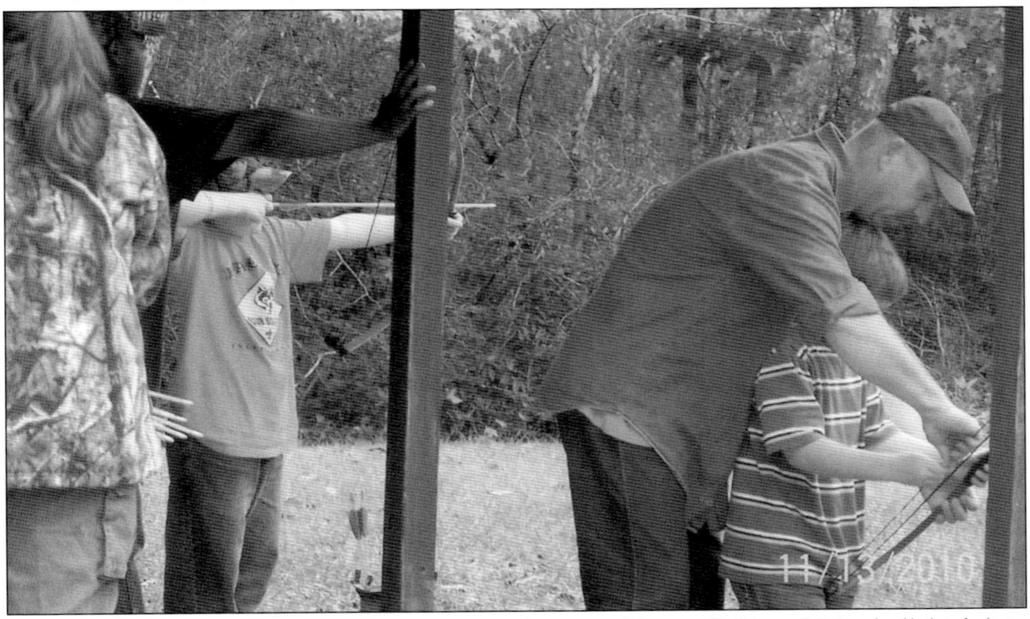

Frank Helm, Cubmaster for Pack 73, instructs his sons Mason (left) and Marshall (right) in the fine art of bow shooting at Camp Urland. For more than 60 years, the Boy Scout camp has contributed to scouting adventures, helped young men develop skills and character, and introduced new friends. To conclude this historical volume with such an image gives the reader a window for seeing future history as it is being made. (Courtesy of Lisa Best Helm.)